Canadian Banks and
Global Competitiveness

© McGill-Queen's University Press 1994
ISBN 0-7735-1138-5

Legal deposit first quarter 1994
Bibliothèque nationale du Québec

Printed in Canada on acid-free paper

This book has been published with the help of a grant
from the Social Science Federation of Canada, using
funds provided by the Social Sciences and Humanities
Research Council of Canada. Publication has also been
supported by the Canada Council through its block grant
program.

Canadian Cataloguing in Publication Data

Darroch, James L. (James Lionel), 1951–
    Canadian banks and global competitiveness
    Includes bibliographical references and index.
    ISBN 0-7735-1138-5
    1. Royal Bank of Canada. 2. Canadian Imperial Bank of
    Commerce. 3. Bank of Montreal. 4. Bank of Nova
    Scotia. 5. Banks and banking, Canadian. I. Title.
    HG2704.D37 1994   332.1'2'0971   C93-090544-X

Typeset in Times 10/12
by Caractéra production graphique inc., Quebec City

Canadian Banks and Global Competitiveness

JAMES L. DARROCH

McGill-Queen's University Press
Montreal & Kingston • London • Buffalo

For my parents, Jim and Bernice,
my wife, Brenda, and our son, Daniel

Contents

Tables and Figures

Acknowledgments

Throughout the course of researching and writing this book, I have had the support of many current and former colleagues and friends at the Faculty of Administrative Studies, York University and the School of Business and Economics, Wilfrid Laurier University. Support from my doctoral committee at York, I.A. Litvak, D.J. Horvath, and D.E. Brewer kept this work on track at the beginning. My subsequent work with Al Litvak has been both an academic and personal joy that few experience. Thanks, Al.

I owe a great debt to Robert D. Cuff for his careful reading and insightful comments over the years. Duncan McDowall was generous in his assistance in clarifying aspects of the Royal. Discussions with Nahum Biger and Richard Wright, McGill University, also helped me to advance my thinking on banking. Especially important were frequent and lively lunch meetings with Dawson Brewer and Sy Friedland which forced me to focus on the flows rather than the stocks. I regret that Sy's untimely death cut short our discussions.

Some other York colleagues merit mention. My understanding of the role of information technologies has been greatly advanced by both my current colleague, Ron McClean, and former colleagues, Larry Dickson and Tim Warner. For opening my eyes to the world of entrepreneurship and small business, my thanks go to Rein Peterson.

Senior executives in financial services firms, public policy makers, regulators, lawyers, and industry consultants were extremely generous with their time. Space precludes listing all the executives in Toronto and New York who generously gave their time to help me with my research. Their lively insights made this a very enjoyable research project.

The librarians at York, the University of Toronto and the Central Reference Library of Toronto made the research task far easier. Without such dedicated people, research would be far more difficult, if not impossible.

Helpful comments and support from the people at McGill-Queen's – Don Akenson, Roger Martin, Joan McGilvray, and Philip Cercone – have helped me to stay the course. Last but far from least, I benefited from a conscientious and talented copy editor, Victoria Grant, and from my indexer, Kathy Sutherland Huard.

Research is not possible without financial support. Support from the Social Sciences and Humanities Research Council during my doctoral years and more recently for my work with I.A. Litvak made this book possible. I would also like to thank the Aid to Scholarly Publication Programme of the Social Science Federation of Canada and the Social Sciences and Humanities Research Council, not only for the grant which made publication possible, but for finding reviewers who helped me to improve my manuscript. I am especially indebted to an anonymous reviewer I fondly refer to as "A."

Support from the Ontario Centre for Research International Business under director of research Alan M. Rugman was of great assistance in furthering and broadening my work on the activities of the banks in the 1980s.

Support from friends and family kept me (relatively) sane and happy. My years at York have been gladdened by many friends – especially Lynn Beard, Hugues Roy, Louise Clarke, and Betsy Duran. Lastly, I have benefited from the support of my extended family.

Canadian Banks and
Global Competitiveness

CHAPTER ONE

The Strategies of Canadian Multinational Banks

In the increasingly global competitive environment, there has been considerable concern for the competitiveness of Canadian industries. The financial services industry, however, is one that can be said to have competed successfully in international markets.[1] Four Canadian banks, the Royal Bank of Canada, the Canadian Imperial Bank of Commerce (CIBC), the Bank of Montreal, and the Bank of Nova Scotia (Scotiabank) rank among the 10 largest in North America, as can be seen in table 1.1. Even more importantly, this table shows that these four are recognized by industry insiders to be among the best in both North America and the world. The non-ranking of some familiar American money-centre banks further calls attention to the sound management of the large national Canadian banks. The status of the major Canadian banks in international capital markets may be surprising to some, since it is disproportionate to the size of Canadian financial markets.[2] However, the international orientation of the major banks from their foundation served to offset many of the limitations imposed by the Canadian market.[3]

The competitive strategies that produced these rankings are the subject of this book. The study examines the lengthy history of each bank from the time that it was founded until the passage of the 1992 omnibus financial services legislation to see how its strategies have unfolded in changing environments.[4] Consideration of this temporal expanse allows us to see the long-term effects of both strategic decisions and public policy that have strongly influenced strategic thinking in this regulated industry.[5] Three of the four banks emerged as industry leaders by the 1920s: the Bank of Montreal, the CIBC, and the Royal.[6] Scotiabank followed a different strategic route, which was characterized by the bank's historians as "non-establishment."[7]

Table 1.1
North America's 10 Largest Banks in 1991

Bank	Assets $ Mil (u.s.)[1]	Euromoney 100 Best Ranking[2]
Citicorp	216.9	Not Ranked
Chemical Banking	138.9	Not Ranked
Royal Bank of Canada	116.9	12
BankAmerica	115.5	39
NationsBank	110.3	81
J.P. Morgan & Co.	108.7	2
CIBC	108.1	34
Chase Manhattan	98.2	Not Ranked
Bank of Montreal	88.1	33
Scotiabank	81.1	71

Source:
1. Farnsworth, "Canada's Mighty Banks on a March South."
2. Euromoney, "The World's 100 Best Banks: Horses for Courses."

At least three of the banks that survived and became industry leaders were international from their origins and compelled other domestic rivals to compete on that basis. But, why was this capacity so valued in the market place? To answer this question, we must identify the goals that guided the banks' strategies. In so doing, we must also recognize that it is important to look beyond profit and growth motives. In this regulated industry, the government has always been an important stakeholder whose interests must be considered if the banks' strategic goals are to be understood.

The Canadian banking industry has a number of important distinguishing features. Canada has regulated its financial institutions in a specific manner. Regulation was designed to ensure service that would be appropriate for a large trading country with a fragmented population in need of capital inflows to develop its natural resource based economy.[8] As a result, the Canadian banks were from their origin involved with the financing of trade – that was their *raison d'être*. In order to provide this service, they had no choice but to adopt an international focus and to develop the skills demanded of a multinational bank (MNB). This required the early establishment of operations in New York, London, and often Boston. In this context, the position of Canada as a natural intermediator between Great Britain and the United States should be recognized.

The majority of scholars of the MNB have focused on the experience of banks from countries with economic structures that are different from Canada. It would be foolish to attempt to refute the position that the primary motivation for internationalization of banks was to follow clients, given the fact that this hypothesis is strongly supported by the experience of British and u.s. banks.[9] However, the hypothesis can perhaps be qualified if tested by a study of the relationship between the activities of both multinational enterprises (MNES) and MNBS in international markets.

The above raises the question: why are Canadian banks different? The answer can be developed by considering the follower hypothesis in a different light: foreign direct investment (FDI) in banking followed FDI in other sectors. If this is extended, then it would seem logical to assume that MNBS will develop during the eras when countries are net exporters of capital, or at least when there are significant capital outflows. Japan is the current major example of this reality. Yet, as we shall see, a major role of Canadian banks has been to facilitate the inflow of capital. Various national policies would seem to have been created to encourage foreign firms to establish operations behind Canadian tariff barriers. The success of this measure may be seen in the number of foreign controlled firms in Canada. But it also makes us question under what conditions significant capital inflows will result in the international expansion of a host country's banks.

The point is not to refute the follower hypothesis, but rather to see what light is shed upon it by the very different experience of the Canadian banks. In this vein, we can well ask why the banks of Great Britain and the United States did not follow their clients into the Canadian market. While there may be many reasons related to profitability or economics, the role of government regulation in encouraging a concentrated and Canadian-owned industry has been critical.[10] It is also important to realize that the influx of foreign firms expanded the market segment of MNES for the Canadian banks. This suggests that an analysis of the strategies developed by the banks must take into account the role assigned to the banks by public policy. The continuing role of government has always played a critical role in determining the environment in which banks compete.

Banking has always been seen as a strategic sector by Canadian governments, and government regulation, sometimes at an informal level, has created barriers to entry that have resulted in one of the most concentrated banking systems in the world.[11] Six clear policy objectives in legislation governing banking can be discerned.

1 The financial sector should be stable, that is provide a safe haven to depositors and investors in order to encourage the inward flow of capital.
2 Federally regulated chartered banks should be among the dominant financial institutions in Canada.

3 The industry should be Canadian controlled.
4 The industry should be able to facilitate trade.
5 An infrastructure should be developed to assist government financing.
6 An extensive system should provide services to the entire populace.

If these observations are correct, then government policy has promoted orderly markets to ensure a stable system. A stable system protects depositors. Public policy has been a major determinant of opportunities, both domestically and internationally.[12] The tremendous role of such regulation on the competitive environment cannot be ignored. However, the manner in which specific aspects of a competitive environment ruled by government regulation could create competitive advantages merits reflection.[13] Regulation was not only a straight-jacket, but a creator of opportunities that led to the development of institutions with specific skills. In turn, these skills have allowed the major Canadian banks to prosper.

COMPETITIVE FORCES AND GENERIC STRATEGIES

Prior to a specific analysis of what constitutes strategic management of a bank, it is important to develop a framework for analysing the competitive forces in banking. The well-known model of competitive forces developed by Michael E. Porter has been employed in this study since it has the merit of facilitating a relatively simple, yet quite powerful analysis of industry structure.[14] The pressures exerted by buyers, suppliers, substitute products, potential entrants, and rivalry within the industry determine the overall profitability of the industry. In Porter's world, relative bargaining power is the major determinant of who benefits from market transactions. The stronger the power of these forces, the lower the profitability of the industry. The weaker the pressures they exert, the higher the level of profitability and the incentive for others to enter this attractive industry.

Essentially, firms can compete in an industry only in two ways. The first is to be the low cost producer in the industry, the second is to be a differentiated producer.[15] The low cost producer's cost structure ensures above average profitability at any price in the industry, while the differentiated producer offers a product whose unique qualities provide protection from price competition. Consequently, the firm is able to charge higher prices that compensate for its typically higher cost structure and generally lower market share. The goal is to find a position that protects the firm from the competitive forces that drive economic profits to zero in perfectly competitive markets.[16]

There can be only one low cost producer, but there are a number of differentiated positions possible. While the above may seem simple, it is far from simplistic. The problem facing any firm is to build sustainable competitive advantage. Successful firms, and even not so successful ones, are known for performing certain functions or delivering certain services. Virtually all firms have distinctive competencies. However, not all distinctive competencies are equally valued in the market place. Consequently not all strategies of differentiation are successful. The challenge for any firm is to develop those distinctive competencies that are valued because these are the foundation of its competitive advantage. With this in mind, we must examine how banks seek to develop distinctive competencies to support their strategy. The dynamic nature of the challenge must also be recognized. Since strategies and components of strategies are copiable, constant attention to market positioning is imperative.

An important issue to determine is whether the two generic strategies are mutually exclusive. Given the logic of Porter's framework, if a company could combine differentiation with the low cost position, the result would be outstanding financial performance. This may have been the case with IBM in the personal computer (PC) market at one time, or American Express Travel Related Services Division of American Express in the 1980s, or with most companies who are rated "excellent" in the popular business press.[17] The considerable variations among these lists from time to time may attest to the difficulty of sustaining the combination of the two positions. In the financial services industry, the relationship between the broad product line that can be bundled into a differentiated position and scope economies that underlie this information-based, technology-driven industry makes this an especially important issue. The fundamental economics of the industry and shifting industry definition and market segmentation further complicate analysis.

Before the Porter framework can be applied to an industry, however, the industry must be defined. The financial services industry is a knowledge-based industry whose purpose is *intermediation* and the provision of advisory and other services. The business of banking is to match savers to borrowers and to provide other financial services. These intermediaries market three very different types of products: loans (assets), deposits (liabilities), and fee-based services.

The definition of any industry is a critical and complicated issue. It is especially complicated in the case of financial services because of the broad range of options facing savers and borrowers, who may not require the services of an intermediary at all but may go instead directly to the market.[18] The commodity nature of "money" must be recognized. This is as true for a company that has the alternative of issuing its own bonds or of obtaining a bank loan, or for a home owner who may choose to borrow funds from a myriad of sources, including family, friends, or RRSPs. Disintermediation, that is raising funds directly rather than through intermediaries, serves to cap profits in the industry. Economists can argue that there is a problem of substitutes in all industries, but the degree of similarity among financial products blurs industry boundaries to a greater degree than in other industries. In fact, as we shall see, "disintermediation" was a major challenge facing all banks in the 1980s and is still a threat in the 1990s.

The importance of substitutes is not limited to the commercial banking sector. An example from retail banking can further demonstrate the importance of "substitutes" not only for theoretical purposes, but for the managerial practice of competitor analysis. In the 1980s, American Express was earning considerable profits from their Travel and Entertainment cards. Banks chose to contest this market with credit cards – a very close substitute from the customer's perspective. However, Travel and Entertainment cards are not the same as bank credit cards such as VISA or MasterCard because the two cards generate revenues in different ways.

American Express is reliant upon fees, while banks primarily seek to earn interest income, as the name "credit" card suggests. Competitor analysis driven by customer benefit must understand how these two compete for space in the wallet and for transaction use by customers. Predicting competitive moves must commence from an understanding of how these cards make money in different ways. For example, American Express has taken to emphasizing the sound financial management practices promoted by their card and the interest costs associated with bank cards. Bank credit cards, on the other hand, make efforts to attract a greater number of merchants by offering more attractive prices or services, since the revenue stream from merchants is only one source of revenues for banks. The focus on customers is essential for bridging the dynamic linkage between industry and competitor analysis.[19]

Fortunately, there is an alternative route to industry definition: government regulation. The Bank Act both created a protected sphere and limited the product scope of the federally chartered banks. Consequently, the competitors in the industry can be defined as those holding a charter. Trust companies, which are provincially or federally chartered, did not compete with chartered banks for corporate

loans,[20] yet the trust companies were competitors in some product markets, such as deposits and mortgages. The banking, trust, securities, and insurance industries – the four pillars of the Canadian financial system – were separated and identified historically through their initial core business. For the chartered banks, this meant originally business loans that were primarily short term, and trade financing. However, growth through diversification into related businesses led to competition among rivals from these different industries. Because the charter allowed banks to compete in essentially different businesses, we are forced to analyse banks as multiservice (product) firms competing against multiple rivals from different sectors.[21]

In Porter's terms, we see how "substitutes" serve to act as a cap on profits, but we should also be aware how regulation affects the distinction between "substitute" and "potential entrant." From a competitor analysis point of view, attractive profits in a product market serve as an incentive for competitors who are formally barred from the market to engineer a close substitute. Financial engineering can make a mockery of formal barriers. However, at the industry level of the blocked entrant, there is still an incentive to end the barriers in order that firms can compete in the most efficient manner possible.[22]

A SIMPLE MODEL OF BANKING

In order to explore the dimensions of strategic bank management, let us build a simple model where we hypothetically consider each bank as a *completely* stand-alone, self-sufficient unit. In Canada, banking needs would be met by a number of different banks, each serving distinct regions with no capital movement allowed between regions.[23] That is, all financial transactions affecting each area would take place within that region. In practice, this corresponds loosely to the linkage between geographic boundaries and regulatory boundaries.

The first question that must be considered in this conceptual exercise is how banks make money as intermediaries. We can frame an answer by examining the sample income statement for the Royal Bank of Canada expressed as a percentage return on assets shown in table 1.2. The major source of bank income is "net interest income," which is the "spread" between the rate paid to depositors and that charged to borrowers. A profitable spread is created and maintained through the matching of loans (assets) and deposits (liabilities). Success depends upon the successful marketing of both types of "products." In general, in this conservative industry assets and liabilities will be matched in terms of maturity and other risks will be

Table 1.2
Revenue and Expenses as a Percentage of Average Assets

The Royal Bank of Canada, 1991

Net interest income	3.09%
Provision for loan losses	(.47)
	2.62
Other income	1.35
	3.97
Non-interest expenses	(2.77)
	1.20
Income taxes and minority interests	(.44)
Return on assets	.76

constrained at manageable levels. That is, prudential management dictates that assets and liabilities should be roughly matched in terms of sensitivity to movements in interest or foreign exchange rates. However, the value of a deposit is constant at 100 per cent of face value, while the value of a loan can vary with market conditions related to factors such as credit worthiness, as real estate and energy loans have shown. Dynamic repricing on one side of the balance sheet is an important source of both firm and industry volatility, as well as of regulatory concern.

As should be apparent, depending upon the attitude to interest rate risk, "mismatching" according to expectations of market movements can generate superior profits and risks.[24] In the trade, this is known as "gap management."[25] Consequently, the net interest income of two banks is the result of management skill, both in terms of marketing appropriate products and managing in different interest rate environments. Given different positions vis-à-vis gap, the net interest income of two banks should not be directly compared without a consideration of sensitivity to interest rates.[26] Acceptance of higher levels of credit risk would also raise interest revenues. In environments where the riskiness of the loan portfolio does not raise interest costs, as when deposits are insured by an independent agency such as the Canadian Deposit Insurance Corporation (CDIC), the net interest income from the riskier portfolio should be higher.[27]

Holding the level of risk as a constant, profits are maximized by increasing the volume of financial flows. Flows can be generated within one broad sector (e.g., businesses) by targeting mature firms generating positive cash flows and young growing firms in need of cash. The bank also matches firms with different cash flow cycles, such as manufacturers of snow skis and those of water skis because clients generally need deposit or cash management service in connection with their credit services.

Another scenario is where the bank develops dual specialization in the corporate and household sectors.[28] Two different units within the bank would each develop the skills and services needed to service its target segment. If the corporate sector is a net borrower and the household a net lender, then there should be a financial flow captured by the two units. Expansion is limited only by the amount of funds to be recycled. Market segmentation is critical for growth because it serves to maximize financial flows within the region.

It is this drive, which is typically for asset volume, that leads regulators to impose restrictions on growth, such as those on the amount of capital needed to support the assets.[29] In the case of small local banks, a variety of different interest rates across Canada would be found, even if one parent bank owned several regional banks.[30] This would be so because each regional unit would need to balance its own portfolio.

The role of additional financial services, or non-interest income, is essential for an understanding of banking strategy. These services may be peripheral ones that are designed to enhance the primary activities of deposit taking and lending, or they may represent profitable growth vectors on their own. One such category is direct financial instruments such as bonds, which are substitutes for indirect financial instruments such as bank loans. Companies can avoid the costs of using intermediaries such as banks by employing investment bankers to take them directly to markets.[31] The relationship between direct and indirect financial instruments therefore has a direct bearing on the relative profitability of investment banks versus commercial banks. In order to understand the strategic actions taken by banks, it is also necessary to consider the specific types of parties that banks are trying to intermediate between and the role of additional services in marketing to these groups. Changing market conditions in the 1980s, which decreased the profitability of commercial banks, increased the desire of commercial banks to enter the field of direct financial instruments.[32] This has been called the movement from "financial intermediation" to "market intermediation." Focus upon capital adequacy to support credit products further served to enhance the attractiveness of fee-based products.

Figure 1.1 illustrates how a bank's strategy and its market scope can be conceptualized by considering three broad ranges of "products" and their inter-relationships:[33]

D-*Deposits* (Liability Products)	S-*Services* (F-*Fee Products*)	L-*Loans* (Asset Products)
$D_1 \leftrightarrow S\text{-}D_1$*	$S\text{-}F_1$	$L_1 \leftrightarrow S\text{-}L_1$
$D_2 \leftrightarrow S\text{-}D_2$	$S\text{-}F_2$	$L_2 \leftrightarrow S\text{-}L_2$
$D_3 \leftrightarrow S\text{-}D_3$	$S\text{-}F_3$	$L_3 \leftrightarrow S\text{-}L_3$
. .	.	. .
. .	.	. .
. .	.	. .
$D_N \leftrightarrow S\text{-}D_N$	$S\text{-}F_N$	$L_N \leftrightarrow S\text{-}L_N$

Figure 1.1
Financial Services "Products" and Their Interrelationships
* Subscripts denote market segments.

1 Loans (asset products)
2 Deposits (liability products)
3 Services

The figure posits three types of services differentiated by their strategic purpose:

1 S-L: services marketed to borrowers
2 S-D: services marketed to depositors
3 S-F: services designed to produce a fee for the bank

It is important to understand what differentiates S-F income. True S-F products are marketed to generate income on their own account. The conceptual distinction is important not only because "services" can be a form of nonprice competition, but because of the implication upon competitor analysis. Fee-based products include the direct financial instruments offered by investment banks or the American Express Travel and Entertainment card. Bank credit cards demonstrate the problem of pure categories because they are a "credit product," but they can also generate relatively pure fee income, depending upon the pricing strategy employed. Direct charges to users and merchants generate fee-based income whereas an emphasis on limiting such fees to promote use of the card as a financing vehicle for consumers emphasizes revenue from the credit side of the card. Any analysis of S-F service products must therefore be made in light of their strategic purpose.

This leads to the observation that a financial services firm may be established entirely to generate fee income. It further draws attention to a possible growth path for the bank: expansion of services. A focus on "services" per se, however, forces a return to the role of regulation and competitive scope. Historically, Canadian regulation has sought to maintain a separation between the "four pillars" of the financial system. In our analysis of the growth strategies of banks, it is imperative to recognize that the regulations concerning the nature of the services that a bank is allowed to offer within a jurisdiction can be as important as the regulations concerning entry into different jurisdictions. Regulation determines the scope of product line within a jurisdiction and geographic locations. In such a situation, changing regulation can create new opportunities for the banking sector to the detriment of the other pillars, or vice versa. Consequently, it is important to analyse how individual firms and trade associations deal with regulatory bodies to promote high entry barriers into attractive markets. The blurred boundaries among competing industries is of practical import, however, for competitor analysis.[34]

RELAXING THE GEOGRAPHIC CONSTRAINT

As soon as capital flows among regions are allowed, the pools of funds increase and a different industry context emerges. Take, for example, the situation of two banks in different jurisdictions where Bank A is paying lower deposit rates and is charging lower borrowing rates than Bank B. Bank A employs this strategy because the area served by it has relatively more savers and fewer borrowers than that served by Bank B. In order to balance its portfolio, Bank A "encourages" borrowers with its lower rates and "discourages" savers with lower rates in order to maintain a profitable spread and a balanced portfolio.

If clients are allowed movement, then borrowers from region B will be attracted to Bank A while savers in region A will be attracted to Bank B.[35] The flow of funds will be dictated by the relationship among interest, exchange rates, and risk assessments between the two jurisdictions. Over time the two regions will establish equilibrium. A similar logic allows for the extension to multiple jurisdictions. Funds will flow into areas as investors or savers seek the highest level of return consistent with their risk preferences. The mobility of customers is an especially strong driving force for harmonization when internationalization of firms is prohibited.

As can be seen, new elements of risk related to foreign exchange have entered the scenario. Since our focus has been on jurisdictions, it must be emphasized that the linkage between jurisdictions and currencies is not absolute, as revealed by federal systems such as Canada or the United States, or by new multicountry arrangements, such as the European Community (EC) that create the possibility of moving to unified currency arrangements. However, as a practical matter, at some time foreign-exchange differences will emerge. While the temporal dimension underlies interest rate risk, jurisdictional or sovereign diversity is at the root of foreign-exchange risk. Yet, where other firms see risks, financial services firms see market imperfections as an opportunity to provide intermediary services to transform the risks, or fee-based products to manage the risk. Increased complexity drives product innovation in the quest for new profit streams.

The above is only one manner of allowing the flow of funds to take place. Another would be to develop alliances between banks or an interbank market. Bank A would lend funds to Bank B, or there would be a pooling mechanism, such as electronic markets. This new source of asset growth means that Bank A would change its savings policy and encourage new deposits until the demand in region B was satisfied. The institutional arrangement could offer some benefits by minimizing transactions costs. These savings would come about in two ways. First, since it seems reasonable to assume that each bank would be better acquainted with the clients in its own region, the costs associated with marketing and credit assessment could be reduced. Second, each bank would have different strategic orientations: one would develop distinctive skills associated with marketing deposit instruments, while the other would develop skills associated with loans. The expanded market opportunities that would develop should increase the number of viable differentiated positions. It seems probable that the potential savings in the area of transactions costs would encourage the development of the institutional over the individual solution.

Allowing linkage between markets allows for an explicit consideration of how strategic drivers affect multijurisdictional or international strategies. Now, the asset-driven bank could develop an international strategy that seeks both loans and deposits, or interestingly, deposits from international markets to fund domestic growth.[36] The deposit-driven bank no longer faces the availability of domestic assets as a growth constraint. One alternative is to develop a private banking strategy that emphasizes security for depositors in different regions. This can be successful, as Swiss banks have shown. There is also the opportunity to raise domestic deposits and then turn to international markets, lending to the cash-short regions. In many ways, this was the situation facing banks in the Organization of

Petroleum Exporting Countries (OPEC). It is this flow dynamic that helps us to understand the role of banks in the international movement of capital. Banks play a major role in facilitating the international flow of capital from savers to borrowers. At the macroeconomic level, a country's domestic financial flows are balanced, in deficit, or surplus. The international sector provides the mechanism that allows for the necessary balancing. Depending upon the situation, the financial services industry of the country will adopt an asset or liability strategy. Moreover, the new market depth increases the opportunity to develop specialization, that is, the core competencies related to target markets. The enlarged market expands the number of bases that can serve as a basis for distinctive competencies and therefore the number of possible strategic positions.

RELAXING THE OWNERSHIP CONSTRAINT

There is a possibility different from the interbank market – that where one bank internalizes the market by operating with branches in different locations. The branches would follow the same strategies as above, but coordination of the markets would take place by "the visible hand" of management. In strategic terms, we would see the corporate-level strategy coordinating two business-level strategies to create a balanced portfolio in a dynamic environment. The advantage of considering the various types of banks now becomes apparent: different units can be assigned different strategic goals. The portfolio is balanced at the corporate level, but not necessarily at the level of each unit. This balancing follows the structural logic of intermediation.

What are the possible transactions cost savings in this arrangement that would make the ownership solution preferable? The first is the ability to achieve scale economies. There is the opportunity to obtain scale economies in all areas of the firm's infrastructure as well as its value-adding operations. Information technology, marketing campaigns, human resource management, and procurement are only a few of the value-adding activities where scale advantages can lead to significant cost advantages for the integrated firm.[37] The new scale would also promote the development of specialized skills, or what economists call human asset specificity. While neither region alone may provide the volume to develop certain specialized skills, the two together could do so. In turn, the increased knowledge base or other attributes gained from the alliance could serve as a further basis for expansion. Specialized skills such as knowledge of an industry allows for improved risk assessment and, in the long run, better loan pricing.[38]

While economists talk in terms of economies of scale, the strategist must also discuss other sources for efficiencies – especially those tied to human asset specificity. With increased specialization comes increased differentiation, or specialization in the organization, and the consequent need for coordination in the organization. These are the costs of managing this arrangement. The focus on organizational features, however, alerts us to information flows – yet another critical area for possible savings on transactions costs.

The ownership solution should provide for a superior flow of information because of the difficulty of properly pricing information, which is the essential input into banking. The two factors of confidentiality and the public good characteristic of knowledge act as a spur to the ownership solution. The public good aspect is an important spur to internalization.[39] A public good is a good whose consumption by one party does not prevent consumption by other parties. The problem for the firm is that knowledge is a difficult input factor to price on external markets because the knowledge would have to be disclosed fully in order to be priced properly. Yet, this disclosure to the public can destroy, or at least damage, the value of the knowledge by making it readily available. To ensure that the firm receives full value for its intangible knowledge assets, they are kept from public view and restricted to internal markets.

It is also critical to realize that within the company, the marginal cost of exploiting knowledge-based competitive advantages is considerably less than *de novo* development in a region.[40] Knowledge of target markets, such as specific industries, types of individuals, or product types, provides a platform for international growth. Implicit in this discussion with its attention to the costs of organization is the notion that dis-economies of scale serve to act as a brake upon bank expansion.

There is an important international dimension for the fee-driven firm. Banks may enter jurisdictions which allow broader product ranges in order to gain experience with new products. Differing domestic regulation that allows firms to develop skills and market knowledge may be a source of competitive advantage in foreign markets. Prior to "the little bang" of 1987 that destroyed a traditional barrier among the four pillars, could Canadian banks compete on a level field with the universal banks of Germany and Switzerland?[41]

From a simple model-building exercise, the importance of understanding relationships among markets, corporate-level strategy and organizational structure in banking has become apparent. Competition among banks can be understood only in relation to the manner in which corporate-level strategy determines the behaviour of each unit and business-level strategies differ. Further, the role of the interbank market as a market mechanism for establishing equilibrium must be taken into account when evaluating the growth strategies of banks.

The existence of global interbank markets and the manner in which they function serves to direct our attention to another way in which boundaries have been destroyed. Changes in telecommunications and technology have linked the capital markets of most advanced countries. Eurocurrencies, that is, foreign currency deposits in different jurisdictions, such as u.s. dollars in European banks, have allowed financial engineers to create products that limited the effectiveness of various jurisdictions to isolate their domestic capital markets. The new financial world is a global market. The dynamics discussed above must be extended to the global flow of funds and the role in this of New York, London, and Tokyo. This means that any genuine analysis of Canadian banks must take place from a global perspective.[42]

In terms of growth strategies, the incentive to expand to markets with different financial characteristics in order to increase opportunities for intermediation or to sell services becomes apparent. When the essential demand of strategy is to balance, the bank is driven to expand either to different areas or to different segments to correct an existing imbalance, or in two different directions simultaneously to prevent the development of imbalances. The alternative is to limit growth by developing a balanced strategy in one area and searching for similar markets. Only by analysing the complexities of global asset and liability management, the relationship of services to this task, and the dynamics of different capital markets within the global system can the strategic management of a bank be understood. At any one time, the optimal balance point between markets and branches will depend upon the development of different capital markets. As markets become more tightly linked, the incentives to internalize may diminish. Consequently, the strategic decision to internalize or to go interbank must be constantly asked and re-asked as capital markets evolve. It should also be recognized that differing public policy regimes are an important factor in this decision. Although globalization may be the dominant theme, borders do exist. The domestic public policy of the financial services firm's home country still has significant implications for both its international strategy and competitiveness.

RIVALRY AND STRATEGIC
DRIVERS

Within the broad market environments discussed, it is important to analyse the nature of rivalry among banks in order to understand what skills and core competencies will constitute competitive advantage. Let us develop a typology of primary strategic drivers:

1 Loans (assets)
2 Deposits (liabilities)
3 Fee income
4 Balance

The significance of identifying the goals that drive the strategy can be developed by considering how the different banks would view the world. While all banks must be "balanced" because loans must be funded and deposits invested, not all banks act as if "balance" were the primary goal.

The traditional, if passé, manner of ranking banks by asset size suggests that assets are the dominant driver. The asset driven bank would constantly be propelled by the marketing of loans to customers and then the seeking of deposits to fund the loans. The aggressive growth strategy demands high quality loan officers and a thorough understanding of the customer, or the "credit" in order to price the risk properly. To be successful, the borrower must believe that the asset-driven bank provides superior service – that is, a higher quality of service and an equal or lower price – than competitors. If growth is secured through simply pricing lower, then the result is a lower earning and possibly a riskier portfolio. However, lower pricing may offset traditional notions of non-price service quality, as the growth of the Japanese banks in the 1980s demonstrated.

In this time-based industry, such a strategy means that the deposit side will always lag the loan side of the balance sheet. The bank will be forced to buy deposits on terms closer to the depositor's preferences, while pricing loans at rates and terms attractive to borrowers. The Japanese banks lent long and funded short in the Euromarkets in the 1980s. While this strategy does provide superior returns when the yield curve is positive, that is, when short rates are lower than long rates, it also exposes the bank to refunding risk. Consequently, as the Japanese and many others have demonstrated, the strategy will probably lead to gap problems.[43] Such conditions give rise to the fear that there could be a liquidity panic in the interbank market as the short-term liabilities are repeatedly rolled over. This concern has caused Alan Greenspan, chairman of the Federal Reserve, to worry about "Japan-based" risk to United States banks.

As is often the case, however, the very nature of this problem also creates opportunities for financial services institutions. In order to manage the interest or foreign exchange risks that arise from the growth strategy, the treasury department of the bank can develop risk management products "to balance" the portfolio. In turn, these products can be marketed to firms that need to manage these risks. The overall riskiness of the portfolio, consequently, depends upon the sophistication of the asset and liability management and the market conditions for advanced instruments. However, not all firms will choose to be fully insured or "hedged" at all times. The degree of risk is a strategic choice, or at least the result of conscious or unconscious strategic choice.

The above calls attention to "core attributes" of the balance sheet that complement the human-resource-based core competencies. The bank must be perceived as sound. Reputation is a key competitive strength. Moreover, asset growth must be supported by capital growth, or the credit rating of the bank itself will suffer. In the event that this happens, the bank's ability to fund its loans will also suffer. Customers select the banks that are viewed as strong to ensure ongoing access to capital. Rumours of problems can lead to a run on deposits that, in the extreme, can become a liquidity crisis. While regulators have focused upon the capital adequacy of banks, runs on deposits more frequently placed banks in a death spiral. It has been asserted that the Continental Bank of Illinois, the seventh largest bank in the United States, failed because of a run on the bank that was sparked by rumours concerning its solvency.[44] Even if the bank recovers, the need to maintain more liquid assets to meet depositors' demands lowers profitability by forcing that bank to make changes in the asset portfolio to include more low-earning liquid assets.

The deposit-driven bank would price deposits attractively to secure growth and be constrained only by its opportunities to find investments (assets). This is a viable strategy and one pursued by a leading North American bank, the Republic Bank of New York. This bank combines an aggressive drive for deposits with a very conservative asset strategy. The bank has few problems finding secure assets to purchase, given the funding practices of major G7 governments and some (once) highly rated corporations. Other aspects of the strategy mirror that for the asset-driven bank. Reputation for stability is perhaps even more important, as the marketing strategy for the Republic Bank emphasizes. To secure this reputation for soundness, the bank will stress its capital adequacy and ensure that there is always sufficient liquidity to meet depositors' needs.

The fee-driven bank would stress its specialized knowledge and find itself constrained only by the size of the market needing its particular services.[45] It has defined a niche and does not necessarily compete directly with the other two types of banks. Some commercial banks have employed this strategy in recent years; for example, J.P. Morgan and Bankers Trust have moved strongly in this direction by offering investment banking services and the four Canadian banks in this study have all acquired investment banks. The key competitive strength here is human-resource-based: the bank with the best people will win most often. However, even here, capital strength matters. Capital strength is needed to do large deals. In addition, a triple A credit rating is a competitive advantage in the markets for many fee-based products.

The balanced-portfolio bank would be driven to correct the imbalances created by the success of any one strategic thrust. This driver can play out in two different manners. One would be essentially reactive. When the bank becomes too deposit-heavy, it alters its emphasis toward loans, or vice versa. Alternatively, there could be an attempt to balance simultaneously deposit and borrowing rates to produce a flow that yields an asset and liability portfolio that is matched according to the bank's risk preferences.[46] While this manoeuvre sounds difficult, it is possible because of the "time" it takes to finalize a deal. While the account officer is marketing the bank to the loan customer, someone else is scouring funding markets or developing new products to fund the loan in the appropriate manner. The bank's ability to link the two markets dynamically is emphasized rather than the time sequence of loan followed by deposit, or vice versa. In advanced electronic markets, this approach is feasible, and even common. An understanding of the temporal dimension in which competition takes place is fundamental to an understanding of this industry.

There are two implications arising from the above strategic drivers (loans, deposits, and fees) that radically differentiate the three major types of bank products. Either customers would coordinate their use of financial services, and/or interfirm arrangements would develop. Given the complementary nature of the services, banks could form strategic alliances with each other to network various products or services as an alternative to market transactions. At the extreme, the three types of banks could even agree to provide their services in a single location, much as many different companies lease space in the same department store.

One option for an independently balanced bank would be strategic alliances. Clearly, it could form an alliance with fee-driven banks where the latter develop specialized products for the balanced bank's clients. Depending upon the economic characteristics of its market, it could also seek an alliance with the loan- or deposit-driven bank. Finally, the balanced bank could become a "bankers' bank," and develop relations with all three types, maintaining orderly markets through its relations with all.

All banks must select target markets and provide the product range appropriate to their market domains. The selection will guide the location strategy and the resources that are allocated to develop distinctive competencies.[47] It is important to recall that since environments change, the distinctive competencies that are the foundation of competitive advantage must also change over time if a bank is to maintain a strategic fit with its environment.[48] In concrete terms, as the environment around the bank's location changes, the bank must change either its location or its positioning. Market size should allow banks to develop different specializations and consequently, different distinctive competencies. Attention must be focused upon the dynamic nature of strategic management because of the relationship between performance, strategy, and industry structure. While many positions are logically possible, not all are economically feasible.

It should be apparent that the range of services and market segments would allow for a considerable number of differentiated positions. However, the question of what the low-cost producer will look like is not immediately obvious. The answer can only be determined by considering the linkages between non-interest expenses and the three broad product lines. While the determinants of the low-cost producer will be explored in more depth later in this study, it is clear that economies of scope play a role in determining the cost-efficient solution of the market or hierarchies problem.[49] It must also be ascertained what forces will drive industry rivalry.

Given the nature of intermediation, homogeneity will force diversification. It is impossible to intermediate between clients with identical needs. Consequently, the fundamental conditions of the market environment that drive industry structural change must be considered. These are basic forces influencing industry economics, such as technology that affects transactions costs, or demand conditions, such as demographic factors. Both individuals and companies go through phases of being cash generators and cash users at different times of their lives. The viability of different strategies in part depends upon the available market. Even in this simple model, time is an important competitive dimension because of market dynamics. Depending upon the choice of strategic driver, the bank will face different asset-and-liability management problems.

STRATEGIC MANAGEMENT AT
THE CORPORATE LEVEL

Observers of the Canadian scene are probably surprised at the discussion of different types of banks, given that Canada has been dominated by large, primarily asset-driven banks operating in national and international markets. But, assuming economic rationality, why have hierarchies been superior to markets as a form of economic organization in Canadian banking? The importance of economies of both scale and scope are critical.[50] Also critical is the risk diversification created by operating in a number of different, though quite similar economies, and lending to a diversified set of companies and industries. This is especially true in an industry where the loss from a bad loan has a far greater impact upon profitability than the potential profits from a good loan of the same size. Unlike many other types of businesses, banks do not make excess profits from their good loans to offset loan losses, as the interest rate is a contractual agreement.[51] This downside sensitivity imposes limits upon a bank's ability to leverage its specialized knowledge. Excessive specialization produces overly concentrated, risky portfolios. Moreover, if one area is in recession, supernormal spreads do not usually occur elsewhere to offset the bad loan loses. This asymmetry between returns from good and bad loans generally produces a fairly conservative corporate culture in commercial banks.

The point of the earlier radical segmentation of bank products and geographic markets was to develop a focus upon the role of corporate strategy as the mechanism for balancing the overall portfolio of the bank. Branch banking is a Canadian phenomenon that developed in response to the environment confronting the first bankers. The public policy decision that a branch system could provide stability to the financial system that would be attractive to foreign investors while efficiently allocating capital across the nation created market opportunity and management challenge. The bankers that have met those challenges laid the foundation for the current successful corporate strategies. Their actions also led to the relatively late development of a domestic interbank market. Industry evolution and competitive dynamics were significantly affected by the development of a distinctive national branch system.

Recently, Porter has suggested four ways in which corporate strategy can add value to different units. Failure to add value means that markets are the more efficient solution and the breakup value of the firm will exceed its market value. To increase shareholder value, management must be adept in at least one of the following areas:

1 Portfolio management
2 Restructuring
3 Transferring skills
4 Sharing activities[52]

Clearly, as discussed earlier, the bank is involved in portfolio management, but the type of portfolio seems different from that discussed by Porter. The "portfolio" of the bank must be considered from two perspectives: first, in relation to both the risk and return structure, and second, how the product line allows the bank to bundle products in order to create differentiated service packages for clients. The bank is also involved in "restructuring" relative to acquisitions strategies and bank workouts. Banks should have experience with restructuring because of their role in assisting troubled customers back to health. It is interesting to consider whether this makes banks shrewd acquirers.[53] The concepts of portfolio management and restructuring both merit further consideration as strategies for banks.

In order to become proficient in the area of transferring of skills, which is essential for the development of competitive advantage in the new unit, the bank must meet three strategic criteria:

1 It must have proprietary skills in activities important to competitive advantage in target industries.
2 It must accomplish the transfer of skills among units on an ongoing basis.
3 It must acquire beachhead positions in new industries as a base.

The first and second points are important because they emphasize that an acquisition strategy must know what the bank will add to the acquisition. The beachhead position can be a costly failure if it does not provide a platform to leverage core competencies of the bank. Management skills, not financial manipulation, are the key to successful corporate acquisition strategies.

"Sharing activities" are essential if the bank is to achieve the synergies that will allow it to create greater value for customers. Four areas merit consideration:

1 They are activities in existing units that can be shared with new business units to gain competitive advantage.

2 The benefits of sharing these activities outweigh the costs.
3 The ease of sharing activities with an acquired company versus entering the market via the creation of an entirely new venture must be considered.
4 They have the ability to overcome organizational resistance to business unit collaboration.

As can already be seen, these concepts of corporate strategy combine aspects of strategy formulation and implementation. Analyses that correctly identify strategic opportunities will not lead to competitive advantage unless certain horizontal sharing can take place in the organization. In an information-based industry, the effect of sharing should be to improve information flows and lower the costs associated with coordination. Throughout the following discussion, what must be kept in mind is how efficient information flows can lower non-interest costs and thereby alter the optimal boundary for each bank.

The "visible hand" must reduce the barriers that inhibit the transfer of information in the market. For this reason, Porter lists the following prerequisites for "transferring skills":

1 Largely autonomous but collaborative business units
2 High-level corporate staff members who see their role primarily as integrators
3 Cross-business-unit committees, task forces, and other forums to serve as focal points for capturing and transferring skills
4 Objectives of line managers that include skill transfer
5 Incentives based in part on corporate results

For "sharing activities," he lists the following organizational imperatives:

1 Strategic business units that are encouraged to share activities
2 An active strategic planning role at group, sector, and corporate levels
3 High level corporate staff members who see their role primarily as integrators
4 Incentives based heavily on group and corporate results[54]

In the increasingly complicated and sophisticated financial services world, banks must integrate product specialists, including those from outside the banking world, to maintain a competitive portfolio. Relationship banking depends upon the provision of such an integrated package. Banks who fail to fit with their market environment will see real earnings decline. Success in the 1990s will depend upon generating earnings from both interest income and fee-based income while controlling costs. Moreover, banks must be wary of excessive specialization to areas, industries, and products as the exposure to increased volatility can produce devastating loan losses. The four case studies presented in this book will show how Canadian bankers developed and implemented corporate strategies to meet the challenge presented by Porter as well as how they managed the complexities that resulted from their need to increase specialization while maintaining a diversified portfolio.

COMPETITIVE FORCES, REGULATION, AND STRATEGY

The historical method employed in this study allows us to examine not only the initial entry decision of the banks, but also the manner in which the roles assigned to the different units evolved in response to changing competitive environments and corporate strategy. The effects of regulation on how the banks competed also needs to be recognized in making an analysis of their returns, or of profitability from different product lines or businesses.

By using a strategy framework, we are forced to recognize the relationships and interdependencies between the different market segments considered by theorists of the MNB. Banks as financial services firms choose to compete in different segments of the industry. Their choices include whether to enter markets that are international or domestic, or retail or wholesale, which asset-and-liability instruments to employ, and which services to market according to a corporate strategy that balances returns, not only through matching of asset and liabilities, but through diversification into fee-based services that are profitable in their own right. As price competition emerges, banks seek to increase the value added in order to protect profitability. Knowledge of customers' industries is critical to adding value and both allows bankers to assess risk and price properly as well as to demonstrate commitment to the industry.

There are two additional factors driving the development of increasingly sophisticated services. First, there are tremendous changes in information technology.[55] Since information is an essential input, changes in relative positions of suppliers of information and information technology impact upon the industry. Second, buyer knowledge has major impact upon both the type and profitability of services. Increasing sophistication among corporate treasurers and other buyers of bank services has effectively turned loans into "com-modities." The two combine to lower dramatically the transactions costs that have historically been a significant part of the economic rationale for financial intermediation. On the other hand, a legacy of recent high inflation environments has been increased sensitivity to deposit rates by retail customers. The combination has placed pressures on interest spreads in the core business of intermediation.

Consider the effects on market structure of the 1980 Bank Act, which allowed for the entry of foreign banks into the Canadian market place. Such banks had not evolved along lines that would conform to the tenets of public policy as previously set in Canada. Consequently, they were able to target specific segments of the market and "cherry pick." Moreover, these banks introduced cost-of-funds lending and thereby engaged in price competition for loans (asset-driven), while seeking to offer additional services as a source of profits and as a way of differentiating themselves. However, such s-f services should not be viewed as a form of non-price competition, but rather as products designed to increase profits.[56] Sophisticated services were bundled with loans to attract a targeted segment. These new services also called attention to the increasing role of product specialists in banking.

The manner in which technology has altered the spatial boundaries of financial services reveals some fundamental differences about this industry. For example, how can one say where a service is delivered when the transaction electronically links London to Toronto? Technological change has severely limited the abilities of public policy-makers in advanced industrial countries to isolate their domestic capital markets. Product innovation driven by technological change has created the impetus for efforts to reform outdated regulation. Increasingly, public policy-makers have frequently been forced to move from a proactive to a reactive position. In many cases, this change underlies basic concerns about the stability of international financial markets. It has also greatly complicated the strategic task of maintaining alignment with product markets.

The development of global electronic markets means that financial services firms not only exist in a world without borders, but also that the very notion of location and service delivery needs to be rethought.[57] Even though the problem may be common to other information industries, it further complicates analysis. Similar concerns arise from the temporal dimension. The implications of maturity or foreign exchange mismatches reveal that financial services firms do not transform deposits into loans. An approach rooted in economics that applies this framework to financial services ignores marketing and strategic issues. If standard industrial models were to be applied, how could a six-month deposit be transformed into a five-year mortgage? The unique spatio-temporal characteristics of intermediation must be borne in mind if the geographic and risk-management strategies of the Canadian banks are to be understood.

A broader perspective concerning the evolution of MNBS, which is taken by Doz and Prahalad, also bears significantly on this study.[58] Their insight that organizations must adapt both to political and economic imperatives is of major importance to understanding banking. Growth through coordinating flows between different economies demands "global" rationalization, while an independently balanced portfolio bank will be very sensitive to local jurisdiction. However, it should be noted that the impact of the political imperative in this heavily regulated industry is not only felt in host countries. Canadian banks have always been exposed to criticism concerning their "desires" to service various communities, as was clear in Alberta during the Depression. Public criticism that the banks transfer wealth from the Maritimes or the West to central Canada has meant that the banks have had to develop organizational capabilities to ensure legitimacy as well as to manage diversity.

The product line expansion of banks has made provincial regulation more important. The establishment of a brokerage unit by Scotiabank in Montreal was possible because of conflict or confusion between federal and provincial regulators.[59] The federal-provincial struggle for authority over securities regulation demonstrates the ongoing importance of provincial politics for banks. Even if in the past, some areas have been strictly subject only to federal jurisdiction, it would be foolish not to consider the influence of provincial politics upon federal politics. Canadian banks have experienced the two forces in their home country and consequently may have an advantage in dealing with sensitive foreign governments. The centralization and decentralization of decision making in so far as it relates to sensitivity to local conditions is the critical organizational issue that must be addressed.[60]

The strategy framework recognizes the importance of this dimension by discussing how the strategies of domestic banks may differ from subsidiaries of MNBS because the actions of subsidiaries are dictated by the parent's global strategy and not simply the domestic market conditions of the host country.[61] The same is true in Canada. A branch of a national bank is different from a stand-alone local bank. In essence, this suggests that the ties between corporate- and business-level strategy be recognized and that the capability to function in international markets be recognized as a base source of competitive advantage. It also calls attention to the value of corporate identity and a national element in different identities. Analysts do talk of Canadian, German, Swiss, or New York banks: public policy has an impact. The constraints discussed earlier do have real world implications in terms of international competitiveness.

The evolution of the subsidiaries of MNBs should be seen from two perspectives. First, participation in the market allows the bank to acquire new competencies. Second, changes will reflect the evolving global strategy of the bank. It is important to see the interdependent nature of organizational change – the parent and subsidiary do not change independently of one another. Discussion of the various bank histories will focus upon how the organization of the banks responds to new strategies, the increasing need to coordinate the actions of different business units, and the need to economize on non-interest expense. Organizational efficiency is an important element in the cost of providing a new service. A bank with superior information-management capabilities will be able to offer new services far more profitably.[62] In this vein, the analysis of decisions to expand the bank's product line will follow Williamson's markets and hierarchies perspective in the belief that the decisions are economically rational.[63] Strategies of globally competitive banks are guided by economic efficiency in the longer run.

In the following four case studies, which are presented in historical order, we will see the evolution of a leading Canadian industry. The creation of such an industry would not have been possible without talented management and sound regulation.[64] The dialectic between regulated and regulator cannot be without tension as managers seek aggressively to grow, while regulators are governed by the need for caution. However, in most market environments, the Canadian emphasis on stability in financial institutions has been an advantage to the Canadian banks. Our domestic stability has allowed banks to tap into global markets. The development of the Canadian banks and the Canadian economy would not have been possible if our financial institutions were restricted to intermediation in our national capital markets. Understanding how international markets removed growth constraints that were imposed by domestic capital markets is fundamental to an understanding of the development of Canadian banking and the Canadian economy. As we approach the twenty-first century, the traditional values of Canadian banking still promote competitive institutions and we must work to ensure that public policy promotes globally competitive institutions.

CHAPTER TWO

The Bank of Montreal

Our offices in the United Kingdom and the United States, acting in close co-operation with our Business Development Department and our branches in Canada, have been able to make a substantial contribution to the establishment of new industries in Canada through the use of our facilities for supplying information and other forms of assistance.

134th (1951) Annual Report, 32.

As Canada's oldest bank, or first bank as it prefers, the Bank of Montreal begins our historical study. The first bank provides an intriguing opportunity to study the effects of selection of competitive domain and its consequent influence on positioning in the intermediation chain and on organizational structure. The bank's choice of customers and its impact upon positioning in the intermediation chain is of critical importance in understanding the strategy-structure evolution of the organization. By focusing on the effect of strategic positioning it becomes possible to understand more fully not only the distinctive character of the Bank of Montreal, but also that of the other Canadian banks. As always, the choice of positioning in the intermediation chain has implications for returns from the asset portfolio, for the cost structure including both cost of funds and organizational costs, and for difficulties of strategic repositioning to meet the demands of changing markets.

THE FOUNDING AND INITIAL EXPANSION: 1817–22[1]

The Bank of Montreal opened its doors on 3 November 1817. The event culminated twenty-five years of effort to form a joint stock bank to service the trading companies of the city. The mercantile system of the British Empire combined with the activities of the Hudson's Bay Company and the North West Company made Montreal an important port for the transshipment of various raw materials, including agricultural produce and furs.[2] Yet, even at this early time, the trade patterns of Montreal were not limited to British-sanctioned trade routes. The city was also the centre for a lively trade with Vermont and other parts of New England, as well as with Upper Canada. Banking services were needed to develop the trade upon which Montreal's prosperity depended.

Despite some old popular beliefs as to the role of the Scots in Canadian banking, the origins of the Bank of Montreal reveal a distinct u.s. influence.[3] Two of the initial founding directors had extensive experience in the United States: Scottish-born John Richardson in New York and the Midwest and Horatio Gates, a New England merchant.[4] The importance of the u.s. connection was such that the bank could not have opened its doors but for resources secured from u.s. sources. However, one key founding director from Montreal, George Moffat, was later to play a far more major role in the development of the bank than these Americans. Of the initial seven paid employees, only one, Henry B. Stone, had any practical banking experience.[5] Interestingly, Stone was not expected to stay with the bank since he was on temporary loan to the bank's directors from mercantile friends in Boston. Perhaps even more importantly, however, the stock issue met with a cool reception in Montreal. The élite in Quebec City and Upper Canada, prominent French Canadians (with few exceptions), and important businessmen such as John Molson and Thomas Torrance in Montreal did not subscribe. Gates was only able to secure the initial capitalization by placing nearly 50 per cent of the stock in New York City, Boston, and other New England centres. Presumably these investors were supportive of Alexander Hamilton's ideas for u.s. banking, which the Montreal proposal closely resembled.[6]

Hamilton had argued for the creation of a strong private national bank with branches throughout the United States. Stability would be ensured by a strong capital base and this stability would allow the bank to manage centrally the government's credit needs to promote a strong currency. A healthy national institution dominating the financial sector would promote private sector economic growth. Although there would be government participation in the bank, it would be a private institution.

In his history of the Bank of Montreal, Merrill Denison attributed the initial success of the bank to its informed foreign-exchange operations and the increased local use of its services, especially by the government. The ties that developed between the bank and the government, coupled with the government's opposition to new banks, made a branch in Quebec City a necessity. The directors acted quickly to pre-empt the market and passed a resolution to establish a parallel organization in the capital ten days after the opening of the Montreal office. Other early moves included the establishment of an agency in Boston in 1818 and the development of close connections with banking houses in London and New York by 1819. There was also some expansion into Upper Canada, as the board offered agencies to Thomas Markland in Kingston and William Allan in York. Legislation of 19 January 1824 that gave the Bank of Upper Canada a monopoly on note issue led to the Bank of Montreal's withdrawal from the market.

The manner in which the bank was founded offers several important lessons. First, the initial opportunity was international and the development of international expertise was essential for success in Canada. Second, u.s. influences played a major role in the establishment and strategy of the bank. Third, government policy promoted the development of branching as a growth strategy. Denison held that branching was not imported, but was rather a response to Canadian conditions. Fourth, government was one of the most important clients, if not *the* most important. Last, restrictions from other "Canadian" jurisdictions promoted a natural focus on other geographically close markets, especially those in the United States.

THE TRANSFORMATION OF
THE BANK: 1824–52

The Royal Charter of 1822 which incorporated the "President, Directors and the Company of the Bank of Montreal" changed the bank from a private to a public company and set forth its powers and obligations. Interestingly, the charter was to continue only until 1 June 1831 unless the government decided to establish a provincial bank. In this event, the charter would be vacated in seven years. Incorporation by means of the charter further gave rise to the distinctive Canadian term of "chartered banking" and a tradition of renewable rather than permanent charters.

Certain clauses in the charter reveal criticisms being levelled at banks. Changes in banking regulations demonstrated concern with foreign control – an important theme in the history of Canadian banking. Fortunately, by this time only 10 per cent of the Bank of Montreal's shares were held in the United States.[7] There was also concern about loans to foreign governments, which were now expressly prohibited in the new regulations. Finally, there was concern that the bank and its two competitors, the Quebec Bank in Quebec City and the Bank of Canada in Montreal, were diverting funds from Quebec City to favoured borrowers in Montreal. Perceptions concerning the relationship between the deposit and loan strategies led to public criticism because the local public believed its funds were being diverted to "foreigners." Such concerns have a long and abiding history in Canada. Examination into charges of favouritism were to lead to important changes in the bank.

As is often the case, financial problems created the impetus for organizational change. Although the bank survived the 1820s better than many u.s. or British banks, there were severe losses in 1824, and the first overall loss led to the suspension of dividend payments in 1826. George Moffat, a founding director of the bank, believed that the losses of 1824 were principally attributable to favouritism to the North West Company group on the part of the bank's president, Samuel Gerard.[8] Moffat moved to limit the power of the president and to clean up lax management practices by making the board of directors truly responsible. While there may have been some personal animus involved, Moffat was making a strategic realignment to establish relationships with the new commercial generation in Montreal, while working simultaneously to improve management. The election of John Molson, Jr. to the board in 1824 recognized these important changes.

The trauma of 1824 affected the presidential chair. In 1826, Moffat charged that Gerard had been guilty of illegal actions on two counts. First, he had granted discounts on his own responsibility and second, he had allowed a borrower to exceed the debt ceiling of £10,000. By a vote of five to four, the board agreed and Gerard was impeached. Horatio Gates briefly succeeded Gerard as president in 1826. It appears that Gates agreed to serve only on an interim basis until his successor, John Molson, Sr. could be persuaded to accept the post. Moffat succeeded in limiting the discretion of officers and with tighter supervision, it became possible to ensure that emerging business sectors received appropriate attention. This centralization of decision making was necessary to restore balance to the loan and deposit portfolios.

It is important to note that the changes in the presidential chair were linked to Moffat's rising power within the bank. Now, he had a board of directors and a president upon whom he could rely. Further organizational change followed. Perhaps the most important was that initiated in 1826 when the by-laws were amended to give the cashier more responsibility and to pay the president, the chief executive officer, an annual salary. The appointment of Benjamin Holmes as cashier in 1827 marked a new style of management, as in effect Holmes became the general manager and was virtually in complete charge of day-to-day operations. The separation of the strategic from the operational within the organization marked an milestone development in the history of Canadian banking.

The new organizational strength led to a wave of prosperity between 1826 and 1860, under the leadership of four presidents: John Molson, Sr. (1826–30); John Fleming (1830–32); Horatio Gates (1832–34); and Peter McGill (1834–60). After Molson had established harmony, the presidents embarked on important strategic initiatives. Fleming's regime witnessed the use of the New York call loan market to employ excess liquidity profitably, which demonstrated the critical importance of the relationship between funding and lending strategies and the need for u.s. capital markets. Gates arranged for the absorption of the Bank of Canada, of which he was a director, by the Bank of Montreal in 1831. He also established an important position for the bank as the "bankers' bank" in 1833 when he marketed its foreign exchange capabilities to the newly chartered City Bank. Sophisticated services were key competitive advantages in the differentiating strategy.

In an era without a central bank, the Bank of Montreal acted virtually as the government bank, a position that demanded a high level of liquidity at all times. Liquidity became a recurring theme in the annual reports and is one that persists to this day.[9] All of the presidents continued to develop correspondent relations with foreign banks and to ensure that the leading commercial houses of Montreal were represented on the board.

One reason for increasing prosperity was the growing British interest in North America, which in 1836 led to the creation of a formidable competitor, the Bank of British North America (BBNA). The operations of the BBNA made an interesting contrast to those of the Bank of Montreal. While this bank initially hired its staff from England, it later recruited personnel from Scotland. In this process it introduced to Canadian banking some Scottish practices, such as offering cash credits and interest on inactive deposit accounts. The hiring practices of the BBNA also helped to stem the u.s. influence on Canadian banking. The BBNA paid its Scottish managers only £400 annually while the Bank of Montreal paid its locally recruited managers £900, plus various perquisites – a sum more in line with u.s. salaries. Recruiting from the old country thus not only offered a way to establish and maintain good relations with the growing immigrant population, it further provided a significantly lower cost of operations. A secondary effect may have been to promote a more internationally oriented corporate culture.

In 1837 the Canadian economy collapsed, largely because of events in Ireland and England that revealed problems in the international credit system. The financial crisis that followed the peak of the business cycle was exacerbated by problems in the u.s. market. As is often the case in times of financial crisis, there was a flight to quality. Paper was being rejected and hard currency was being demanded. These global demands for hard currency created the threat of a species drain on the Quebec banks. The Bank of Montreal recognized the dangers early and organized the other banks to act together to suspend specie payments to avoid a run on the banks that would have damaged the banking system.

Such was not the case in Upper Canada. The lieutenant-governor of Upper Canada, Sir Francis Bond Head, demanded that the redemption of notes in specie be continued as a matter of national honour. The immediate effect was a run on the banks and commercial collapse. The Bank of Upper Canada requested help from the Bank of Montreal in the form of £40,000 in Bank of Montreal notes against interest-bearing notes of the Bank of Upper Canada, payable in Montreal. This was the only hope of the Bank of Upper Canada to meet their customers' demands. After careful consideration, the Bank of Montreal advanced £50,000. The Bank of Montreal's actions limited the disaster consequences that resulted from Head's policy.

The crisis demonstrated the importance of the bank in two ways: first, it provided assistance that was critical for the survival of the Bank of Upper Canada and second, it acted to ensure that proper banking practices were followed throughout the crisis. This was done even when the government of Lower Canada requested it to modify the strict and sound policies on specie payment it had adopted to prevent a financial crisis from precipitating further economic crises. Not only was the bank the "bankers' bank," it acted as the leading financial institution in the Canadas.

Benjamin Holmes, the general manager, was granted a leave of absence to serve in Parliament as a new era in Canada was ushered in by the Act of Union (1841). Public spirit was not the sole motivation, as it was hoped that Holmes would secure three objectives: the renewal of the Bank of Montreal's charter; the circumvention of the intention of the governor-general, Lord Sydenham, to establish a provincial bank of issue; and the opposition of the designs of the lords of the treasury to have sterling adopted as the Canadian standard. This last point attested to the importance of the ongoing and extensive u.s. relationship with the Bank of Montreal.

Holmes was appointed to the currency and banking committee which drafted the new currency and banking legislation passed by the first parliament of the Province of Canada in 1841. The legislation met with the Bank of Montreal's wishes. Unfortunately, Lord Sydenham reserved royal assent on the the bill renewing the Bank of Montreal's charter and others, including one which would allow province-wide branching for banks originally chartered to operate only in either Lower or Upper Canada. Lord Sydenham's accidental death led to a difficult situation that lasted until Sir Charles Bagehot arrived in Kingston and proclaimed the currency and banking laws on 27 April 1842.

The Bank of Montreal had acted in anticipation of the political changes. In 1840, it had acquired all the stock of a private bank, the Bank of the People (Toronto). Since legislation prior to the new act proclaimed in 1842 prevented the Bank of Montreal from operating a branch in the province, the Bank of the People was operated as a wholly owned subsidiary. In 1842, the bank responded to the new conditions and amalgamated the Bank of the People with its operations in Amherstburg, Cobourg, St Catharines, and St Thomas into the parent bank. By the early 1840s, the bank was reorganized and prepared to participate fully in Canada West.

Public works projects, such as the Welland Canal, which were largely financed by foreign capital, created economic growth and tremendous lending opportunities in Canada West. Although a newcomer there, the Bank of Montreal was successful in obtaining a majority of the loans. The result was expansion of the Toronto and other Canada West branches, as well as a raising of their credit limits. The expansion necessitated that central controls be developed to direct the far flung operations. In 1844 head office staff increased from 7 in 1817 to 16 and William Gunn began the process of branch inspection, although the formal position of Inspector of the Branches was not adopted until 1852.

The bank's ties with the government strenthened in 1843 when it aided the government in the practical administration of the canal loans. At roughly the same time, the bank became involved with Montreal's municipal finances as it expanded its involvement with the public sector. As has often been the case in large and complex public works projects, expenditures began to exceed what many viewed as already excessively large budgeted amounts. After hearing from the bank's manager in Hamilton that collections from the government on the canal contractors' notes were slow, Holmes investigated and learned that the funds from the Imperial loan that provided the funds for the canal were nearly exhausted. He subsequently informed the government that the bank would instruct its agents to refuse further advances to contractors. The problem did not go away and in late 1845, an order-in-council listing the banks eligible to receive deposits for the receiver general did not contain the Bank of Montreal's name. A heated and public debate, including personal attacks upon Holmes in the newspapers, followed. Eventually, although he was personally vindicated of any wrongdoing, Homes resigned from the bank stating that hostility directed against him in the public press made his connection detrimental to the bank's interests.

The intense and hostile public scrutiny had its effect on the bank's public image. In response to the battle, the bank would no longer advertise in the press beyond statutory requirements and even refused to have Holme's rebuttal to his attackers published. This withdrawal from the public arena contributed to the image of an institution that did not view itself as accountable to the public. The new aloof reputation stayed with the bank.

Changes in u.s. policy and the development of the Erie Canal had important implications. By 1845, the u.s. government had begun to treat Canada as a separate entity, and not merely as an adjunct to Great Britain. With the opening of the Erie Canal, there was a shift in trade routes: grain from the Canadian West no longer had to be transshipped through Montreal. u.s. connections became even more critical for financing Canadian trade.

By 1859, the Bank of Montreal was the third largest bank in terms of capitalization in North America. The New York Bank of Commerce was the largest at $9 million, followed by the Louisiana's Citizens' Bank at $6.7 million, and then the Bank of Montreal at $6 million. The inflow of foreign capital that developed the economic infrastructure of Canada, the Crimean War and reciprocity trading with the United States all played a part in creating the environment that fostered the bank's growth. Estimates of foreign capital entering Canada in the 1850s range from $60 to $100 million for the railroads. The sources of the inflows were varied. One was $10 million in military payments from Great Britain. There was also significant u.s. investment in lumbering and manufacturing.

At the same time as capital was flowing in, the conditions under which banks could lend were changing. Changes in banking legislation requested by the business community and the banks allowed banks to accept a wider variety of security as the first steps to a broader level of commercial financing were taken. In 1859 the Act Granting Additional Facilities in Commercial Transactions allowed banks to lend on bills of lading and warehouse receipts and to acquire ownership in the pledged goods and hold ownership for up to six months in case of default.[10]

The effect of the above was to ensure that the bank's strategic orientation was to the West: it had little to do with the West Indies or to other aspects of Canadian trade. A further change came with the acquisition of the Montreal Savings Bank in 1856. A new market was entered: that of the small depositor. The increased complexity that resulted from this expansion of services led to efforts to increase control over the staff. In 1852, the office of Inspector of Branches was formally created and staffed by branch managers on a two-year rotating basis. This proved to be unsatisfactory and the board looked for a full time person. They found one in the person of Edwin H. King, who was then assistant general manager of the BBNA.

THE KING YEARS: 1852–73

Merrill Denison considered that the arrival of King was a "red letter" day for the bank. Not only did he end the lax practices that had developed during the recent period of growth by instituting new control systems, but he also established the basis for a new training system. Previously the bank had followed a policy of providing essentially life-time employment. Under King, however, while dismissals were rare, the frequency of promotions and transfers to other branches was increased. Efficiency was improved by offering training programs and making efforts, such as increased pay, to keep the trained employees on staff. In the expanding market of the 1850s, this was an important move.

Growth created pressures for organizational development. Increased complexity brought about another change in the organizational development. The cashier was relieved of his duties for local Montreal business and a new manager was appointed for the branch. By 1860, it was clear that head office was not like any other branch, but was responsible for the entire bank. The organizational changes showed continuity with the expansion of the head office staff in 1844 and that the bank was adapting to its new environment.

Increasing trade with the United States made it economical to open an agency in New York. In many ways, this was not a radical move, because the bank already had extensive international experience and had been operating in the Chicago grain markets since the 1840s. Nonetheless, the decision to make loans against commercial name paper (with the approval of head office) signalled a new assault on the U.S. market.

By 1861, Charles Smithers was appointed agent in Chicago and the bank found itself in possession of real estate properties, security for loans that had gone sour as the effects of the American Civil War hit the u.s. economy.[11] While the bank was prohibited by legislation from lending to the Union, a foreign government, it did take advantage of opportunities created by the conflict in foreign-exchange markets. A distinctive competence that had developed from the bank's origin contributed handsomely to profits.

A signal event occurred for the bank on 19 November 1863 for it was on that day the bank captured the business of the government. The bank was selected for five reasons: it had a large capital base, an extensive branch system, and experience in government finance. It also had established and respected facilities in New York, and connections in London. A solid relationship was established between the bank and the government since the latter was on shaky standing and needed the support of the bank's sterling reserves to maintain its credit in London. Sir Alexander Tilloch Galt, the minister of finance, and his government would remember the debt incurred and continued to favour the bank in better times.

King recognized the importance of the bank's international connections for its domestic business. The two largest accounts, the government and the Grand Trunk Railway both depended upon the London money market. Consequently, during his 1866 trip to England, King reorganized and strengthened correspondent relationships with the Bank of Liverpool (a connection that had been established in 1838). He also extended the international reach of the bank into India and China via ties with the Oriental Bank, into Ireland via the National Bank of Scotland, and the Caribbean via the Colonial Bank.

Following the end of the American Civil War, the bank had to adjust to various changes, such as the advent of Greenbacks and Galt's decision to end the privilege of issuing notes in Canada. In essence, Galt's action freed up $3 million of the bank's assets for other purposes. Merrill Denison held the view that the terms of the agreement with the government made the Bank of Montreal both treasurer and overlord of the other Canadian banks. As such, the bank more closely resembled England's central bank, the Bank of England, than any North American bank. The closeness of the ties was demonstrated in 1866 when the government requested that the bank send officers to St John and Halifax to receive revenues and make disbursements.

The bank acted in what was virtually an "official" capacity during the crisis of the Commercial Bank in 1867. While the bank offered assistance, it could not convince a sufficient number of other banks to join in and save the Commercial and the government would not intercede. In the aftermath of the failure, E.H. King argued for stricter banking regulation to prevent future failures. The Bank of Montreal had credibility because it had criticized the unsound banking practices in Canada West and had avoided engaging in the disguised real estate loans that were the cause of the bank failures. In addition, King made significant contributions to government policies designed to secure a sound currency. Such actions, of course, created entry barriers that promoted a sound Canadian system.

Under King there was a significant expansion of international operations. The bank was second only to Brown Brothers and Co. of New York in supplying foreign exchange in New York. After a visit from King, assets in New York jumped from $1.2 million to $8.85 million, over half of which represented gold obtained from head office. Canadian banks supplied almost half of the available gold on Wall Street and of the $10 million that was supplied by all Canadian banks, the Bank of Montreal supplied roughly $7.8 million. Such actions marked the leader.

King was spurred on by a unique contract that featured profit sharing. The approval of this feature by the board of directors demonstrated an unusual understanding for the time and for commercial banking of the entrepreneurial spirit. It must be stressed that the move to New York was profit-driven. Denison concluded:

A major cause of its expansion had been given in the annual report of 1866, where it was stated that the Canadian usury laws "encourage the banks to prefer foreign and mercantile transactions rather than advances depending on local industry for repayment, with the object of keeping surplus funds more under command for employment in better money markets as occasions arise." Later that year, the Provincial Note Act had provided the Bank with further "surplus funds" for use in the more sophisticated New York market.[12]

We can only wonder what effects this outflow of savings had on Canadian industrial formation and entrepreneurship.

In 1869, President T.B. Anderson resigned and King became president, the first professional banker to become the chief executive officer. Unfortunately, his early tenure was marred by a change in relations with the government occasioned by the introduction of reserve requirements in 1870. King saw this as nothing more than a tax and expressed his displeasure. This created a certain tension with the government officials responsible for the policy.

Confederation expanded the domestic market and the result was an expansion of the banking system. The Bank of Montreal, however, did not pursue growth for the sake of growth, but rather limited itself to governments and large clients in the railroad, lumber, or industrial sectors of the economy. The bank was intent upon maintaining its reputation in foreign trade and as a "bankers' bank."

International operations were expanded with the opening of a branch in London in 1870.[13] The purpose of this move was to facilitate the transfer of stock and payment of dividends in England, to develop and facilitate two-way trade, and to provide safe employment for surplus funds. The branch was managed by a London committee and employees were recruited locally. Growth was rapid as the Franco-Prussian War created money market opportunities similar to those in New York during the Civil War. In addition, booms in the Chicago grain market led to the reopening of a Chicago agency. Changes in banking legislation that allowed the bank to lend to foreign governments led to a growing involvement in the u.s. bond market and growth of foreign assets.

PUBLIC FINANCING, MERGERS, AND MANAGEMENT CHANGE: 1873–1935

King's resignation in 1873 did little to slow internationalization.[14] The new president was David Torrance, a man of Scottish parents who had been born in New York City. He inherited an experienced management team in New York, Chicago, and London and in 26 branches. One reason for the international outlook of the bank may have been its willingness to hire foreign nationals, especially u.s. citizens. Although 1873 was not a good year for banking because problems in the small commercial discounting sector created a panic, the bank found itself relatively unscathed due to its lack of participation in those markets. The continued involvement, and even expansion, of the bank's role in public finance was demonstrated in 1874 when the bank acted as underwriters for a loan on the London market for the Province of Quebec. This was followed by a similar transaction for the city of Montreal.

Upon Torrance's death in 1876, George Stephen, later Baron Mount Stephen, became president. Stephen was responsible for expanding the bank's role in underwriting when an issue for the Province of Quebec was placed on the New York money market. The bank had outbid London bankers in order to place the issue on its merits in the New York market. This was an historic first and showed the tremendous vitality of the institution.

The growth of the international sector enhanced the bank's image as the "bankers' bank." During a rash of business failures in 1875–78, the bank used its foreign reserves to assist Canadian banks and industries. In addition, the $14.4 million balance maintained by the bank in New York gave it the ability to provide trade services to others, since it clearly had the resources to do large deals. Operations in New York helped to ensure the orderly flow of capital between the two countries.

In 1881, Stephen resigned as president in order to take over the Canadian Pacific Railway (CPR) and C.F. Smithers was appointed president. This signalled the beginning of an ongoing relationship with the CPR that involved acting both as a lender and as an agent for the government. Interestingly, the bank kept the Grand Trunk as a client, although its loans to the CPR totalled $11.5 million. Fear of losing business from the Grand Trunk had inhibited the actions of other banks. As was typical with Canadian development, the CPR served to bring massive inflows of capital into Canada. Fifty per cent of its shares were held in the United States, 15 per cent in Great Britain, 15 per cent in Europe, and only the remaining 20 per cent in Canada. The bank's involvement with this massive Canadian project as well as its cautious lending practices to the railway, were typical of its activities at this time.

In 1887, Donald A. Smith, Baron Strathcona and Mount Royal, became president of the bank and shortly came to realize the practical importance of portfolio diversification. Poor harvests in the years 1889 and 1890 created economic problems in Canada that were somewhat alleviated for the bank by its ability to repatriate $6.8 million from abroad. There were also organizational changes when a pension plan for employees was introduced in 1884 and the Bank of Montreal was appointed as the clearing bank for the clearing-house established in Montreal in 1889. The major result of the new clearing operations was to reduce the time taken for clearing from half a day to under one hour. The improved operations were similar to the experiences of clearing-houses in Halifax (1887), and Toronto and Hamilton (1889); they resulted in a drop of cash balances at the branches and promoted a more efficient use of funds. The Canadian industry was thus becoming an efficient one.

The 1890s saw two other important changes. First, savings deposit collection was extended to all branches in 1891, expanding the service line. Second, the bank scored a major coup when it was appointed the government's fiscal agent in London in 1892. The government believed, or had become convinced, that the bank could provide the same services that had been offered by the government's London bankers.

As the new century dawned, there were tremendous banking opportunities available because of burgeoning western development as the prairies were being developed.[15] By 1905, the bank felt the need to have a president who was resident at head office. Lord Strathcona, who was then the president, had been resident in London since 1896 when he had been appointed high commissioner. During his tenure, he had done an excellent job of attracting British capital to Canada and had contributed to the bank while living in London. His successor as president was Sir George Drummond. Under Drummond, the bank, as was typical, did not seek to open branches in every possible location but rather limited itself to those of strategic importance. It had established closer relations with the Royal Trust Company in 1903 by appointing it as agent for the issue and registration of Bank of Montreal stock. The bank recognized that the increased volume of various financial transactions could support further specialization in capital markets.

The Bank of Montreal had achieved an impressive stature by 1908 and had 142 branches and agencies. Mergers with the Exchange Bank of Yarmouth (1903), the People's Bank of Halifax (1905), and the takeover of the Ontario Bank (1906) had served to increase branch coverage within Canada. Staff had increased from 300 in the 1880s to over 1,000 by 1908 and had led to the building of a new head office in 1905 in Montreal. In addition, the development of the Mexican Light, Heat and Power Company under its president, James Ross, formerly of the CPR, led to the opening of a branch in Mexico City to take advantage of foreign exchange opportunities. An eleven-storey building in New York was also acquired to accommodate expanded operations there.

In 1910 Drummond was succeeded by R.B. Angus, who ably guided the bank until 1913, when he was succeeded by Sir Vincent Meredith. Meredith's tenure was marked not only by the task of guiding the bank through World War I, but also by an important administrative change. Meredith and his general manager, Sir Frederick Williams-Taylor, functioned together as a management team and pooled their complementary experiences. In addition, Meredith's appointment marked the end of an era when managers without experience in New York could rise to the top; after World War I, the importance of New York as a financial centre was significantly greater. Despite their lack of experience in New York, however, both Meredith and Williams-Taylor did have international experience.

Prior to the outbreak of the war, Meredith had occasion to announce some other developments. In 1913, external auditors were appointed to assure shareholders that proper banking practices had been established and were being followed. The BBNA had been using such auditors for several years and had demonstrated the efficacy of such a measure. Moreover, the change was required under the new Bank Act since four out of six Canadian failures had involved fraud.[16] The onus was placed upon the banks to appoint auditors because the government feared it would be held liable if it acted as the supervising agency. The use of private means was meant to ensure that the government was not held directly responsible by outraged depositors and shareholders for bank failures.

A new London branch was opened to service travellers and, followed by a second branch to assist servicemen. From Denison's account, it would seem that the branches served as both a meeting place for Canadians and a convenient mail drop. Once again, the bank saw its mandate as extending beyond the mere provision of banking services. By 1913, the tremendous boom of capital flowing into Canada was subsiding and the bank's rate of growth was slowing.

The war years were an impetus to the banking system. The branch system was seen by the nation as a convenient conduit for selling securities to support the war effort, and the value of the distribution network was recognized. As a result, although there was growth in the system, there was a fundamental shift in asset portfolios as banks increased their securities rather than their loan portfolio. At the same time, there was a general expansion of deposits as savings increased. The performance of the chartered banks during this difficult period demonstrated to the nation that a central bank was not necessary.

In 1918, the bank merged with the BBNA and thereby acquired good personnel and 79 new branches, including one in San Francisco that had been established in 1864. The merger in conjunction with the demands created by the increase of deposits and a new agency in Paris led to reorganization of the bank on a regional and client basis. The executive ranks were expanded from one to four assistant general managers: one for Quebec, the Maritimes and Newfoundland, one for the BBNA, one for London, and one for Ontario.

During the 1920s, Meredith was responsible for guiding the bank through several important mergers. First, in 1920, a substantial interest in the Colonial Bank was purchased to fill out the branch network and to provide representation in the West Indies and West Africa. In 1921, the financially troubled Merchants Bank of Canada with its nationwide system of over 400 branches was acquired.

Approximately one-sixth of the branches were deemed either unprofitable or redundant and were promptly closed. Finally, the Molson Bank was taken over, a major acquisition that was ratified at a special meeting in 1924. This move resulted in the addition of 117 branches in Ontario and Quebec, as well as 8 new branches. By 1925, the branch system of the Bank of Montreal totalled 617 service outlets.

Postwar growth led to major internal reorganization. Commencing in 1920, the need was recognized for specialized departments to provide both increased efficiency and improved customer relations. In 1919, the Foreign department was created, and in the 1920s, Foreign Exchange, Routine Efficiency, Bank Premises, and Special Debts departments were all created. The importance of New York was signalled in 1926, when the Montreal Company of New York was created as a wholly owned subsidiary to engage in the underwriting and distribution of investment securities in the United States.[17]

Another tactic used to improve relations with both clients and employees was the production of new publications. The bank had issued circulars during the war to improve employee morale and continued this practice afterward. However, the real change was with the bank's attitude to the public. The move was made necessary by expansion of the branch system that followed the acquisition of the Merchants and the Molson banks. Following the dispute mentioned earlier between Holmes and the government, the bank had maintained an aloof posture. But, at the 1926 annual meeting, the general manager, Williams-Taylor, called attention to a number of popular pamphlets on topics as diverse as business conditions and scientific farming: "Not all of these services perhaps are directly remunerative, but we believe they have all been of very definite value. They are broadening the facilities available to our clients, creating goodwill, and demonstrating that the Bank is keenly concerned in the public welfare and in furthering the general interests of this country."[18] As was often the case, the bank took a statesman-like position while promoting its public image. In a more pedestrian manner, these pamphlets could be seen as a form of marketing or non-price competition.

Sir Charles Blair Gordon became president in 1927, but that year marked extensive changes in the executive level. Sir Vincent Meredith retained the position of chief executive and became the first chairman of the board and chairman of a newly created executive committee. At the same time two vice presidents were elected: Huntly R. Drummond, the son of a former president, and S.C. Mewburn. The four men constituted the new executive committee that was intended to strengthen the management of the bank.

The Depression was a difficult time for all, especially for banks who were seen as refusing to lend the money that they had. The Bank of Montreal maintained that it would lend to creditworthy borrowers, but that such were hard to find. In such a situation, low-yielding securities came to play a more major role in the asset portfolio. In addition the Bank of Canada Act of 1934, in creating a central bank, created a changed environment. Denison held that this Act closed one chapter of the bank's life and opened a new one. The bank would no longer fulfil many of the roles played by central banks such as the Bank of England. It would have to find an identity other than the government's bank.

DEVELOPING A NEW STRATEGY: 1935-59

President Gordon was challenged to develop a new strategy during the tail-end of the Depression. The asset portfolio was adjusted by increasing the percentage share of government securities which lowered the profitability of the banks. However, he also directed attention to some major strategic themes. The bank stressed the importance of mining and natural resources to the future of Canada in conjunction with the need for maintaining trade with the United States, as well as the importance of obtaining foreign capital for Canadian development.[19] The bank built upon its competitive advantages in international trade promotion to become an active participant in the development of the mining sector.

Government connections continued to play a role as the bank participated actively in the government-backed Home Improvement Loan Programme.[20] Naturally, by the end of Gordon's tenure in 1939, war financing had led it to increase government securities in its asset portfolio. During the war years, any portfolio adjustment toward corporate lending was difficult. There was further evidence of increased government involvement when the bank was appointed as an authorized agent of the foreign-exchange control board.

The period was also interesting because of changes in personnel practices. Remarks such as the following taken from the 120th (1937) Annual Report indicated early attempts to employ internal marketing: "Permanency of employment, in particular, is a feature of this Bank's policy." In addition, the policy of internal promotion and the importance of training for advancement were stressed. The annual reports of the period addressed employees as well as shareholders.

Huntly R. Drummond, president from 1939 to 1942 and chairman of the board from 1942 to 1946, guided the bank through the war years. The erratic nature of appointing chairmen of the board should be noted, as Drummond filled a post that had been vacant since 1929.[21] During this period, the contribution of George W. Spinney, president from 1942 to 1948, and his government work should not be minimized in recognizing the continuity of the bank's close ties with the government.[22]

As could be expected, World War II led to a highly liquid portfolio and to staffing problems. The extent of such problems were apparent in the 123rd (1940) Annual Report where it was observed that 500 people had been hired to replace the 300 who had joined the service.[23] However, there did appear to be some benefits from the necessary increase in training. The 129th (1946) Annual Report praised the teamwork of the staff, but conceded that increased mechanization and routinization were instrumental in the bank's ability to process increasing volumes of work. The bank also rationalized its entire branch system inspired by the federal government's policy of conserving manpower.[24] This critical examination of the system fostered by the external crisis of the war improved the efficiency of operations and demonstrated the importance of environmental fit for successful strategies. Economic efficiency demanded that the services that were provided matched customer's actual needs.

The war years had major implications for lending practices. The 127th (1944) Annual Report commented upon changes in banking legislation that widened the scope of lending activities to farmers, fishermen and businessmen. The legislation meant that banks would now be allowed to play a broader role in financing. The importance of this measure was made clear near the end of the war in the 128th (1945) Annual Report, which discussed a move toward longer-term notes to finance plant conversion and other capital expenditures of business. Both the effects of war on industry and the high liquidity in the banks made such a change feasible and desirable. The 129th (1946) Annual Report discussed new markets. Increased commercial and personal loans were being marketed and were assisted by an advertising program rated the highest in North America by an independent agency.

In 1947, President Spinney commented upon the nature of banking and the changing environment:

I might also add that it is at a time like the present that the practical value of the highly personal relationship between banker and customer becomes most fully apparent. One speaks of the "extension of credit" in abstract terms, but banking can never be conducted impersonally with a rule book and on a production-line basis. Every situation has its individual aspects, and in meeting each one intangible factors of character and personal knowledge arising out of experience are given due weight. I know of no business less fitted to the routine techniques of bureaucracy than banking.[25]

Only experienced bankers with a knowledge of the client were capable of adjusting to this type of lending.

A new, or renewed, interest in Latin America surfaced in the 124th (1941) Annual Report. The 128th (1945) Annual Report informed the reader that a review of foreign operations was under way which had included making a tour of Latin America and the West Indies as well as developing new thinking on the Far East. Since the bank believed that most countries in these areas would develop their own banking institutions, its intent was to establish correspondent relations with them. This strategic move was strongly reinforced in the 129th (1946) Annual Report, which also emphasized how the bank's presence in London, New York, Chicago, and San Francisco provided a strong base for expansion. The decision to go with a correspondent strategy became a major determinant of the bank's international location strategy.

B.C. Gardner became president in 1948 and was chairman of the board from 1952 to 1954. The traditional emphasis on the importance of trade and the need for Canada to combat inflation in order to stay competitive in global markets was a recurring theme in the annual reports of these years. Perhaps the most visible change could be seen on the cover of the 1950 Annual Report where the promotional phrase "My Bank" was used. This signalled a conscious effort on the part of the bank not to appear solely interested in big business and government. The annual reports, however, continued to stress how intimate knowledge of the client's business needs was a prerequisite to providing "constructive advice" to the larger and even some some smaller customers. There was also discussion of "decentralization" in conjunction with the emphasis on new types of lending. The general manager, Gordon Ball, asserted in the 131st (1948) Annual Report that 99 per cent of the bank's loans were being made at the branch level. At the same time, it was recognized that "decentralization" and new services increased the necessity of training staff. The annual reports often linked discussions of global competition and Canada's need to improve productivity. In this context, the bank recognized that it must increase its own efforts to control costs and to increase efficiency. At the same time, dispersed operations and product-line expansion produced strong forces of centralization in order to maintain balanced portfolios and operational efficiencies.

The most interesting statements of this era concerned international banking. There was an almost continuous concern with inflows of u.s. capital and the need to maintain such capital to finance Canadian development. Ball made the following statement in the 134th (1951) Annual Report: "Our offices in the United Kingdom and the United States, acting in close co-operation with our Business Development Department and our branches in Canada, have been able to make a substantial contribution to the establishment of new industries in Canada through the use of our facilities for supplying information and other forms of assistance."[26] The bank saw attracting foreign investment to Canada as a key business opportunity and as part of its social mandate.

When Ball became president in 1952, few strategic changes were initially made. Some new ideas did appear, however, such as promoting the efforts to service small businesses and individual borrowers.[27] The revision to the 1954 Bank Act opened two important markets. A new type of customer appeared in the 137th (1954) Annual Report now that automobiles were to be accepted as security. Perhaps even more importantly, the Act simplified oil and gas lending by allowing banks to lend against the security of hydrocarbons in the ground.[28] An ongoing interest in the mineral industries quickly developed. The 138th (1955) Annual Report revealed the continuing growing importance of small business, the personal borrower, and resource industries.

There was emphasis on bringing foreign firms into Canada and the value of strong correspondent relations.[29] Branches were established on NATO bases in Europe, showing ongoing renewal of strong government ties. There was a new twist evident in the 140th (1957) Annual Report where there was discussion on how new security issues were being floated by Canadian borrowers abroad because of the high value of the Canadian dollar. The creation of the Bank of London and Montreal (BOLAM) to meet new trends in trade with developing countries was discussed in the 141st (1958) Annual Report. The general manager, G. Arnold Hart, also noted an appreciable increase in foreign currency deposits. International operations were becoming increasingly important and were perceived differently as the name change from the Foreign department to the International department in 1957 signified. Connections between international and domestic operations were made clear in the 141st (1958) Annual Report, which described how changes in British banking were being monitored with an eye to introducing new services into Canada. Such activities provoked the need for increasing cooperation between domestic and international with the result that head office services had to be expanded in order to bring all departments under one roof.[30] Increased interdependencies resulted in a demand for improved internal information flows to provide efficiently the appropriate levels of service.

THE INTRODUCTION OF NEW
INFORMATION TECHNOLOGY:
1959-82

During this period, the management team, at least as expressed in statements given in the annual reports, was the president, G. Arnold Hart, and the general manager, R.D. Mulholland. The major domestic concerns were slack loan demand,[31] the ever-present need to improve efficiency,[32] the effects of such improvements on banking operations,[33] the positive benefits of government support of small business,[34] the development of a new department title, Administration and Legislation,[35] and ongoing decentralization.

In addition to these recurring themes, there were some important additions. The bank wanted to be a leader in the petroleum industry and paid greater attention to Edmonton as a centre of this activity.[36] In addition, it acquired modern computerized information equipment from IBM and began to automate banking in 1963 with a system called GENIE, GENerates Information Electronically. This integrated system was implemented in Toronto and some other centres prior to its full introduction throughout the system. Interestingly, the name was the result of a staff competition. This was a clever way of acclimatizing the staff to the introduction of technology as non-threatening. New technology granted wishes to make life easier: it did not take away jobs. Such a message was credible because of the bank's long tradition of offering employees job security.

There was also explicit discussion of a location strategy that weighed the advantages of a branch on the campus of the University of Western Ontario and on subway lines.[37] Attention to service was further stressed with emphasis on how every customer must be treated as an individual. A clear marketing orientation came through the addresses made by the executives in the annual reports.

Internationally, the key themes were expansion of Latin American operations via BOLAM, the development of publications on foreign exchange issues,[38] the continuation of a door-knocking campaign to generate business in Europe, the Far East and Latin America,[39] and the establishment of agencies in Tokyo, Dusseldorf, and Houston.[40] Clever use of the international network and the historical legacy was made when "Canada's First Bank Abroad" was highlighted on the back cover of the 143rd (1960) Annual Report.

A.C. Jensen was promoted from vice president to chairman of the board and served as chairman from 1959 to 1964. These years were ones of growth, both domestically and internationally, and were accompanied by increased decision making at the branch level in order to adjust to new environments.

The Hart years, president from 1959 to 1967, CEO from 1959 to 1974, and chairman of the board 1964 to 1975, marked what should be seen as a major change in strategic orientation. In the 147th (1964) Annual Report, he warned that banks would have to choose, and presumably carefully, what new services to offer. By the 157th (1974) Annual Report, many things had in fact been implemented, as this passage under the heading "Banking with innovation" on the cover shows: "The scope of services offered by the Bank continues to widen. Our objective is to offer our customers the most complete range of services ever made available by a Canadian financial institution."

A strategy to utilize fully the expensive branch distribution channel was being developed. This strategy capitalized advantage on the strengths offered by the decentralized structure in which 99 per cent of the loans were being authorized at branch or regional headquarters.[41] If the expertise for credit assessment was there, then the skills to market other services should also be there. A change in the understanding of the customer was taking place. The addition of a general manager for marketing in 1966 was instrumental in creating and maintaining impetus toward implementation of the concept of "convenience banking" discussed in the 158th (1975) Annual Report. The bank began to understand that a broad product offering was a prerequisite for creating a customized product package for each customer. The ability to offer advice based upon knowledge of the client's needs was a source of pride and demonstrated the advantages created by product-line expansion.

Yet, it would be foolish to see marketing as the sole factor responsible for the new orientation. Behind the scenes, the introduction of new information technology was dramatically changing the nature of banking. State-of-the-art computer equipment was now imperative for operations, as was demonstrated by the discussion in the 149th (1966) Annual Report concerning the purchase of third generation computer equipment.[42] Vancouver, Montreal, and Toronto had this equipment by the following year, and Calgary was slated to receive it. The 152nd (1969) Annual Report revealed the five-year plan to bring all branches on-line and the signing of a contract described as the biggest ever for IBM Canada.[43] A critical element in implementing the computer strategy was the signing of a contract with AGT Data Systems to develop a training program that would empower personnel to better serve customers. The bank realized that it needed outside specialists to assist in implementing the new technology. By 1973, it could report that it was on target with its five-year plan and that the system was undergoing final debugging with 24 branches on-line. The computer age had arrived.

As we have already seen, the economies of scale made possible with modern data processing also allowed the bank to extend its services. In fact, an increase in services, such as MasterCharge, was required in order to maximize use of these expensive capital assets.[44] In addition to various marketing firsts designed to improve customer convenience, the bank continued to stress its role in resource development. Since the scale of resource projects was expanding, the bank needed to employ new techniques for financing. It discussed an agreement between Bethlehem Copper Corporation and Japanese purchasers that seemed to be a version of project financing based upon long term contracts.[45] It took pride in its pre-eminent position in Canadian development when it acted as the lead bank for the development of Churchill Falls hydroelectric project.[46]

The importance of increasing the number of services to serve customers properly and to generate revenue was made clear in the 155th (1972) Annual Report when the bank's strong financial performance was attributed to controlling costs and increasing other operating revenue. The changing information technology altered the cost-structure of banking and also made it possible, if not necessary, to increase other revenue by adding services. Modern technology was thus having a major impact on both sides of the income statement.

The bank began to alter its strategy for international operations by focusing on the development of foreign loans.[47] It deliberately set about to develop its international activities. Between 1967 and 1971, international operations were the bank's most rapidly growing area; its 25 per cent annual growth meant that a quarter of all assets were international.[48] By 1975, growth of 35 per cent in international assets was announced. Another change in strategy was evident, as commercial loans went from being 39 per cent of the portfolio to 58 per cent.[49]

Growth was facilitated by new offices in Venezuela, Germany, Milan, Melbourne, Amsterdam, the Caymans, and by expansion in Singapore. There was some specialization, as a wholly owned subsidiary, Hochelaga Holdings, N.V., was created in Amsterdam for Euromarket dealings. The Australian venture, the Australian International Finance Corporation, was interesting in that it was undertaken with four partners: two from the United States, one from Japan, and one from Australia.[50] Computer-based information systems dramatically assisted the suceess of such on international operations.

With the increasing speed of information transfer, it became both possible and necessary to develop a new type of Money Desk that could instantly provide quotations to clients on such matters as foreign exchange, interest rates, and bond prices. This was a service in which the bank took pride, as the 158th (1975) Annual Report showed.[51] Modern information technology was changing virtually all facets of banking.

For students of business-government relations, the period 1959 to 1982 was interesting because of the conflicts that emerged between the banks and the regulators. The bank argued that the public good would be served by allowing banks to provide more services because they could do so at a price lower than other institutions currently providing the various financial services.[52] But it also complained that near banks, such as trust companies, had advantages in competing for deposits and that all deposit-taking institutions should be treated equally.[53] The importance of a deposit strategy was made clear. After 1969, there was increasing discussion of the widening gulf between the business community and the government. The 154th (1971) Annual Report reported that the erosion of the banking industry's share of deposits was halted by changes to the Bank Act that made the playing field more level between banks and trust companies. The 1967 Act had ended restrictions on interest rates and lowered the reserves on savings deposits, although trust companies were still not bound by reserve requirements. Something was wrong with the consultative process between business and government when legislation penalized a key enabling industry.

The annual reports during the period also revealed an increasing effort to deal with social concerns. In 1964, the 147th Annual Report included a statement in French addressed to the employees. The report of 1966 showed an increasing awareness of women as a distinct market segment when it described how "Le Salon" had been opened in Montreal to cater specifically to the banking needs of women. Perhaps a more important gesture was made in 1967, when Pauline Vanier became the first woman appointed to the board.

With all these pressures and strategic changes, the structure of the organization itself had to change. There was increasing pressure to improve both service and training and recruiting practices.[54] It was now recognized that the largest impediment to growth in the international field was the lack of trained staff. Given the demand for such people, in-house development was a logical method to solve the problem.[55] However, the bank also acknowledged that it was difficult to retain trained employees and it embarked on a plan to improve salaries. At the same time, it sought to improve its overall profit through better planning.[56] The 150th (1967) Annual Report stated that the employees should share in the increased profits generated by efficiency gains,[57] while the 151st (1968) Annual Report featured a policy statement on personnel practices signed by Hart.[58] These communications made it clear that the annual reports were addressed to the employees, as well as to the shareholders.

To summarize, increased international involvement and commercial loans were major changes in the growth strategy. However, this must be related to changes in the domestic market and the impact of new information processing technologies. While the bank's organizational structure allowed the role played by the branches to expand in order to adapt to growth, the new information technologies greatly increased the capacity to centralize information. These two trends were important for understanding the future evolution of the bank.

Fred McNeil was appointed president in 1973 and later served as CEO from 1975 to 1979 and chairman of the board from 1975 to 1981. The period can best be put into perspective by considering the following statement from the 165th (1982) Annual Report: the bank noted the need to develop services "to counter the erosion from non-bank competition."[59] During these years, competitive pressures mounted, not only because of the competition from other financial institutions, but because the world had become virtually a single financial market.[60] In this competitive environment, services had to be increased to meet the competitive threat from non-bank competitors, while geographic expansion was necessary to deal with the internationalization of banking. An environment that exerted pressures for expansion of both product line and geographic coverage at the same time was the new reality.

Domestically, the bank was confident that its investment in real time computer technology,[61] its focus on other operating revenue,[62] and an asset portfolio that increased concentrations in personal loans[63] and larger corporations, especially in the resource sector,[64] was paying off. The growing demand for specialist knowledge and the complexities of corporate accounts led the bank to create a new Corporate Banking Group headquartered in Toronto. It was the role of this group to maintain continuity of client contact as well as to join with branch managers in various locales to provide services beyond the capacity of a single branch. The changing nature of banking forced a closer integration of head office with operating units that were geographically diverse. The bank saw itself in a strong position for further expansion; because of its ability to tap foreign markets for capital. It was able to raise one billion dollars of capital in 1982.[65]

International operations were a source both of asset growth and increasing profitability. The bank sought to increase non-interest income in international operations by striving to be a leader in loan syndication.[66] Past history may have helped the bank achieve success in the field as it was the lead manager for various government loans, both Canadian and foreign. However, increased international activity and advances in information processing continued to create further pressures to reorganize. By 1976, a new International Banking Division emerged to coordinate international activities.[67] Without the organizational capacity to centralize information flows, it became impossible to understand the net exposure to movements in different capital markets, or to broader social forces.

By 1982, international operations were responsible for 46 per cent of net income, up from 33 per cent the year before. These were not only a source of revenue but they allowed the bank to diversify its risk exposure through participation in different national economies that were not perfectly correlated. Interestingly, we should also note that in some years the driving force for increased profits was not higher margins, but rather asset growth, because the spreads were often narrower as capital markets became more integrated and competitive.[68] The opportunities offered by international markets both for asset growth and risk reduction made them highly attractive, since growth and earnings could be more stable.

Once again, however, it is important to realize that international operations could not be radically separated from domestic operations. This was recognized in the 160th (1977) Annual Report when it was stated that there was a need to improve the interface between the two spheres of operation.[69] The need to improve the level of advice available to Canadian businessmen led to the opening of an additional International Banking Centre in Winnipeg.[70] As an intermediary between Canada and other countries, the bank needed the capability to provide information about Canada to foreign interests and information about foreign practices to Canadian business. The very nature of intermediation between the two markets created real organizational stress.

The effect of the government's anti-inflation program was discussed in the 159th (1976) Annual Report.[71] The legislation which imposed measures such as a ceiling on profits, restrictions on certain discretionary expenses and interest spreads, and the freezing of service charges to the level of 13 October 1975 applied only to domestic operations. Therefore if banks were interested in increasing their profitability, they had little choice but to focus on international operations.

In the same year, the entry of foreign banks into Canada drew attention. The Bank of Montreal took the position that foreign banks should not receive more favourable treatment in Canada than domestic banks, nor treatment more favourable than Canadian banks enjoyed in the home country of the foreign bank in question. In some respects, the statement asked for reciprocity, but also seemed to suggest that foreign banks had been operating in Canada and they should be forced to carry out business under the same regulations as Canadian banks.

By 1979, 1,050 branches were on-line.[72] Computerization had progressed well. Perhaps even more important was the effect of the new information technology. The 165th (1982) Annual Report revealed that considerations concerning the new technology were critical in the decision to structure the banks corporate and government banking operations on a worldwide basis.[73] It was now more logical to structure around the type of client than on the basis of geography. The need to integrate information overrode the importance of geography and even political boundaries. Time and the advantages of real-time computer operations had had a decisive impact.

WILLIAM D. MULHOLLAND AND THE BUILDING OF A NORTH AMERICAN BANK: 1981–89

William D. Mulholland became president in 1975, CEO in 1979, and finally chairman of board in 1981. The 172nd (1989) Annual Report provided an eloquent summary of Mulholland's years with the Bank of Montreal. While he maintained continuity with McNeil's initiatives in the area of technological transformation, Mulholland also staked out important new directions for the bank. He instituted key organizational changes, such as the creation of the Treasury Group and the Corporate and Government Group, which modernized international and financial market operations in order to enhance the bank's ability to arrange large corporate financings. Mulholland drew upon his background with the New York investment bank Morgan Stanley, as well as his experience as CEO of Brinco, Ltd in order to target large prime customers.[74] The 1987 acquisition of Nesbitt Thomson, one of Canada's leading investment dealers, was another key component in this market strategy. The announced acquisition of the Harris Bankcorp of Chicago in 1983 was an even more important strategic move during this period. Mulholland, perhaps influenced by his American background recognized that global success depended upon a strong North American base. Even before the era of the Free Trade Agreement (FTA), Mulholland developed a North American bank. The 166th (1983) Annual Report provided an intriguing look at his emerging strategy. The following statement in the foreword to the report showed the clear link to the past, but also looked to the future: "The Bank's continuing role in promoting trade abroad and in securing foreign sources of capital for development projects has contributed significantly to Canada's growth."

The chairman presented the view that the bank's basic strategy must take a long-term approach. The most significant trend for the future was the increasing integration of capital markets promoted by trade and the development of the transnational Euromarkets. Such integration gave rise to two major strategic implications. First, as barriers to the Canadian banking market fell, being competitive within Canada meant becoming competitive internationally.[75] The Canadian market was too small to support the level of investment needed to achieve the economies of scale and the skill levels required by the new competitive realities in banking; therefore the Bank of Montreal would have to expand its operations to become even more of a global competitor. Any competitive strategy for the 1980s had to be a global competitive strategy.

Second, Canadian trade patterns and capital markets were affected more by the United States than by others. Consequently, responding to the new global realities meant an increased focus on the United States, the world's largest banking market and Canada's largest trading partner. Mulholland was clear that the acquisition of the Harris Bankcorp of Chicago was part of the new *global* strategy.[76]

But *why* was the Harris chosen? Mulholland explained that the Harris and the Bank of Montreal had complementary networks and skills. The Harris' business was in the Midwest, while the Bank of Montreal's strength was in the East and the Far West. Interestingly, while there were powerful banks in New York and California, the Midwest, headquarters for many MNEs, was relatively vacant. In addition, the skills were complementary. The Harris had greater expertise in trust and investment management while the Bank of Montreal had superior information-processing systems. The new parent also added a greater international presence and capability to the Harris. The fundamental importance of the acquisition was made clear in 1984, when Grant Reuber, the president of the Bank of Montreal, asserted that the acquisition had created something unique: a bank with complete operational capability in both Canada and the United States. The addition of the Harris therefore meant that the Bank of Montreal had become a truly North American bank, perhaps fulfilling the visions of the first shareholders. International operations had been developed in order to gain competitive advantage within North America.

The need to focus on international networks had organizational consequences that revealed the importance of efforts to create a centralized data base for all operating units.[77] The marketing strategy of "relationship management" meant that account managers had to be able to link the different units of the bank to meet all the customer's financial services needs.[78] To maintain and build such relationships, account managers needed to know the client's needs and then mobilize the bank's capabilities to create a unique service package for that client.[79] The strategy demanded a broad product-service range of more or less generic products.

Only the development of advanced management information systems (MIS) could empower the account managers to accomplish this task. Computer terminals had the capability of portraying the complete relationship for the account manager, while also providing the customer with timely, if not immediate, access to banking services.[80] In addition, the use of MIS facilitated the assessment of the profitability of each relationship. The significance of new information technologies for competitiveness was signalled by the creation of the Electronic Data Processing Group in 1987.

A further implication of the strategy focusing on large North American borrowers was the need to improve the skill level of employees. The services offered by the Treasury Group could generate significant amounts of non-interest income for the bank, but such activities demanded highly trained professionals.[81] In the competitive world of corporate banking, account managers could no longer wait for clients to come through the door requesting credit, they had to sell their services as financial advisors aggressively.[82] The increasing sophistication of clients had turned loans into low-profit, commodity-like products and the only effective defence against such forces which drove down profitability was to augment the service, or non-interest, component and develop a strategy to secure lower cost funds.[83] Such a strategy sought to increase value added by improving the skills of bank's employees.

With this view of the market, it became reasonable to organize around clients with similar needs. The bank developed the following organizational divisions: Corporate and Government, Canadian Commercial, Personal, Bank of Montreal Mortgage Corporation, Banco De Montreal Investimento S.A., Treasury, and Operation and Systems Division.[84] The relative importance of the different divisions can be seen from the composition of the asset portfolio. In the 166th (1983)

Annual Report, the breakdown of lending was set out as follows: Corporate and Government was responsible for 60 per cent of bank lending, Canadian Commercial for 20 per cent, and Personal for 13 per cent of assets (60 per cent in instalment loans). The 167th (1984) Annual Report provided the following breakdown of Corporate and Government: 48 per cent to commercial and industrial corporations, principally in North America; 21 per cent to banks, governments or government related; 19 per cent to natural resources; and 12 per cent to real estate.[85]

The above provides a fascinating portrait. Once the concentration on large customers with multinational service needs was recognized, then the growing importance of Treasury with its knowledge of capital markets became apparent. Treasury not only managed much of the liability strategy, which had to be in tune with the asset strategy, but it was also the source of expertise for underwriting, swaps, and other sophisticated financial engineering services demanded by clients.[86] In 1987, these corporate banking capabilities were deepened when the Bank of Montreal acted aggressively and became the first bank to acquire an investment dealer, Nesbitt Thomson Inc.[87] The addition of investment bankers dramatized the degree to which the new strategy of relationship banking forced product line expansion. However, for the strategy to work, closer coordination among diverse groups, often with quite distinct cultures, was necessary.[88] The realities of the market strategy forced a streamlining of management. While this was consistent with the focus on productivity, it was just as important for breaking down the bureaucracy that hindered the speedy flow of information and coordination of efforts. It should be noted that the reorganization created some upheavals that were discussed in the financial press.[89]

In more recent years, the bank has shown strategic continuity with the emphasis on resource industries, especially petroleum,[90] government financing, and efforts to develop non-interest income. The organizational focus upon customer types served to develop competitive advantage in other markets. Expertise in the petroleum industry was fundamental to winning the Texas-based United Gas Pipe Line Company as a customer. However, the price of this expertise was steep, as revaluation of the energy portfolios in the mid-1980s was a significant factor in driving the bank's loan loss figures.[91] Expertise in mortgage-backed securities was exploited in the U.K.[92]

Mulholland took the lead in challenging the Dome Petroleum takeover and in announcing increased provisions on LDC loans. Perhaps even more important were internal organizational changes sparked, at least in part by LDC debt problems. In order to improve risk management and control, systems within the bank were revised. A two-track, decentralized process was developed in which the risk assessment was separate from line credit procedures. To ensure overall prudential management, centralized monitoring and control was also firmly established. The Bank of Montreal was trying to regain its former position of leadership. The creation of an International Advisory Council as reported in the 1986 Annual Report added lustre to the bank's image. Rather than being the largest bank, the bank hoped to restore its reputation as the "bankers' bank." It is in this light that Mulholland's public statements concerning debt for equity swaps as a solution to Brazil's debt crisis should be considered. Mulholland proposed a flexible plan in which the bank would convert its loans to Brazil into equity investments. This change would help to remove the crippling debt service charges that hindered Brazilian economic development. The bank wished to be a leader among international banks.

During this period, the Dome incident and the LDC writedown were also interesting because of the manner in which interconnections between international and domestic banking were revealed. While Dome was a Canadian company, the financing for it was international and several major foreign financial institutions were involved. LDC debt has had an impact on the growth potential and profitability of virtually all major banks. Pessimistic forecasts concerning revenue from these loans raised the cost of equity and thereby restricted growth domestically as well as internationally. In addition, the cost of debt increased as agencies lowered the credit rating of all the major Canadian banks.[93] Nervous depositors may also have increased the cost of attracting deposits in some markets. In the modern global world, it became increasingly difficult to separate domestic performance from international effects, and vice versa.

In 1987, Mulholland made an aggressive move to restrict asset growth in order to focus on profitability. That year was a landmark year as the bank acquired 75 per cent of Nesbitt Thomson, one of Canada's leading investment dealers. The Bank of Montreal now provided full services to its large corporate customers. Perhaps even more importantly, the future CEO, Matthew W. Barrett, was named president.

The reduced role of credit products in the large corporate segment served as a natural brake upon asset growth. The bank sought to achieve greater profitability based upon success in fee-based products, and growth in other areas such as financial institutions and government.[94] It also increased its focus on personal banking: "Individual customers have never been more important to Bank of Montreal. Their business provides the solid foundation for activity in all major markets. To maintain its position in the Canadian market, the Bank will continue to make the substantial investment required in staff training, technology and premises."[95] While the above may sound like rhetoric, there was strong evidence to support the importance of the new direction toward retail during this period. In 1984, Matthew W. Barrett moved from Treasury to Domestic. New strategic thrusts occurred, such as breaking ranks from the other major banks in marketing MasterCard rather than Visa and then not charging annual card fees, which by 1987 won the largest share of the credit card market among the banks.[96] That same year, plans were being made to enter the trust business in order to service better retail clients in Canada, as it was anticipated that the traditional "four pillars" separation was soon to be a relic of the past. The Canadian commercial sector, including independent business and specific subsegments such as automotive dealers and franchises, were also receiving greater marketing attention. Sophisticated information systems and credit procedures facilitated the increased decentralization of credit approval. The FTA signalled once again that the needs of smaller clients were not restricted to Canada. Their trade needs created pressures for integrated international and domestic operations, especially with the integrated North American market. To this end, centralized systems and supporting information networks and data bases were developed. The agreement with a retailer, 7 Eleven, to share automated teller machine networks was a first among banks and demonstrated the vitality of the commitment both to retail and commercial.

Mulholland thus created a North American bank that was able to meet the needs of large corporate clients with sophisticated systems that were designed to ensure both service and profitability. Despite some turmoil in the executive ranks, a bank poised for profitable growth was created. However, the prime segment that seemed so desirable would not be sufficient to ensure the Bank of Montreal's future. The phenomenon of disintermediation, customers going directly to credit markets rather than using traditional intermediators, banks, forced strategic reorientation. Even viewing the segment as a source of fee income became problematic as chief financial officers (CFOs) became more knowledgeable and transaction-oriented. Only relationship management or a low-cost strategy could provide protection from heightened competitive pressures in this segment. Alternatively, a new direction could be found.

MATTHEW W. BARRETT: 1989–

Matthew W. Barrett was appointed to the board of directors and to the position of president in 1987.[97] At forty-four he was not only a young CEO, but his personal style and background stood in sharp contrast to his predecessors. He was an Irishman who had spent twenty-eight years working his way up through the ranks after joining the bank as a clerk in its London, England office. His education and therefore his training came primarily from the front ranks, not from patrician institutions.[98]

As CEO, Barrett faced a formidable challenge. the Bank of Montreal's financial performance lagged behind the other banks and it was widely believed that there were significant internal problems, especially in morale. The importance of corporate culture to a service industry must be recognized, as Barrett remarked: "You can't have a rotten internal climate and then expect people to be warm and friendly with customers."[99] The pressure for improved performance meant internal reforms had to proceed simultaneously with any changes in market strategy.

By 1988, Barrett had been successful in increasing the importance of the domestic banking segment. Sound economic reasons motivated a move toward Canadian retail banking, and it was clear that low-yielding foreign currency assets were a drag on profitability.[100] In 1990 Barrett announced six priorities in his first report as CEO:

1 Improving customer service
2 Moving to a higher-yielding asset mix
3 Focusing on higher yield assets, especially Canadian dollar loans
4 Focusing on non-interest expense
5 Improving profitability
6 Avoiding product lines where there was no synergy

The order and implied change in targeted segments indicated an interesting shift from the priorities that had been announced by Grant Reuber in 1986, which ranked prudence and integrity first, profitability second, and customer service third. The service organization was becoming market-driven as back-room systems were developed to empower employees to deliver high quality service.

The 1990 report opened with a statement on how the strategic *vision* would meet the expectations of diverse stakeholders, which were presented in the following order: customers, shareholders, employees, and communities. The challenge was to create value for all. Barrett defined the scope of operations as follows:

Our business is to satisfy customers who seek assistance and advice in meeting their financial goals.

Our primary emphasis is traditional banking services, namely deposit, loan, payment and collection, custodial, information and risk management services. We will selectively enter new areas that broaden our range of services, logically extend our existing strengths and match or surpass competitor offerings.

A life-time banker, Barrett's challenge was to establish a solid core. The first step was to ensure that all knew what was expected and what were the priorities. It was in this context that his clear statement on market scope was fundamental:

North America is our principal market-place. Offshore we will select regions of strategic importance for trade and investment flows affecting our North American customers.

We will focus on three main customer groups:

• The first priority is individuals and small and medium-size businesses across Canada and in selected u.s. markets.
• The second priority is selected segments among large national and multinational businesses and governments and financial institutions in Canada and the u.s., including their international operations.
• The third priority is individuals, corporations and institutions with investment interests in North America, located in selected off-shore markets.

The bank's aspirations to global status have disappeared, as Barrett remarked: "It's arguable whether Canadian banks can still legitimately aspire to world stature. Besides, how can we possibly compete in our cost of capital with Germans or Japanese? We're at a major disadvantage trying to price international deals, and if you were to combine all the Canadian banks into one $400-billion institution, our competitiveness wouldn't change one iota."[101] However, this change was not a retreat, but a strategic refocusing upon North America. It made no sense to suffer low profitability in international markets, when the bank could succeed in the United States. A goal of raising the percentage of profits from the United States from 20 per cent to 50 per cent announced by Barrett set a new standard for the North American bank.[102]

The hallmark of Barrett's approach to date has been to involve the bank's employees in his vision through increasing personal contact via tours, meetings, and videos.[103] His charismatic leadership style has been successful, as earnings have improved and both Barrett and the bank have received increased and favourable press coverage. Patricia Chisholm described Barrett for *Maclean's*: "Smiling and gracious, Barrett's Irish charm also marks him as an anomaly in a world where many executives bolster their authority with a stern personal style."[104]

The anomalies were not restricted to personality. The rejuvenation of the bank required aggressive strategies to woo back lost customers, as well as to develop new relationships. Even before becoming CEO, Barrett had shown that he was prepared to break with the mainstream when under his direction MasterCard refused to implement annual user fees when the other banks did so. A front-page report in the *Financial Post* discussed the new competitiveness on loan rates he brought to the bank as CEO.[105] The cuts were not restricted to prime customers, because rate cuts were also used as a competitive weapon in the small business and agricultural sector.[106] More recently, a new lower rate credit card was introduced that targeted people who carry a balance from month to month.[107] Perhaps even more significant was Barrett's independent position on the retailing of insurance. He announced that struggling to get into insurance was "bananas" because the "traditional banking service pillar is going to constitute 85 to 95 per cent of major bank's earnings for the next decade."[108] However, he was clear that banks should not be artificially restrained from entering any financial services area.

Unlike some charismatic leaders, Barrett has been willing to share the stage. The rate cuts were generally announced by executive vice-president and chief economist, Lloyd Atkinson. Tony Comper, the president and chief operating officer wrote the introduction to the high profile report from the bank's task on women in the bank and announced policies to erase barriers to women.[109] Promotion of women in banking received a significant boost when Sylvia Ostry was appointed to chair the prestigious International Advisory Council. More recently, Vice-Chairman Alan G. McNally has been outspoken on Native issues and has seen an aboriginal services program established. A "team" spirit has been encouraged by the new leadership. Indicative of the new spirit was the expansion of the office of the chairman in April 1992 when Brian J. Steck was appointed vice-chairman, investment banking, and Keith O. Dorricott, vice-chairman, corporate services. Yet, it is an unusual team: a key member, Nesbitt Thomson has retained its own identity, even though the bank has sought 100 per cent ownership.[110]

Strategic changes were reflected by the senior executive structure. A reorganization was undertaken to improve the performance in the prime market, which, despite new emphasis on retail, had not been abandoned. J.S. Chisholm was appointed vice-chairman, corporate and institutional services with the mandate of ensuring that his bankers know their clients and can act as advisors on an ongoing basis. Bankers no longer wait for the customer to call.[111] New capabilities, such as 24-hour currency trading, have also been added.[112] Organizational change and renewal was necessary to restore competitiveness in the prime segment. Mr. Chisholm has also been outspoken on the need to improve the u.s. regulatory system, a real concern because of the implications for using Harris as a growth platform.[113]

Signs of a new aggressiveness were also evident in personal and commercial financial services under Vice-Chairman Alan McNally. To improve customer service by increasing local decision making, 36 vice presidents and 8 senior vice-presidents were located in 24 cities across Canada.[114] In anticipation of entering the trust industry, an arrangement was struck with the trust subsidiary of Sun Life Assurance. Rather than pursuing an ownership strategy with its attendant problems, the Bank of Montreal opted to "network" trust products through its retail network.[115] To build capabilities in this new area, an equity stake in a financial planning firm, PerCor Financial Consultants, was taken.[116] The bank has prepared itself for developing more extensive and profitable relationships with its retail customers. An initiative with subsidiary Nesbitt Thomson to offer a joint account integrating a customer's investment and banking needs and cutting mortgage renewal fees are further proof of innovation at the bank. The move was also interesting because it took place despite complications arising from jurisdictional overlap between the federal and provincial levels. The complexities of relationship management have multiple strategic implications.

While the public affairs department has done excellent work in ensuring press coverage of the bank's initiatives, there is a new reality emerging at the bank. The bank is attempting to show that it is genuinely committed to stakeholders in the community beyond the elite and has made important symbolic gestures such as holding the first full board meeting in Chicago and dropping the sponsorship of equestrian events.[117] Speeches on national issues demonstrated the depth of community involvement.[118] The bank has opened an impressive new educational centre that will help to develop the employee skills needed to deliver upon the implicit service promises. This image repositioning has been of fundamental importance, not only in the efforts to win a retail franchise, but to instil a new service spirit in the staff. Barrett's "nice guy" image was not built upon being soft. Central to the new vision of the bank was the "benchmarking" of the bank's performance against its major competitors in both the 1990 and 1991 annual reports. We will now examine how the bank has done in this regard.

STRATEGY AND FINANCIAL
PERFORMANCE

When Barrett became CEO, the Bank of Montreal decided to benchmark its performance against its five major competitors on seven
criteria. The key measures were:

1 Return on shareholders' investment
2 Profitability (return on equity (ROE))
3 Earnings growth
4 Productivity (expenses as a percentage of revenues)
5 Capital
6 Asset quality (provision for credit losses as a percentage of average
  non-LDC loans)
7 Liquidity (cash and securities as a percentage of assets)

In 1990, the bank ranked first in asset quality, liquidity, and capital
while it placed in the middle of the pack on the other measures,
except for productivity, where it ranked last. In 1991, it fell to fourth
on capital measures and there was relatively little change on the
others.

The interrelationships of the measures must be considered. For
example, consider the relationship between profitability and capital.
If a constant return on assets was maintained, then the volume of
profits will fluctuate directly with volume growth. Unless new capital
is raised, increased profitability and earnings growth will be directly
tied to decline of capital ratios. Rather than viewing such a decline
as an indicator of poor performance, however, the bank saw it as a
strategic decision related to efforts to gain market share in asset and
fee-based product markets and to a consideration of the timing, or
need to raise capital on markets. The first place ranking in asset
quality demonstrated that growth occurred without taking on excessive risk in a hostile environment. However, "safer" assets may have
also been a drag on profitability because of their lower risk premium.

The recent improvements that have taken place need to be placed
in context. First, consider the growth that has occurred. Since 1981,
asset growth of roughly 60 per cent has been supported by capital
growth of over 120 per cent, as can be seen in figure 2.1, which
employs logarithmic scaling to call attention to the significant capital
growth.[119] The soundness of the bank was confirmed when its credit
rating was raised by the Canadian Bond Rating Service at a time
when other banks were being downgraded.[120] The number of
employees has increased by under 10 per cent and the number of

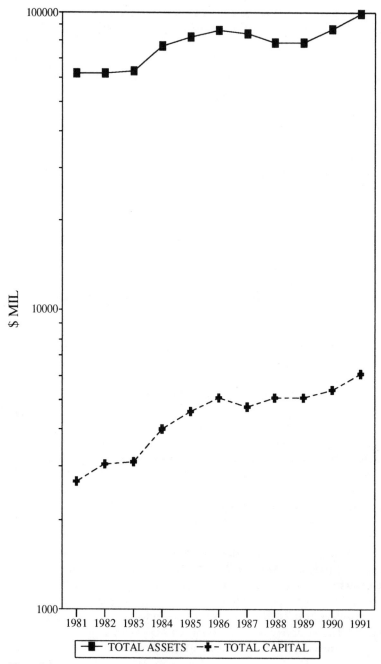

Figure 2.1
Bank of Montreal Asset and Capital Growth

service-delivery units has seen a slight decline, although the latter is barely detectable in figure 2.2. Given the bank's laggard performance on productivity measures, such a pattern suggests that significant changes took place in the industry.

Statements made by Barrett indicated that there had been a fundamental restructuring of the asset portfolio toward retail banking and toward North America. Figure 2.3 provides a history of asset portfolio by geographic classification. The dramatic growth in Canada and the United States is evident as is the retreat from Latin America. In the main, this reflects loan loss provisions rather than complete withdrawal. However, there seems to be no rush to do business in Mexico despite North American Free Trade Agreement (NAFTA) talks. This is not to say that NAFTA will not provide opportunities, but rather that correspondent relationships with Mexican banks and trade financing may be the preferred vehicles. It should also be remembered that the classification is by ultimate risk, so that loans could be made to companies, especially Canadian who are operating or intend to operate in Mexico, but that the risk falls upon the parent company.

The shift to North America is not synonymous with a shift to retail, although a strong linkage would seem reasonable, especially when the bank owns the Harris. The extent of the shift to retail can more clearly be seen in figures 2.4 and 2.5, which provide a breakdown of the asset and deposit portfolios. The level of measure precludes fine grained analysis; however, the tremendous growth of mortgages reveals a dramatic change. In 1982, mortgages accounted for only 11.8 per cent of the portfolio, while in 1991 they accounted for 28.1 per cent. The story is similar on the deposit side. Deposits from individuals accounted for 40.9 per cent in 1982 and 51.6 per cent in 1991. The shift of the portfolio to higher earning assets can also be seen in the declining percentages of day and call loans and loans to banks. Another significant growth area has been small business. A recent study found the bank to be the favourite of the big five among small businessmen.[121] Changes in international markets, especially sovereign lending, are the probable source for changes in bank deposits. The bank has returned to more traditional intermediation between savers and borrowers, as Barrett stated. This strategic change places changes in revenue patterns.

Figure 2.6A provides an analysis of income employing the standardized measure of return on assets (ROA). Over the period, certain trends stand out. First, the increasing importance of non-interest income is obvious. Banking has changed. Increased fee income is a two edged sword. On the up-side, the growth of non-interest income

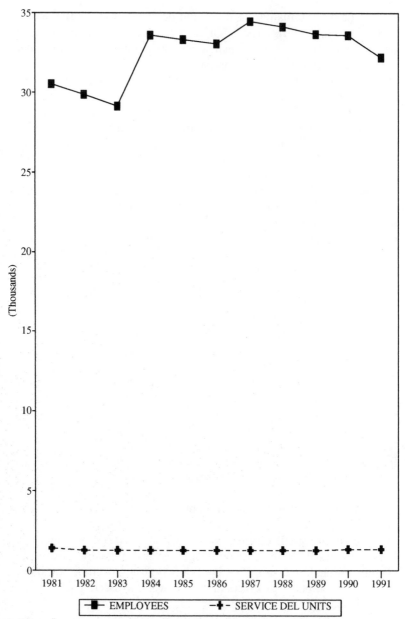

Figure 2.2
Employee and Branch Growth

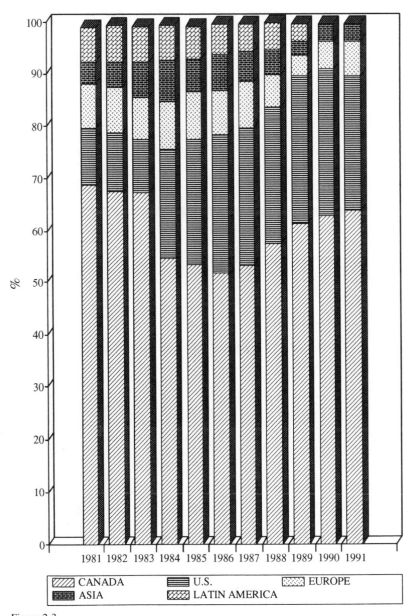

Figure 2.3
Location of Assets

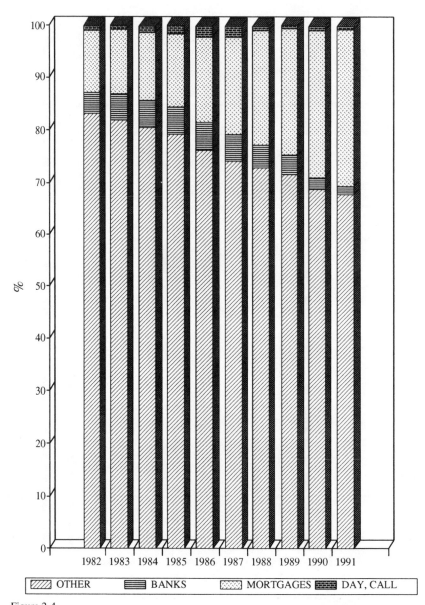

Figure 2.4
Asset Portfolio

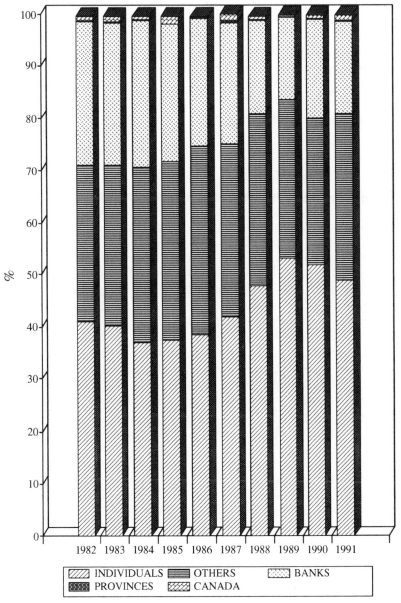

Figure 2.5
Deposit Portfolio

provides evidence that relationships were being built on the basis of services. On the other hand, this was also a result of disintermediation as former clients went directly to markets. The second major trend is the increased non-interest expense. On a percentage basis, it will take significant effort to return to 1979 levels. A decline commenced in 1982 that was not reversed until 1991. Nonetheless, the new team does have the curve pointed in the right direction.

Figure 2.6B presents the varying fortunes of international and domestic ROA. The classic benefits of portfolio diversification can be seen by the manner in which the returns frequently moved in offsetting directions. However, the ongoing problems created by low levels of international earnings in recent years can also be seen. Interestingly, the bank decided not to segment international from domestic for 1991. Perhaps this reflected the integration of North American banking combined with the diminishing presence in other markets. To a North American bank, it does not make sense to see the United States as international.

The importance of other income merits further discussion, especially in the light of changing portfolios. Figure 2.7 provides a breakdown of the contribution to other income made by five major product lines and consequently, does not sum to 100 per cent. In percentage terms, the most significant changes reflect the addition of new services, such as trust, securities, and safe-keeping. The effects of "the little bang" and other regulatory changes are also evident. For example, while revenues from credit cards increased over five times, its percentage contribution to other income has declined.

While the level of non-interest expenses remained high relative to other banks, the composition of expenses remained relatively stable. An examination of figure 2.8 reveals only one interesting trend: a fall from 60 per cent to 55 per cent by salaries and staff benefits. Presumably this was the result of the telecomputational revolution, although computer expenditures have fluctuated between 5 per cent and 7 per cent throughout the period.

All of the above factors coalesce in the analysis of income presented in figure 2.8 where two trends leap off the chart: the increases in fee income and non-interest expenses. Beginning in 1982, the two are almost mirror images of one another, although the decline for non-interest expenses in 1991 seems larger than the decline in other income. The linkage is reasonable. The bank had incurred costs to generate new revenue streams. However, given the relatively poor productivity performance and assuming roughly similar costs in servicing markets, the level of non-interest expenses must continue to

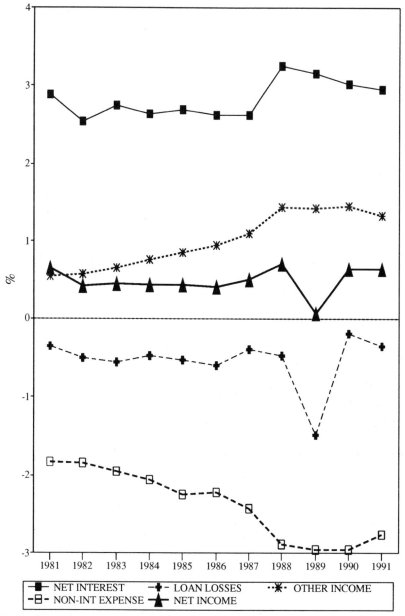

| NET INTEREST | LOAN LOSSES | OTHER INCOME |
| NON-INT EXPENSE | NET INCOME | |

Figure 2.6A
Analysis of ROA

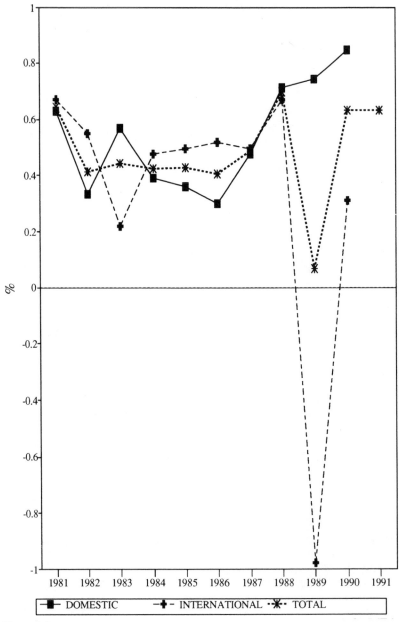

Figure 2.6B
Analysis of ROA

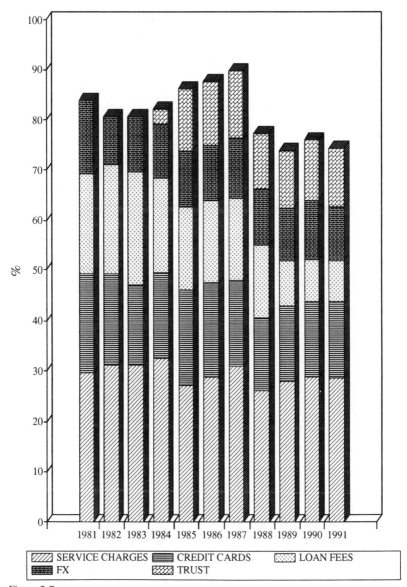

Figure 2.7
Other Income

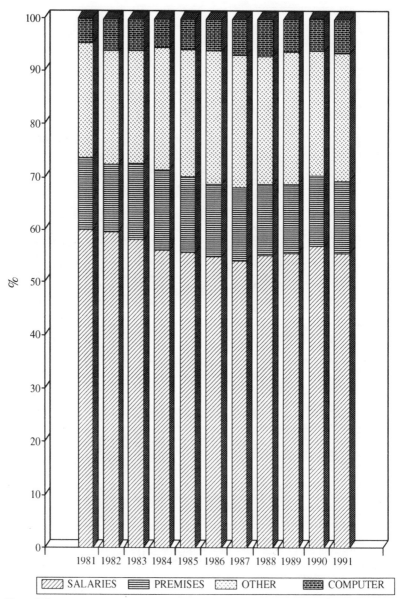

Figure 2.8
Non-Interest Expense

be cut. The bank's executive team must work to help the trend that may be emerging in 1991 to continue. Any improvement would have a dramatic effect on net income. Just as the 1989 loan loss blip is mirrored by net income, so will blips in the other direction.

The relatively narrow fluctuations in net interest income over a period that has seen extensive changes in interest rates strongly suggests that the bank is carefully managing differences in its interest rate and foreign exchange positions to maintain reasonable matches.[122] While the bank would take trading positions on interest rate or foreign exchange movements, prudential management limits the extent of these positions. Perhaps more important are the efforts to lead the competition in cutting the prime rate. With its high-liquidity position, the bank is positioned to increase its profitability by engaging in price competition. However, in the long run, the strategy will be problematic if productivity does not improve.

Perhaps the most significant measure of the degree of Barrett's success and expectations for the future has been the stock-price performance. While it is virtually impossible to isolate this from other factors, the relationship between the closing price and book value of the shares over the period was interesting. Under Barrett, the market price frequently exceeded the book value, as figure 2.9 shows. The gap between market and book that developed was a tribute to the ability of the new team to create shareholder value. Moves to compete for new loan business and lower liquidity have met with market approval. The bank presents its results with pride, and it shows. The 1991 Annual Report was judged to be the best in the world in a study by London-based Lafferty Business Research.

CONCLUSION

There were several interesting features in the bank's history. First, geographic expansion was only possible with the development of the systems necessary to manage the portfolio centrally. Second, Mulholland's rise to CEO, the acquisition of the Harris, and Barrett's commitment to generating 50 per cent of earnings from the United States were in keeping with a longstanding tradition of involvement with the United States. Third, foreign-entry decisions were always primarily influenced by trade patterns and access to capital markets.

Moves by both Mulholland and Barrett demonstrated a desire to be the "First Bank." The old strategic position of the "bankers' bank" or the government bank meant an emphasis on sophisticated services and liquidity, a legacy that still influences the bank. Up to Barrett's time, it has been the tradition to refrain from pursuing

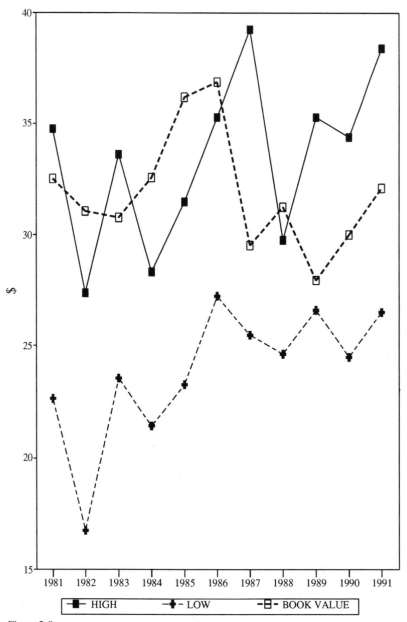

Figure 2.9
Stock-Price Performance

growth for its own sake, and to concentrate on specific types of financing. Mulholland's corporate strategy was founded upon a belief that while areas of expertise might lead to a portfolio of lower-yielding assets, service fees could generate healthy profits. The position that had been sought in the intermediation chain forced the bank toward increased sophistication in its service offering and internationalization from its very founding. The decision to limit international branches and to pursue correspondent relations was critical and confirmed a position of bankers' bank. Barrett's emphasis on retail marked a historical strategic change.

Ties between the bank and the federal government have been extensive. While this was obvious in the bank's early history, it was an ongoing tradition with people such as Jack Warren, vice chair of the bank from 1979 to 1986 whose career in government culminated in being ambassador to the United States (1975–77) or Grant Reuber, who had been deputy minister of finance (1979–80) before becoming president of the bank. The connections were important not only in Canada, but in international markets. In the same vein, the International Advisory Council chaired by Sylvia Ostry developed connections that could be a source of competitive advantage. Interestingly, Alan Gottlieb, another former ambassador to the United States, and Allan J. MacEachen, former deputy prime minister are also members of the council.

Just as internationalization was necessary to finance trade or bring capital into Canada, and later globalization was necessary to compete, now domination of a region has become critical in order to compete in a globalized world. In reality, the Bank of Montreal's strategy says that only a "domestic" base as large as North America can support the investments required for global banking. It is incorrect to see current changes as a "retreat" from international activities. Rather the bank is seeking to maximize returns from its most important assets, its people, by focusing upon the markets in which its knowledge base allows it to create value. The North American strategy that was initiated under Mulholland showed an early recognition of the fact that strategy must be developed in a global context, but as Barrett's strategic reformulation demonstrated, the strategy need not be global in operation. In 1991, the Bank of Montreal has positioned itself to profit from increased North American economic integration. Other moves to develop strong franchises and capital base augurs a bright future. While outside the scope of this study, 1992 was a good year for the bank. Assets grew by 11 per cent and both ROA and return on equity (ROE) fell only slightly while those of the CIBC, the Royal, and the Toronto Dominion fell considerably. Barrett is having an effect.

CHAPTER THREE

The Bank of Nova Scotia

From our beginnings as a maritime trade bank in Halifax, we at Scotiabank have always looked outward in the knowledge that opportunity is a word without borders ... Today we are one of North America's largest financial institutions, with assets of more than $88 billion. We offer a full range of services to retail, commercial, corporate and international banking clients alike.

1991 Annual Report, 1

Schull and Gibson made it quite clear in their history of the Bank of Nova Scotia, or Scotiabank, that in order to appreciate its recent strategies, it is necessary to understand the evolution and culture of the bank. They state that "The tradition of The Bank of Nova Scotia is non-conformist and non-establishment ... As a non-member of the establishment, with only a limited number of big accounts, The Bank of Nova Scotia has had to scurry for a living. Since it was difficult to obtain more big accounts in Canada, the Bank pursued big accounts abroad. If life had been comfortable the Nova Scotia might not have been a leader in consumer credit or international wholesale lending."[1] This chapter examines the historical formation of Scotiabank's strategy and the importance of its historical legacy by considering how the results of earlier strategies affected its later positioning.

In many ways, Scotiabank is the most international of the Canadian banks and perhaps the least typical because of its past domestic strategies. Not only does it have a higher percentage of its total assets in international, but it has also frequently enjoyed above average profitability from these assets compared to other Canadian banks. In addition, the branch strategy for international offers a sharp contrast to that of the Bank of Montreal. Thus an examination of the history of Scotiabank's development helps to explain both *why* Scotiabank became so and why it has been successful.

WILLIAM LAWSON AND THE FOUNDATION OF THE ENTERPRISE: 1831–76

The early founders of the bank had no difficulty in identifying a market niche. The strategists could see that the rapidly growing commerce of Halifax created an increased demand for banking services. What the early bankers did not fully understand, however, was the extent of the resources required to pursue the opportunity. The struggle to develop the organizational form appropriate to the banking environment posed a formidable challenge.

The Halifax of the 1830s required increased banking services to ensure the easy flow of money and commercial credit necessary to sustain and to expand the maritime trade upon which the city depended. The first bank in Nova Scotia, the Halifax Banking Company, was largely controlled by the merchant and political elite of the province. Dissatisfaction with the service it provided provoked 184 people to present a petition on 31 January 1832 for a public bank to be formed along the lines of the joint stock corporations operating in Scotland and New York. The new bank, the Bank of Nova Scotia, received its charter on 30 March 1832.[2]

The founding was important for several reasons. First, as was the case with the Bank of Montreal, the market need was in large part created by foreign trade, giving Scotiabank an international orientation from its inception. Moreover, one reason for this international orientation was especially interesting – water routes between Halifax, Boston, and New York allowed for faster communication between these centres than between many towns of New Brunswick and Nova Scotia. Because banking was (and still is) an information industry, the viability of growth opportunities was dependent upon communication lines. The international orientation, with an emphasis on the Caribbean, was confirmed with the choice of the first president, William Lawson, who had had extensive dealings in the West Indies. Further, two other original subscribers had had international connections: Henry Bliss of London and Rupert Cochran of New York (although Cochran was a former Haligonian). The foreign joint stock model that was adopted also suggested an international awareness.

Second, the origins were non-establishment. The early officers showed themselves prepared to pursue opportunities in hostile environments. Finally, the importance of government regulation for banking should be noted. Not only were early regulators concerned to protect the establishment, but to ensure stability of the banking system. For that reason, the capital holders were subject to double liability – that is, they were liable to pay twice their equity – and the bank was excluded from mortgage lending because of the volatility of land prices.

The major problem facing the first officers was their lack of practical banking experience. Their solution was to import manuals and supplies from the only available source in North America, New York. Once again, an American influence can be seen. In the early days, the work of Cochran, the New York agent, played an essential role in securing supplies, including cash, in New York. Unfortunately, he went bankrupt in 1836 largely because of confusion in the u.s. banking world following President Andrew Jackson's vetoing of the charter of the Bank of the United States.

The use of agents was an organizational response to the problem of control. In order to be profitable, any organization that dealt with cash had to have tight controls. Since it was extremely difficult to control operations that were separated by great geographic distances and hindered by poor communication, control could be more easily exercised by limiting direct involvement. The level of responsibility placed upon the agent served to lessen incentives to exercise opportunistic behaviour.

These early years saw some other interesting developments. First, the two Halifax banks came to a truce and established a clearing house once they realized that their early battles resulted in the strangulation of trade which was damaging to both banks. Some level of cooperation among competitors in the banking world was essential for the smooth running of the financial system. Second, international operations were expanded by employing agents who were situated in London and Boston to carry on foreign exchange business.

The period 1840–70 was marked by the appearance of many new banks in Nova Scotia, including the Bank of Montreal. This in turn resulted in slow growth for Scotiabank. Despite this, it maintained its position as the leading bank in Nova Scotia and established relations with Samuel Cunard, who would become its most important client. The first loan to Cunard pointed again to an important aspect of banking: cooperation among competitors. In 1842, Cunard had requested a loan of £45,000, which amounted to one-third of Scotiabank's capital. Such an amount clearly exceeded Scotiabank's prudential practices and ceiling on loans. It was not possible to syndicate the loan, but when the BBNA agreed to accept and hold Scotiabank's notes for a stipulated time, it became possible to make the loan. Without this cooperation, this important link would never have been forged.

The importance of internal control was brought dramatically to light when it was discovered that James Forman, the cashier for the bank, had embezzled $315 000 over twenty-five years. Forman had been taking the books home with him at night and making fraudulent entries. To quell the crisis, a new cashier, W.C. Menzies, was appointed. He was a well-trained Scottish banker who had originally been recruited by the BBNA. The Scottish connection stood in contrast to the Bank of Montreal. As an immigrant banker, Menzies fostered an international perspective different from the competitor, the Bank of Montreal.

The early years of Scotiabank clearly demonstrated the need to make necessary adaptations to the environment. No bank could survive without control systems that would thwart the larcenous impulses of employees. The bank found a solution by hiring the necessary person from abroad. The need for distant representation and the ensuing control problem was solved through the use of agents who were personally responsible for their accounts. Imprudent actions by these agents, so difficult to monitor in those days, would not unduly endanger Scotiabank.

ENTER THE LEGENDARY
THOMAS FYSHE: 1876–97

Once the appropriate organizational form had been recognized and achieved, it was easily adapted to other locations.[3] In service industries such as banking, location was a key strategic variable, since clients seek to minimize inconveniences that create transactions costs for them. In addition, the very nature of the intermediary service provided by banks, matching savers to borrowers, means there are advantages to linking diverse areas with different economic characteristics. Geographic expansion that allowed for a pooling of capital and a diversification of risk promoted the efficient allocation of capital in the Canadian and global economy. However, expansion was impossible unless centralized control systems could be developed to manage decentralized operations. The improved nature of such controls permitted the bank to expand during this period, but expansion also created the demand to provide ever more sophisticated information systems.

Thomas Fyshe was another Scottish banker who left a lasting mark on the bank. He furthered the expansion program that had been initiated by Menzies. In order to attract the personnel necessary for the expansion, Fyshe adopted innovative personnel policies that stressed adequate pay, a pension fund, and a policy of training young employees for promotion. Internal development of talent created a pool to staff the growing branch network. Attention to the role of human resources in strategy implementation was critical to success in this period.

Despite difficult economic conditions in shipbuilding, lumber, and fishing, the bank continued to prosper as it adapted to financing the new manufacturing industries that emerged as a result of the 1879 "National Policy" which increased tariff protection to domestic industries. This, combined with the demands of the railway and shipbuilding industries, attracted new manufacturing industries to the Maritimes. Schull and Gibson made the following assessment:

At the same time that the Bank of Nova Scotia was expanding, two other Maritime banks failed and several others made little headway, succumbing in the next decade. The Nova Scotia, because it had developed wider connections and a more diversified business than the small local institutions, was better able to adapt to the financing of the new industries which came into being in this period. And it was eminently successful in its operation of a branch system – a system which, with rapidly improving transport and communication, was becoming best suited to Canadian conditions.[4]

Even in the early stages of Canadian banking, diversification of lending and funding sources was necessary for survival, and diversification without a wide network was impossible. A branch system was the obvious strategic response to these market forces.

Fyshe displayed an entrepreneurial drive to recognize and pursue new opportunities. In 1882 the Canadian growth market was in Winnipeg where a substantial land boom was taking place. Following a quick inspection of the market, Fyshe ensured that the bank quickly established a presence. When the land-boom psychology driving the growth proved unstable and the venture unprofitable, he manoeuvred a quick exit from the market in 1885. Following this abortive attempt, Scotiabank did not reopen in Winnipeg until 1899. The entrepreneurial orientation of the bank stood in sharp contrast to the more staid policies of the Bank of Montreal.

During this period, important changes were taking place in Canadian banking. In 1882, two Maritime banks drastically reduced their capital because difficult conditions in the Maritimes meant that the funds could not be employed locally and these banks lacked the resources to employ them at a distance. Fyshe, on the other hand, with his growing branch system, was aggressively seeking new opportunities. Small markets strangled banks that lacked Scotiabank's initiative.

In 1885 the first foreign branch was opened in Minnesota at a time when there was no representation in Canada outside the Maritime provinces. Although the Winnipeg venture had been a failure, that operation had alerted the bank to the development of Minneapolis as the largest flour milling city in the United States, a wheat trade second only to New York, and a growing manufacturing sector. Winnipeg and Minneapolis had always had close ties, and the recent development of railroad connections had dramatically improved communications between the two cities. This proximity was responsible for the bank becoming aware that most Minnesotan businesses were forced to employ eastern bankers – a fate lamented by the Minneapolis Chamber of Commerce in 1884. The area was under-banked. Knowledge gained from the Winnipeg venture and an extensive network of contacts in Canada facilitated pursuit of this profitable opportunity. Two of the bank's top men, H.C. McLeod and James Forgan, were sent to investigate the market in the fall of 1885 and by 20 October 1885, Scotiabank's services were advertised in the *Minneapolis Tribune*.[5] However, by 1893, there were 12 other new banks in Minnesota and the bank withdrew from this newly competitive market.[6]

A presence in the U.S. Midwest was maintained because in 1892 an agency had been opened in Chicago, the hub of the Midwest and a central reserve city. The foreign-exchange opportunities that would result from the Chicago Exposition were the specific attraction, and the success of the office was based upon competitive advantages in foreign-exchange expertise. The following comments to the Maritime managers by Fyshe were telling: "The Bank's loans in the lower provinces have increased by nearly $400,000 since the 15th of May. All this money had to be brought from Chicago where it might have been earning 10% or more."[7] This remark echoed the complaints made by the Bank of Montreal.

Fyshe not only pursued asset growth and outlets for surplus funds, but he was also concerned with managing the deposit, or liability side. In 1888, he decided to open an agency in Montreal to utilize better floating balances and to have greater access to funds when money was tight in the Maritimes. The move was further precipitated by the news that the Merchants' Bank of Halifax had opened in Montreal. In this industry, firms followed each other as well as clients: an exchange of hostages helped to maintain orderly markets.

International operations were increased in 1889 and as Scotiabank became the first Canadian bank to enter the West Indies when it opened an office in Kingston, Jamaica. A letter to Fyshe from a former colleague in New York had convinced Fyshe that Jamaica merited investigation. Although the bank had extensive connections in the area because of the substantial trade between Halifax and Jamaica, Fyshe had resisted opening a branch because he believed the area was unprogressive. However, a trip to Jamaica convinced him that economic changes presented opportunities because of increased exports to the United States. The Kingston office marked the beginning of an important connection for Scotiabank.

Fyshe left an impressive list of accomplishments when he resigned in 1897. During his leadership, foreign operations had increased, total shareholders' equity had gone from $1.2 million to $3.1 million, and total assets from $3.5 million to $15.1 million. Such achievements were made against a background of increasing industry concentration, since between 1870 and 1890 the market share of chartered banks other than the 9 major banks fell from 56.1 per cent to 46.4 per cent, although they had grown in number from 15 to 27.[8] Between 1880 and 1900, Scotiabank increased its share of the total assets held by Canadian chartered banks from 2.2 per cent to 4.5 per cent. Fyshe also left a lasting impact on the bank's market strategy through his opinion that the growth of large companies endangered the future of banking because large firms would become self financing. A bank that become too reliant on large customers risked its long-term survival.

H.C. McLEOD AND THE MOVE TO TORONTO: 1897–1909

The consolidation movement of the era demonstrated both the flexibility and appropriateness of the Canadian branch system. It had not been difficult to integrate failing banks into the structure because of the centralized control systems developed through earlier experience with the branch system. However, Scotiabank's growth strategy had shifted the centre of gravity westward and had strained its capacity to exchange and process information because the communication technology of the day was limited. Given the slowness of communication, it became imperative that the bank move its headquarters closer to the centre of its operations.

Following Fyshe's resignation, H.C. McLeod was chosen to lead the bank. McLeod had been the Chicago agent and his experiences there as well as in Winnipeg and Minneapolis had convinced him of opportunities in the West. Yet, in order to become a national bank, Scotiabank would have to develop a means of minimizing communication delays. For that reason, the board of directors decided that the general manager's office should be moved to Toronto.[9]

Growth in the West was now given priority over that in the Maritimes. This expansion provided diversification by geography, customers, and industries in the loan portfolio. As had been previously shown in Winnipeg and Minneapolis, the bank never hesitated to close an unprofitable branch, unless it was located in a key centre. It also expanded its operations in the West Indies and commenced operations in Cuba where the sugar and tobacco industries were booming due to u.s. investment.

The McLeod years saw a continuation of Fyshe's concern with internal operations. To improve the social life of employees in the West Indies, the Acadia Club was built on an attractive 143-acre tract just outside Kingston. The club expanded the number and variety of leisure pursuits available to the bank's employees. Scotiabank was also the first Canadian bank to do extensive cost analysis as the basis for determining the appropriate fee for services when it initiated its "Unit System of Work" in 1901. This new attention to fee, or non-interest income, as a revenue source was an important change in strategic orientation.

The non-establishment nature was again demonstrated in 1899 when withdrawal from the Canadian Bankers' Association (CBA) was prompted by the CBA's accusation that the manager of the Winnipeg branch was engaged in the improper practice of "raiding" another bank's clients. Competitive forces had sharpened and agreements on deposit rates in both Winnipeg and Halifax showed signs of weakness. McLeod not only desired this accusation to be withdrawn, he further expected an apology.[10] This was eventually offered in 1904. The CBA's role promoting cooperation, or orderly markets, was clear. Competition must not threaten stability.

H.A. RICHARDSON AND THE AGE OF AMALGAMATIONS: 1910-23

Under H.A. Richardson, the number of branches grew from 97 to 306 and assets from $53.5 million to $227.8 million. Behind this rapid growth was the increasing concentration of the banking industry: between 1910 and 1930, the percentage of assets controlled by the two largest banks increased from 30.5 per cent to 52.8 per cent while the percentage controlled by the five largest went from 48.0 per cent to 85.5 per cent.[11] It became apparent that only the large would be able to survive and grow, yet the difficulty of obtaining staff and the expense of opening new branches made expansion difficult. Fortunately, the same forces exerted far more severe pressure on smaller banks. As a result, the bank grew significantly via mergers with the Bank of New Brunswick, the Metropolitan Bank, and the Bank of Ottawa. Since most of the branches added from the amalgamations opened up new markets, the branch network of 127 in Ontario compared to 86 in the Maritimes continued to shift the centre of gravity further westward. The complementary nature of the additions, which were the result of a clear strategic vision, limited the need for branch rationalization, and demonstrated the flexibility of the branch system.

Expansion in the Caribbean continued as four branches were added in the British West Indies, three in the Dominican Republic, and two in each of Puerto Rico and Cuba. As trade increased, competitive advantage created by early presence in the market was leveraged. Scotiabank, the fourth largest Canadian bank, followed the lead of the other "establishment" banks and opened an office in London, England.[12] J.A. McLeod was brought from Chicago to Toronto in order to assist Richardson. Richardson prepared for the future by grooming his chosen successor. McLeod was appointed assistant general manager (AGM) in 1917 and upon Richardson's death in 1923, rose to general manager. He consolidated Richardson's impressive gains and carefully managed through the Depression. But, until the end of the World War II, there was little dynamic activity.

HORACE L. ENMAN, F.W. NICKS, AND GROWTH THROUGH PRODUCT DIVERSIFICATION: 1945-72

Growth via geographic expansion led to organizational slack because new resources were not being fully utilized. In this type of service industry where there were relatively low profit margins and high costs associated with each branch, it was imperative that each branch process a number of transactions. Increasing the range of product offerings in each branch was the simplest method to increase the volume of transactions. In order to implement this strategy, however it was necessary to decentralize to move decision making closer to the market and to provide more sophisticated control systems to manage centrally the total portfolio. The struggle during this period was to adapt the structure of the organization to the increased complexity of information flows created through the expansion of the service line.

Horace L. Enman became general manager in 1945 and brought new vigour to Scotiabank. Under his leadership, the scope of local decision making increased, and staff was recruited from Scotland to support new growth initiatives, such as consumer lending. The booming Canadian economy attracted significant capital inflows and placed pressure on exchange rates. In late 1950 when the government moved to floating rates in response to these pressures, Scotiabank rebuilt its foreign exchange trading skills and thus developed an important skill for entry into foreign commercial banking.

In the early 1950s, Scotiabank began to target aggressively the domestic consumer market. Scotiabank introduced the Personal Security Program (PSP) to attract new deposits. This program was an insured savings program in which a saver would announce a savings goal of up to $2,000 (later $5,000) and endeavour to deposit one fiftieth of the amount each month. If the depositor died prior to completing the fifty month contract, the heirs received the full amount. The PSP was patterned after a similar idea that the Bank of America had introduced earlier in the United States.[13] The bank also had assistance from the Bank of America in preparing to enter the consumer loan segment. By 1955, it was prepared to enter the market, but declined to make the move in a tight-money environment. Economic conditions changed and in 1958, Scotia Plan Loans were unveiled. This major undertaking required hiring almost 100 additional experienced consumer credit staff from outside companies. This domestic strategy was clearly different from that of other major competitors who in general still targeted large accounts. The willingness of the bank to go outside in order to gain the skills necessary to compete indicated a shrewd and self-confident management team.

The boom in the Canadian economy combined with the new market offerings limited international growth. The 127th (1958) Annual Report, which described a Western tour of the bank directors, echoed remarks made in the 109th (1940) Annual Report concerning the desirability of expansion in the West.[14] By the late 1950s, the priorities of the bank were changing. While Western expansion was still on, the 126th (1957), 127th (1958), and 128th (1959) Annual Reports all attested to the considerable growth in international markets in terms of branches, loans, and deposits. The international arena was becoming the focus for growth.

Growth in the Caribbean continued in the late 1940s because of expanded trade opportunities.[15] But in 1954, when F.W. Nicks became general manager, a search for new external business in the general area was initiated. Scotiabank innovated in sovereign lending to the Dominican Republic, with sufficient success to inspire other banks to follow. This success was somewhat offset by increasing political pressures being exerted in Cuba and Jamaica. As a result, the bank began to turn away from politically sensitive retail operations and move toward international commercial banking, thus demonstrating the importance of the political imperative.

In 1958, the Bank of Nova Scotia Trust Company (Bahamas) was created in partnership with British financial interests to carry out transactions not open to a Canadian bank in Canada.[16] the Bank of Nova Scotia Trust Company of New York opened the following year,[17] while entry into the gold market provided yet another opportunity to expand the bank's international scope. In association with Samuel Montagu and Company of London, a firm with extensive experience in the gold markets, gold certificates that were redeemable in London or Toronto were developed.[18] The fact that Americans were prohibited form holding gold in their own country provided the bank with a market opportunity. Proximity to the United States and its regulation has always played a role in the strategic thinking of Canadian banks.

Although Scotiabank had opened a London branch shortly after World War I, there was little activity there until after World War II. In the mid-1950s Nicks made calls on the continent which resulted in the development of important connections in West Germany and Holland. Later the same technique of personal calls by one CEO to another was also practised in London. Nicks' role in developing a substantial base of clients in the United Kingdom and on the continent who were interested in entering the Canadian market should not be downplayed. It was a good example of the manner in which Canadian banks successfully attracted foreign clients into Canada. This was in contrast to U.S. and many British banks, whose principal strategy was to follow clients into foreign markets. International capital flows mattered as much as trade flows, especially as Canada was open to foreign direct investment, but domestic capital markets were protected. CEO to CEO contact was an important tool for developing new markets.

The original (informal) rules governing the London banking scene were important. Banks were able to handle and to invest sterling from their other foreign operations and could approach British companies that were considering entering the foreign bank's home country. As long as many countries prohibited foreign banks, there was an important role for banks from such countries in channelling international capital flows. However, foreign banks were not supposed to approach British companies for British business. This could have been a critical determinant in how the Canadian banks came to view foreign operations. In this market structure, foreign banks could be expected to form alliances with British banks. Scotiabank developed cordial relations with the Midland Bank and gained the opportunity to assist the Midland's customers desiring to establish Canadian operations.

Operations in New York were essential because it was the centre of a lively call loan market and an important source of U.S. dollars, which were increasingly important in international lending. A strong presence there meant the bank could take advantage of any unusual situations in foreign exchange markets, as the 126th (1957) Annual Report asserted. Scotiabank increased its participation in the New York call loan market and its penetration in deposit markets with some success, as shown by the considerable growth in U.S. dollar certificates of deposits.[19] It maintained its grain financing and its other traditional markets, but also sought clients, using in part techniques that had worked in Europe, that of CEO calling on CEO.

In 1958 in order to cope with the rapid growth and increased complexity of product offerings and geography, the bank was reorganized and eight general managers were appointed. Five of these dealt with credit and were in charge of regions: B.R. Calder for foreign, G.C. Hitchman for Quebec, C.L. Bowlby for the West, G.J. Touchie for the Maritimes, and C.J. Ash for Ontario. C.G. Webster in New York and Harry Randall in charge of the international division were also promoted. In addition, a new player and position emerged as W.S. Bond was appointed assistant general manager, administration with responsibility for personnel and premises.

Other strains had also become apparent: by 1948 there was public pressure concerning the conduct of the banks and talk of "nationalizing" the banks.[20] Through the vehicle of the annual report, the general manager assured the shareholders, and presumably the public at large, that the decennial review of banking legislation provided a suitable mechanism for ensuring that banking was regulated in the public interest. The discussion raised the all-important point of business-government relations in this regulated industry. While Scotiabank clearly felt a need to respond to the public, its statements suggested cordial relations with the regulatory body. Regulation was described as "informal" and carried out through a small book of rules. There was no hint of antagonism between bankers and regulators at this time; rather the public was assured that the regulators were doing their job. Industry and government cooperation had created a strong industry.

The period between 1960 and 1965 saw impressive growth as 104 new branches were opened in Canada, and 27 abroad. The bank's increased attention to the international scene was demonstrated by the greater volume of its foreign currency business, which grew at 14 per cent per year over the period, while domestic business grew at only 9.5 per cent.[21] By 1965 foreign currency assets amounted to 40 per cent of Canadian assets and by 1967, to roughly 50 per cent. The bank's policy related to international markets was articulated by Executive Vice-President and Deputy Chairman J.D. Gibson in 1962: "We have found that participation in this international market opens doors to much worthwhile business and is directly profitable with careful management."[22] The strategy for success was to deal in large volumes and always to hedge foreign exchange risk. Gibson's inference of indirect profits attested to the difficulty of analysing the profitability of individual products.

Success in penetrating international markets was due to many factors, but of critical importance was the emergence of the international banking division as an operating unit. Scotiabank made determined efforts to establish a base in the United States, primarily to seek deposits and to develop some loan business because this was seen as the greatest market opportunity.[23] The large u.s. balance-of-payments deficit situation also meant that funds were readily available not only in the United States but almost everywhere. The bank followed a niche strategy focused on asset growth in areas that were not of interest to the American banks, such as finance companies and call loans against stock securities. In addition, u.s. banks were content to allow Canadian banks to supplement loans to their clients when money was tight. The nature of banking promoted a degree of cooperation, as well as competition. Presumably foreign banks were not perceived as formidable a competitive threat as were other domestic U.S. banks.

A substantial percentage of the funds raised in the United States was channelled to u.s. companies entering the European Common Market. Scotiabank was developing corporate clients in the United States, not only because of its dedicated "door-knocking" campaign, but because of its ability to offer important services to corporate treasurers, who were shown how to secure a higher yield than they were obtaining from T-bills.[24] But even more importantly, the bank developed a competitive advantage in the chief accountant's department: A.B. McKie, the British tax expert. McKie, once described by an American banker as the bank's "secret weapon," instructed American companies on the optimal manner to structure deals. In 1965, all tax expertise was brought into one department under McKie in order to focus the bank's skills on both its own and its customers tax problems. His expertise combined with Nicks' personal touch created a formidable competitive weapon for business development.

The bank opened a business office in Tokyo in 1962 under the direction of a former Japanese Canadian, George Korenaga. By 1964, substantial u.s. funds were also being directed to large Japanese firms.[25] Interestingly, expanded trade between Japan and Canada created a demand both for traditional and new services. Product lines had to be expanded in order for the bank to be competitive internationally.

Business in the Caribbean was changing. The Cuban revolution demonstrated the importance of political forces in the area of international banking. Moreover, the plantation economy was declining and was being replaced by new resource industries and tourism was developing. Lessons learned in financing Canadian resource industries could be employed to develop these new markets. In addition, Edgar Felsenstein, the representative in Latin America, and Harry Randall, a deputy general manager, were able to obtain for the bank substantial deposits in the form of gold and u.s. dollars underemployed by several central banks in Central and Latin America. Perhaps Canada's more neutral reputation was instrumental in facilitating this intermediation.

Domestic growth was also impressive. Large corporate borrowings in the 1960s put to rest the ghost of the fears of Fyshe and Patterson that large companies would become self-financing. However, the original market strategy still had impact as was revealed in the 130th (1961) Annual Report which stated that larger clients were being led towards bond markets so that services could be provided to smaller and medium-sized domestic firms.[26] The creation of Markborough, a fully integrated real estate investment and development corporation was a first for Canada. But again, this product was copied from British models, and provided further evidence of the international nature of financial services. Domestic growth was further stimulated by Scotiabank's early entry into the personal lending market. This was an important move that was intended to increase the revenue-generating capabilities of the retail branch network.

The resultant branch expansion created significant organizational pressures and led to discussions of decentralization in the 133rd (1964) and 134th (1965) Annual Reports. Further, to maintain this growth the 1964 report placed an increased emphasis on marketing.[27] It also discussed transferring headquarters functions to the field and establishing profit targets for the decentralized units. The chief accountant's office was responsible for developing the profit-planning system that was key to decentralization. A major player was the future ceo, C.E. Ritchie, who was the chief accountant at the time. In addition, the bank established a job evaluation program to clarify lines of command within the institution and employed outside experts, such as the Hay Group, to cope with the new demands created by the deposit revolution. The Hay system provided a tool for measuring the relative importance of each job by giving points for know how, problem solving, and accountability. The system provided the base for a comprehensive and consistent compensation and benefits policy. Perhaps most significant, however, for the future of the financial services industry was the installation of a computer in April 1965.[28] The impact of the new information technology was to be enormous.

The need to increase the deposit base led to another interesting development in the early to mid-1960s: discontent with regulation. Throughout the period the annual reports painted a rosy picture for international operations, but complaints about the effects of regulation on the domestic market began to surface. Discontent with restrictions on lending rates and participation in the mortgage market appeared in the 133rd (1964) Annual Report and was strongly reiterated the following year. The real sore point was competition from other deposit-taking institutions, such as trust companies, which were subject to different regulatory regimes, frequently provincial ones. Near banks did not have to meet reserve requirements and consequently had a lower cost of funds than the banks which were saddled with the hidden tax of reserve requirements.[29] The following statement by Nicks in the 134th (1965) Annual Report revealed a quite different posture from that of the 1940s: "Over the years there has always been an inherent public policy problem in the banking sphere – how to reconcile the basic need for regulation (in the interests of a sound financial system) with the equally vital need to encourage initiative and flexibility in the supplying of bank services."[30] While the potential for conflict had always existed, the development of the ability to provide an ever increasing range of services combined with domestic growth strategies was bound to create conflict over the role of near banks and other financial services firms.

While it was fairly clear how geographic expansion promoted decentralization, it was less obvious, how the growth strategy focusing on international also promoted centralization. The relationship between the domestic and international portfolios and the integration of capital markets were powerful forces buffeting the organization. Perhaps even more important, however, were the changes in information technology that facilitated the integration of capital markets. The computer revolution had a dramatic impact on the opportunities open to Scotiabank, as well as a tremendous effect on the organizational structure. The need to coordinate information in conjunction with the expense of acquiring the technology were both powerful forces that limited decentralization. In addition, the scarcity of people who understood the complexities of rapidly changing financial markets served to limit decentralization further. Strategic thinking was dominated by efforts to find an appropriate structure that balanced the forces promoting centralization and decentralization, yet allowed for an aggressive internationalization strategy. Between 1966 and 1971, international growth was rapid; in 1969, for example, 11 new foreign branches were opened.[31] These openings were especially important since Scotiabank had always maintained that a direct presence in foreign markets was an essential part of their success.[32] Joint ventures were also employed.[33] International assets increased at an average annual real rate of 16 per cent (20 per cent nominal), while domestic assets increased at a real rate of 7 per cent. Schull and Gibson believed that the early work of Nicks establishing foreign connections had given the bank a considerable advantage over its Canadian rivals. Nicks' personal attention was now directed toward increased participation in the German market and the Greek shipping industry. The latter seemed a fitting move for a concern whose first major client had been Samuel Cunard. In addition, the bank became more active in the u.s. wholesale market and opened a new agency in San Francisco.

Domestic operations improved because of the efficiencies generated as a result of prior organizational changes.[34] However, the growth and profitability of international operations were limited by the quality of loans available and the practice of large commercial banks to maintain 40 per cent or more of their assets in the form of deposits with other banks. In the absence of regulation, the market was enforcing practices that would reduce risk both through diversification and a de facto limit to risky loans. By 1971, the bank believed that it had sufficient experience in the market to adjust its portfolio strategy towards greater profitability. A cautious shift towards commercial loans and foreign securities from bank deposits in the portfolio was made. At the same time, the bank's foreign-exchange trading developed into a profitable business.[35]

Important changes also took place with the organization. Since 1965 all credit applications for the international wholesale market went through the international credit department following the recommendation of the General Office Methods Group (GMOG) that had been set up in 1964. By 1967, Randall was general manager of the whole international division and had under him four AGMs in Toronto. There were two in charge of credit, one for the Caribbean, and one for business development. In addition, there were two AGMs in New York and one in London. By 1968, when future CEO C.E. Ritchie became head of international, organizational problems were obvious. A banking division was created to facilitate the efficient matching of assets and liabilities over the wide range of currencies represented. Expansion demanded greater centralization. Credit approval was formalized and discussed at regular meetings rather than as the requests came in. The sheer volume of information required that decision-making procedures be streamlined. Computer services were updated to accommodate the ever-increasing flows of information.[36]

Not only growth but the increased complexity of international banking in the Euromarkets forced change. In domestic banking, competition for loans and deposits was separate. But such was not the case in the Euromarkets where the two processes were simultaneous.[37] While this procedure did facilitate better matching, it demanded closer integration of information processing. To complicate matters, it was recognized that the conduct of firms was serving to increase the complexity of the environment. The increased flow of communications was seen as a possible factor in making market fluctuations more volatile.[38]

Such difficulties were recognized by the GMOG which recommended the closer coordination of the money-market operations of the investment department and the foreign exchange operations of the international division. However, lack of political support delayed implementation of this proposal for over a decade. The proposal made clear that one source of increased complexity was the relationship between international and domestic. The two were becoming less separable as capital markets became more integrated.[39]

In domestic markets, earlier decentralization had created difficulty in controlling the quality of loans. Perhaps the shortage of skilled assessors led to the merging of Eastern and Western Canadian credits into one office under Deputy General Manager H.R. Younker. The problem of risky loans may also have been exacerbated by the continuing focus on middle- to small-sized clients.[40] Conversely, however, the strategy of concentrating on smaller loans encouraged decentralization, because it required a more hands-on understanding of local conditions. But even in domestic markets, centralized control over the asset portfolio was necessary to ensure an appropriate diversification strategy.

Politics continued to have an important influence on the bank. Scotiabank moved to allow increased national participation in its Jamaican operations, since it believed that this was the appropriate behaviour for multinationals. The goal was that operations should become completely self-managed.[41] Shares were also offered in Trinidad and Tobago.[42] Domestically however, discontent rather than satisfaction seemed to be the rule. There was dissatisfaction that changes in the Bank Act failed to create equal competition between banks and near banks.[43] In addition, the bank argued that agencies of foreign banks would make a positive contribution to the Canadian market and should be allowed entry.[44] The non-establishment nature of Scotiabank was still in evidence.

Perhaps even more important than concerns over banking regulation was the general feeling that the government was intervening excessively in the economy. From 1968 on, the annual reports emphasize the theme that government must get its own house in order – especially the growing deficit. At the same time, guidelines on wages and prices were seen as desirable in order to awaken the Canadian public to the dangers of declining productivity, vis-a-vis the United States.[45] By 1970, there was also discontent over how the restraints affected both spreads and service charges.[46] As a conduit of foreign capital into Canada, the bank was not impressed by government policies that neglected the benefits of foreign investment and focused on the ownership issue.[47] It is impossible to read the annual reports from these years without becoming aware of a widening gulf between government and the business community.

C.E. RITCHIE AND THE CHANGING FACE OF BANKING: 1972–80

When C.E. Ritchie became CEO in 1972, the major forces driving change within the financial services industry were developments in information processing made possible by the expanding capabilities of computers. As more on line terminals were installed and the goal of one central information file became closer,[48] business at the branch level began to shift from being people-intensive to technology-intensive. Once again, the need for cooperation among competitors was made apparent by research into the "cashless" society and the practical aspects of the Chargex system.[49] Scotiabank delayed its entry into the Chargex network until 1973, even though the card had been started by three other Canadian banks in 1966. However, it believed that a follower strategy was appropriate:[50] late introduction would not significantly affect the customer base, and the bank would be able to offer the best service at a lower cost by letting others pay for the development costs of this easily copied service.

The organization also found that increased specialization worked against the regional structure. Corporate banking, liability management, and foreign exchange trading were all specialties that cut across regional divisions.[51] The increasing complexity and integration of capital markets in conjunction with more sophisticated information-processing capabilities was forcing change within the organization in order to provide a competitive level of service to customers.

The impact of changing markets and social mores on organizations was also demonstrated by increasing attention to the personnel function and the development of the educational facility, Spencer Hall, in association with the University of Western Ontario. Changes in employee attitudes were having an impact. During the period, it became necessary to respond to the changing role of women in Canadian society.[52] As well, decentralization efforts benefited from decreased mobility among employees. Good employees had not always been anxious to move and it became easier to maintain qualified personnel in diverse locations. In a similar vein, MBAS were found to be better suited to certain environments, principally Toronto and international. The challenge was to manage human resources in order to maintain the proper fit with the environment.

Scotiabank enjoyed a period of high growth between 1971 and 1981, to which international operations more than contributed their share. Domestic operations saw an average growth of 21 per cent per annum (11.5 per cent real) while international grew at 25 per cent (15 per cent real). In 1960, Scotiabank held 17 per cent of the total international assets of all Canadian banks. By 1980, it held 24 per cent and was second only to the Royal. This impressive growth was the result both of expansion in former markets and new initiatives. In 1979, the balanced diversification strategy was declared a success. In general over the period, domestic and international spreads did move in offsetting ways and reduced the volatility of the total portfolio.[53]

The familiar U.S. market provided new opportunities, especially after 1977 when the bank had some concerns about its international portfolio.[54] Consistent expansion within the United States made it clear that the U.S. market was targeted as a major growth vector, and that commercial loans were becoming a more important component of the international portfolio.[55] The portfolio was expanded by building upon relationships with shipping and other multinational industries. In addition, the bank increased its presence in the Euromarkets and developed specialized spheres of interest for different branches. For example, Frankfurt worked on Euromark loans, while London specialized in the Eurodollar ones. The overall development of such European markets resulted in greatly increased importance for London.[56] Changes in markets also led to the creation of a Special Loans Department focused on loan syndicates.[57] Scotiabank, in company with other banks, was increasingly seeking to differentiate itself through its ability to provide a full line of services. The annual reports discuss the Pacific Rim as the developing area and reveal plans to open a Hong Kong office in 1972.[58] Ritchie's trip in 1973 to the Far East was further evidence that this area was viewed as a major growth area. While Scotiabank had followed Canadian clients to some areas, it had also shown itself adept at identifying new growth areas.[59] There was a certain entrepreneurial verve in Ritchie's addresses during this period. It should also be noted that there was little reluctance in joining consortia to promote market entry, as Asian and Indonesian forays demonstrated.[60]

The expansion of gold dealings led to an interesting change.[61] In 1975, connections with Samuel Montagu and Company of London were severed as the bank believed it had sufficient knowledge to go it alone in the gold markets. In a knowledge-based industry, such a move should not be unexpected since a number of temporary joint ventures will end when at least one partner has acquired sufficient information capital to act on its own.[62] The success or failure of international joint ventures or strategic alliances must be evaluated against the original and subsequent strategic goals. Cessation does not equal failure.

Why was Scotiabank successful? In part, the age-old skill of the personal touch in service industries was important. C.E. Ritchie's 1974 trip to China was instrumental in eventually securing an office there. But the Canadian banks were also able to take a lead because of their experience with a branch network spread out over vast distances and their experience with floating rates.[63] Products designed to help corporate clients deal with the problems that arose because of the geographic expanse of Canada provided valuable experience in developing services for multinational firms.[64]

The strategic importance of a good name was recognized. As early as 1974, it became clear that banks that appeared risky were losing deposits.[65] At that time, Scotiabank began to address the problem of its soundness. By 1978, international success was attributed to its strong capital base, which allowed Scotiabank to take advantage of some opportunities unavailable to weak banks.[66]

Success in international was in part required because of the bank's continuing focus on small- to medium-sized clients in Canada.[67] In response to public pressure, Scotiabank also asserted that less than 3 per cent of its loans were to large subsidiaries of foreign corporations and that only interim financing was provided in takeovers.[68] If Scotiabank was to have a base of large clients, such clients would have to be in the international portfolio. However, it is important to note that foreign funds, swapped and hedged, were employed when money was tight in Canada.[69] In order to be competitive in the Canadian market, access to foreign funds was necessary.

The strategy of balanced diversification to smooth out earnings was supported by a regionally based organizational structure. In 1979, the Western Hemisphere division was split into two: North America and Latin America. The other regions were London, the Caribbean, and the Pacific. While in theory all regions were equal, it was clear that North America and London handled far larger volumes than did the others. Another dissonant feature of the organization was the fact that there were two head-office divisions whose responsibilities could conflict with the autonomy of a regional division. T.A. Healy as general manager of the treasury at head office had the responsibility of coordinating the movement of money, foreign exchange, and gold. In order to ensure the overall profitability of the bank, centralized planning and control was essential. P.S. Dodd had the responsibility of determining exposure limits to countries and companies. Both Healy and Dodd had to overrule their regional counterparts from time to time. The nature of banking required that the field officers have two bosses.

There were other factors that served to limit increased regionalization of credit. Increasingly, head office became responsible for a number of specialized services. Moreover, as in any business where individual analysis of data is critical to success, there was a shortage of qualified people. Despite training programs designed to overcome this problem, it was at best ameliorated. Finally, the rapidity of change in financial markets as well as in the world economy exposed the bank to increased levels of risk. The rational response to such downside risk was more analysis. Given the shortage of qualified people, the necessity of assessing the riskiness of any individual asset was related to the total portfolio, and the improvements in information processing meant that increased centralization was both possible and desirable.

The ties between the bank's domestic and international operations became more apparent. Six international banking centres were established across the country to coordinate international and domestic services for its clients. An interesting sidelight was the manner in which André Bisson, vice-president and general manager in Quebec, and Ritchie leveraged international expertise to improve the bank's presence in the Quebec market, a traditionally weak area. Scotiabank wished to create the impression of "a large international bank serving Quebec with its international expertise." The success of the strategy was demonstrated in 1979 when the bank acted as lead manager of a Quebec government debt issue and again in 1980 when it acted as agent and was one of three lead managers in a one billion U.S. and Canadian dollar issue. Moreover, the bank's operations in Haiti were used cleverly to provide international exposure for francophone employees.[70] International expertise was a competitive advantage in domestic markets, especially as capital markets become more integrated.

Throughout the period, a certain level of disenchantment with the federal government can be detected. The bank continued to see that it was advantageous for Canada to be the host for foreign investment, including foreign banks, since the present back-door entry was seen as unsatisfactory.[71] Moreover, there was discontent with banking legislation since it had failed to create a level playing field.[72] The Anti-Inflation Board (AIB) was also seen as hindering bank profitability. However, it was recognized that changes in the 1967 Bank Act created new opportunities, especially in consumer lending,[73] and that new changes would make raising capital easier.[74] Given the strategic importance assigned to a sound reputation, the latter change was especially welcome.[75]

Schull and Gibson offer a pertinent appraisal of Scotiabank's success. In the 1970s, money was always available and the bank achieved an asset growth of 11.5 per cent per annum. This was all the more impressive when it is noted that staff grew at only 5 per cent per annum. Throughout the decades, returns from the international sphere offset declining margins at home. In order to maintain a steady return on equity of roughly 12 per cent, holdings of government securities, an expensive source of liquidity, were reduced and leverage was increased. Without its impressive international growth and diversification, the bank would have been hard pressed to increase its leverage and maintain its return on equity.

C.E. RITCHIE: THE GLOBAL NORTH AMERICAN BANK

History had left its imprint. The early assumption that large companies would become virtually self-financing had led to an asset portfolio with relatively few large domestic clients and pressures to seek large clients internationally.[76] While the Bank of Montreal became a North American bank, Scotiabank continued to develop its global network with an increased emphasis on North America. However, by using a strategy similar to the one later developed by Barrett, retail banking came more to the forefront. A move by all banks toward greater strategic homogeneity in the late 1980s should not be surprising as deregulation, new technologies, and product innovation destroyed traditional boundaries within the financial services marketplace. All banks faced a new and far more intensely competitive market in which chief financial officers (CFOS) made few distinctions between domestic and international capital markets.

Activities during this period are most easily examined by employing the market categories used in the annual reports:

1 Domestic Retail Banking
2 Commercial Banking
3 Corporate Banking
4 Investment Banking
5 International Banking
6 Private Banking

The increased emphasis on retail banking was obvious, even though Scotiabank's shift in this direction was not as dramatic as that of the Bank of Montreal, given the earlier importance of personal loans and other products. The following passage from the 1988 Annual Report echoes similar statements from the Bank of Montreal: "We sharpened our focus on customer service in Retail Banking through the ScotiaService program. Retail Banking is the long-standing basis of Scotiabank's strength."[77] Programs to improve service were an ongoing theme. A Customer Satisfaction Index that employed a systematic sampling technique was introduced in 1989 to monitor ScotiaService's progress. Other initiatives included the testing of new products, such as debit cards, and increased market segmentation and target marketing in the credit card market. New products reflected not only advances in information technologies, but fundamental shifts in the market, such as the aging of Canada's population. An aging population meant an increased demand for retirement and investment products.[78] Scotiabank's announced entry into the trust industry demonstrated its attention to the changing market.[79] The sharpened focus was also evident in its introduction of private banking and the marketing of these services in the Orient. In 1988, the acquisition of Mcleod Young Weir, investment dealers and the subsequent creation of ScotiaMcLeod in that same year meant that the bank now had the capacity to offer full investment banking services to corporate customers. Perhaps even more important was the ongoing expansion of the branch network; between 1981 and 1991, 119 new offices were opened.

Discussions concerning reform of financial services regulation also served to focus discussions upon retail banking. While "the little bang" of 1987 seemed to promise speedy reform, the promise was not fulfilled as sweeping financial services legislation failed to be passed until early 1992. Delay resulted from disagreements over retailing of certain products with the insurance industry and ownership rules with the trust industry. Caution in light of the collapse of equity markets in 1987 may also have played a role. Whatever the reason, the bank was outspoken in its criticism of the government, as these comments from the 1989 Annual Report made clear:

It is hoped that long-awaited federal legislation to further liberalize the financial services industry in Canada will be enacted so as to bring significant new benefits to consumers. Unfortunately, the government has indicated an unwillingness to permit banks to retail a range of insurance products through branches or to engage in the lease financing of automobiles. In our view, *these decisions lack any valid public policy rationale* and work to the disadvantage both of consumers and of your Bank.[80]

A heightened notion of service led to the development of services to the front-line employees. Investment in systems and services was a driving force in non-interest expense. Moreover, there was a recognition of the importance of information processing for organizational design. In 1991, regional data centres for cheque and statement handling centralized activities that had previously been performed at the branch level.[81] Improved customer service instead of simple efficiency was the driving force behind the change. Distinguishing between front-line and back-room processing activities meant that the front-line people would have more time to devote to customer service in the branch. Expanded educational and training efforts in the human resources section provided additional and necessary support for the implementation of the service strategies.

The commercial group served small- and mid-sized businesses, especially in the agricultural, equipment financing, leasing, and franchising segments. Service was the priority: "Adding value for the customer by emphasizing convenience, specialized staff skills and technology-based services lies at the heart of our approach to commercial banking."[82] A decentralized approach was taken to provide quality service, especially in sophisticated fee-based services such as cash management, foreign exchange, and trade financing. Information technologies became more important in this sector. In 1990, two new products based on personal computers (PCS) were introduced,

ScotiaCustody and ScotiaNote, which gave customers new tools to manage commercial paper and securities portfolios. In the same year, the bank participated in one of the industry's first electronic data interchange (EDI) projects. During the period, 42 new commercial centres demonstrated the bank's strong commitment to this sector.

New technologies and product innovation had dramatically changed corporate banking. In addition, fundamental changes in capital markets had led to strategic challenges for the bank. Intense competition placed severe pressures on margins. Competitors included not only other banks, but large multinationals such as IBM or Kodak, whose understanding of their own banking requirements limited their needs for intermediaries, or in the case of GE Capital, created a base for diversification into the financial services industry. Without some basis for differentiation, which could only be grounded in information capital, banks would be limited to competing in an essentially commodity-like business in the prime market segment. To some extent, the fears of Fyshe had came to pass. To compete as an "international financial services corporation," Scotiabank continued to invest in information technologies.[83] North American Corporate Banking and the international division combined to develop a $35 million computer system to automate global transactions.[84] The system, developed by Internet Systems Corporation of Chicago, had been purchased by 7 of the world's 200 largest banks. Competitiveness demanded leading-edge telecommunications technology.

In addition to investing in information technology, the bank integrated some aspects of affected organizational structure. By 1986, it had the following divisions: Corporate Administration, Canadian Commercial and Retail Banking, North American Corporate Banking, Investment Banking, and International. By 1987, North American Corporate Banking and International Corporate sector of the International Division had merged into Corporate. The integration of global capital markets was mirrored by other changes to coordinate marketing, as authority for investment banking for Europe and the Far East was centralized in London. A further sign of globalization was evident in 1992 when Bruce Birmingham was appointed vice chairman to oversee the bank's entire corporate loan portfolio.

Such changes revealed complex forces driving the organization toward both centralization and specialization. The move toward specialization was evident in the targeting of specific industries, such as communications, media, forestry, real estate, and oil and gas.[85] The strategy was successful as in 1986 the bank ranked among the largest lenders to the communications industry in North America.[86] Other groups were also developed to increase the bank's expertise in government lending and project financing.[87]

The bank's decision to add investment banking services was imperative if it was to meet the needs of large customers who increasingly replaced bank credit products with direct financial instruments, such as bonds and commercial paper. In 1988, the acquisition of McLeod Young Weir enabled the bank to create the customized debt products demanded by sophisticated CFOs. Fee-based products became a major source of revenue and required integration across functions to cross sell the various services and products. In the corporate division, each client had a relationship manager. The manager was required to have both a broad knowledge of services and an indepth understanding of the client in order to create the proper service bundle by coordinating the efforts of different product specialists. Scotiabank's presence in Tokyo was increased to ensure the global reach of the group and was evidence of the belief that the potential of Asian-Pacific markets was only beginning to emerge.[88]

Scotiabank still remained true to a certain non-establishment tradition as was shown in its creation of a wholly owned securities firm in Montreal. While a complex set of negotiations on the future of the securities industry was occurring between Ottawa and Ontario, Scotiabank acted pre-emptively to create Scotia Securities, apparently gambling on a position taken by Barbara McDougall when she was minister of state for finance. According to the *Globe and Mail*, the move infuriated both Ottawa and Ontario, but was seen by the other major banks as "a master-stroke of timing that forced both levels of government to play their hands prematurely."[89] In the 1987 Annual Report, the event was proudly recounted: "According to *The Economist*, the establishment of this subsidiary [Scotia Securities] 'lit the deregulatory fuse in Canada,' bringing fundamental changes in securities legislation that will provide many new opportunities for the Bank."[90]

By 1990, the International Banking Division, which since the 1987 reorganization was responsible for sovereign lending, correspondent banking, and most subsidiary and branch activities outside of North America, was guided by three aims:

1 Further reduction of LDC exposure as a percentage of capital
2 Diversification of international operations and sources of revenues
3 Improvement of sales and service capabilities throughout the international bank[91]

Unlike the Bank of Montreal, Scotiabank remained committed to a broader notion of global operations: "As nothing before, the debt issue and stock market volatility demonstrated the interconnectedness of markets and the need to operate on a global basis, a need we have long recognized as essential to protect the long-term interests of the Bank and to profit by the opportunities change casts up. The reality is that we now operate in a single, complex and often contradictory world market."[92] Entrance into the Philippines linked both expansion and the LDC debt problem as acquisition of a 40 per cent interest in Consolidated Bank and Trust with its 57 branches was accomplished via a debt-equity swap.[93] Activities in other markets, notably Japan, Hong Kong, Taiwan, Thailand, and India also increased.[94] Interestingly, the Caribbean, an area of traditional strength, continued to provide growth opportunities.[95] Along with such expansion, capacities in trade financing and foreign exchange continued to grow.

Once again, the bank's executive was not hesitant to take bold steps and be outspoken. Unlike some other banks, Scotiabank did not liquidate its LDC debt portfolio, because it believed prices were unrealistically low.[96] Significant loan loss provisions and improved capital ratios ensured both that the bank was both sound and perceived as such. The decision appeared wise in 1991 when the market value of the LDC loan portfolio exceeded the book value.[97] Key to the rise in value were changes in Mexico and the development of a practical framework for the LDC debt problem that was exemplified by the trading of Mexican loans for thirty-year 6.25 per cent bonds. Scotiabank had always pushed for a framework for debt relief realizing that provisions or increased capital ratios were not the answer. The success of this position caused many to revise earlier opinions and regard Mr. Ritchie as Canada's top banker.[98]

The frustration vented over the financial crisis of 1987 in a section of the annual report entitled "Muddling Through No Longer Enough" could have as easily been expressed about LDC debt restructuring: "The challenges ahead are not solely those of financial technique: they are those of old-fashioned political economy and need to be addressed as such – with a political will and leadership of a much higher order than has been apparent in the last few years."[99] More recently, even more serious charges have been levelled by Mr. Ritchie. At the 1992 CBA conference, "The Regulatory Environment: Obstacle or Opportunity," he stated that the events surrounding the final form of the new Bank Act, which limited bank participation in insurance, may have broken the trust that used to facilitate discussions between policy-makers and bankers. It would be a national tragedy if long-standing relationships between public policy and this enabling industry were permanently damaged.

STRATEGY AND FINANCIAL PERFORMANCE

Between 1981 and 1991, assets increased by almost 80 per cent, employees by roughly 10 per cent, and branches by slightly under 10 per cent as figures 3.1 and 3.2 show.[100] Capital grew by almost three times to support the asset growth and has placed Scotiabank on solid footing for the future. The risk-adjusted ratio of 8.62 means that there is the capacity to expand in an environment where credit from major American and Japanese banks is tightening.

Similar to the Bank of Montreal, the geographic distribution of the asset portfolio shown in figure 3.3 has changed significantly: the percentage of Canadian assets increased by 10 percentage points to 59 per cent and American assets from 14 per cent to 19.6 per cent. Again, part of the change can be explained by the effect of provisions for LDC debt, especially the decline in Latin America, but more importantly, the movement to retail and the effects of the FTA are revealed. While the number of opportunities taken to develop the global network distinguished Scotiabank from the Bank of Montreal, the shift of the centre of gravity towards North America was evident. The bank has prepared for NAFTA and beyond. In 1991, Scotiabank used a debt-equity swap to obtain 24 per cent of Chile's sixth largest bank, the Banco Sud Americano and in 1993, it was the first Canadian bank to move into Mexico with the purchase of 5 per cent of Grupo Financiere Inverlat SA. However, it should be noted that the dollar volume of assets in Asia has increased, while the decline in Europe is marked. The regional figures do not total to 100 per cent because the bank uses one adjustment figure to update the portfolio to 31 October from 30 September.

The strategic shift toward retail is demonstrated by figures 3.4 and 3.5. Mortgages as a percentage of the asset portfolio changed from 10 per cent to over 24 per cent, revealing the increased importance of retail banking. Growth in "other" as an asset category would be consistent with the movement from sovereign lending towards retail and commercial in North America. The marked increase in individual deposits and decline in deposits by banks is further evidence of the shifts taking place in strategic position.

With the exception of a dip in 1989 that appears to be driven by loan losses, net income was steady or slightly improving over the

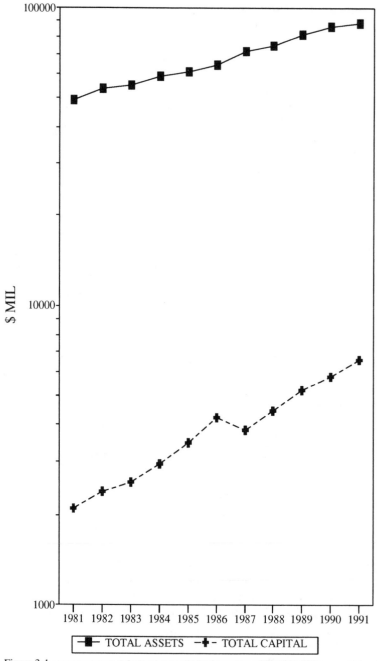

Figure 3.1
Bank of Nova Scotia Asset and Capital Growth

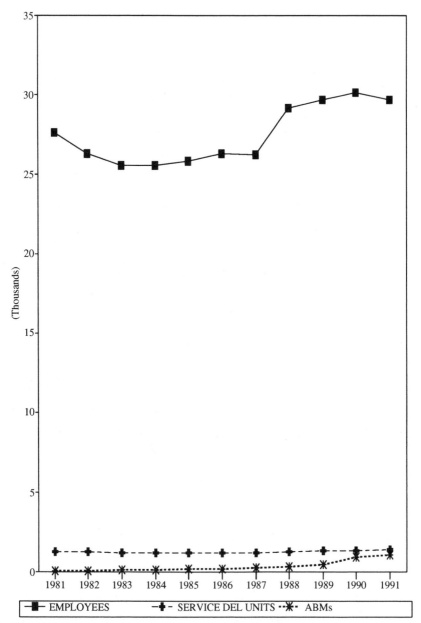

Figure 3.2
Employee and Branch Growth

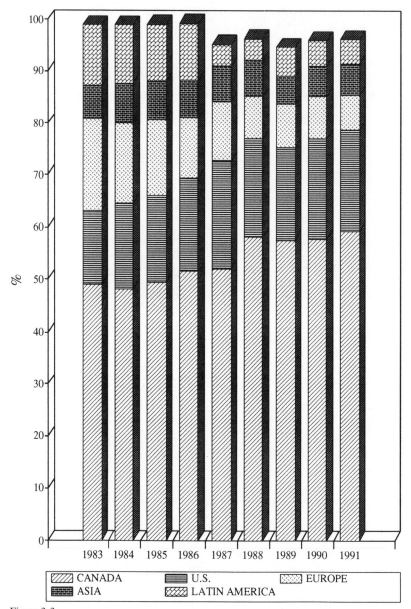

Figure 3.3
Location of Assets

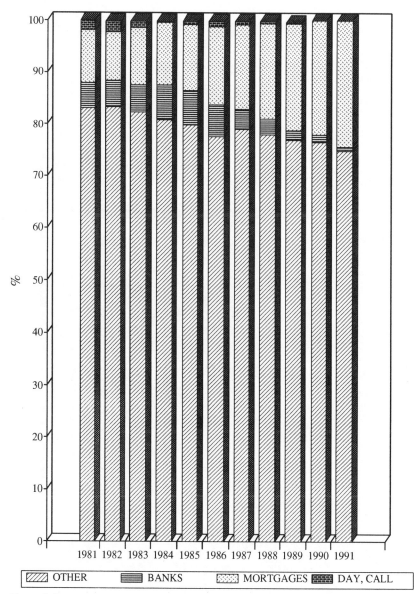

Figure 3.4
Asset Portfolio

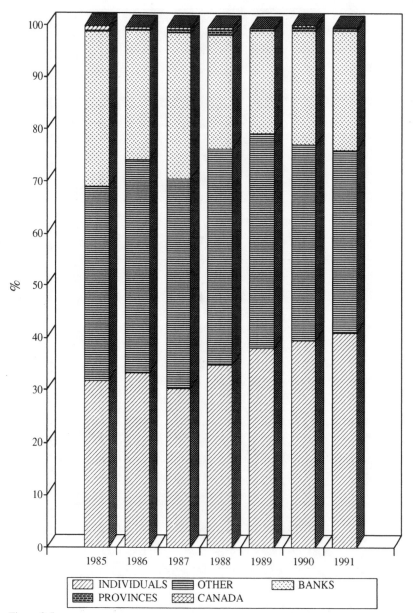

Figure 3.5
Deposit Portfolio

period, as can be seen in figure 3.6A. A distinguishing feature of Scotiabank was the performance of net interest margin. For example, improvement in 1991 performance was the result of the fact that the bank had a larger volume of floating rate deposits than assets. Consequently, falling interest rates led to improved profitability.[101] As expected, other income increased, although there was a levelling off in 1988. This increase was not linked to rising non-interest expense, which was stable until it increased slightly from 1987 on. Generally rising loan-loss provisions reached a high in 1989 and then improved to levels reminiscent of the early 1980s. The overall picture was one of improving profitability with sensitivity to loan losses and interest rate movements.

Perhaps no Canadian bank's performance better portrays the varying fortunes of international and domestic markets than does that of Scotiabank, as figure 3.6B shows. For virtually the first half of the period under consideration, international performance was superior to domestic. By 1985, there is scant difference in ROA between the two broad markets, and then severe loan losses began to impact upon international. Now that the portfolios are basically clean and with the new Bank for International Settlements (BIS) capital regulation levelling the playing field and hopefully restricting unrestrained asset growth by some international banks, the future performance of Scotiabank merits watching. Yet, it must be remembered that the return figures alone do not truly reveal the contribution of international networks. While diversification effects can be seen in the offsetting movements of the two trend lines, business generated in Canada by international networks, or low-margin business, possibly of domestic origin booked abroad for various considerations, cannot be easily broken out. Consequently, focus should be on total return and how linkages between domestic and international networks were critical for Scotiabank's overall performance.

Figure 3.7 presents the contribution of six major product lines to other income and consequently they do not total 100 per cent. The steadily increasing role of service fees, loan fees and ScotiaMcLeod over the period is clear. The fairly steady role played by Foreign Exchange (FX) attests to Scotiabank's far-flung international activities. Due to space limitations, the full categorization of FX could not be given. FX for Scotiabank includes precious metals. One characteristic of Scotiabank that differentiates it from other Canadian banks is its continuing activities in the gold market. Figure 3.8 shows very few changes in patterns of expenses over the period. At the broad level presented, Scotiabank seems content with its pattern, if not level, of controllable costs.

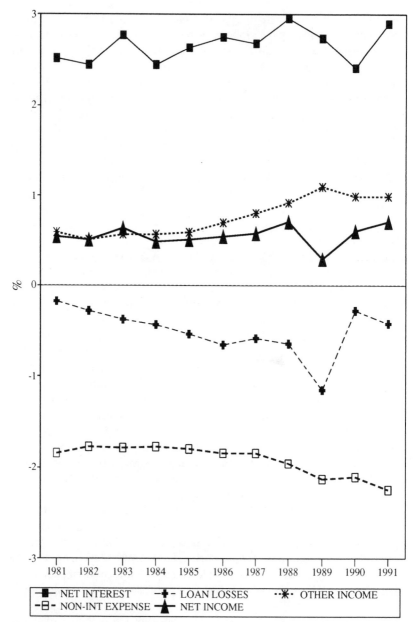

Figure 3.6A
Analysis of ROA

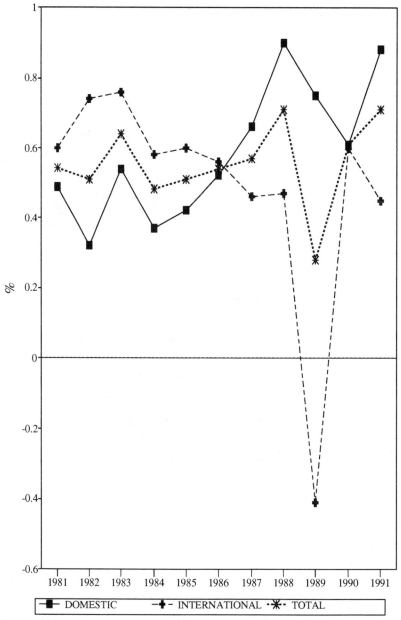

Figure 3.6B
Analysis of ROA

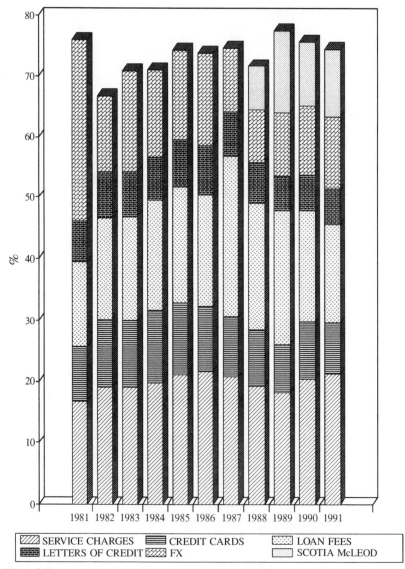

Figure 3.7
Other Income

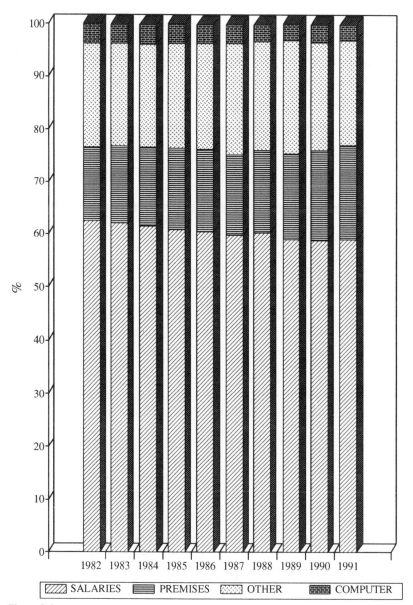

Figure 3.8
Non-Interest Expense

Figure 3.9 displays the results of Scotiabank's efforts to create shareholder value. As can be seen, while the stock frequently has highs that exceed book value, the lows have never exceeded book. The trading range is also interesting, especially as very wide ranges can be seen to occur in some years. On the whole, however, shareholders should have been content, as the stock closed near its high in 1991. Mr. Ritchie went to the annual meeting with numbers that attested to positive market perceptions over Scotiabank's performance.

CONCLUSION

The analysis of financial data offers support that Scotiabank has followed a strategy of balanced diversification. The diversification was not only along geographic lines, but also in terms of the types of assets that it holds. The bank has adjusted to market realities and has taken advantage of changes in communication systems. In the same vein, does the shift in focus to retail, the u.s. market, and efforts to target specific industries suggest a less global outlook? In its early international experience in Minnesota, Scotiabank did not hesitate to withdraw from unprofitable ventures and search for new opportunities. In today's world of global banking, networks must be focused and coordinated in order to be profitable.

The performance levels suggest that the efforts to develop a profitable competitive strategy and to maintain an internal organization that "fits" with the market strategy have been largely successful. A reading of the annual reports and of Schull and Gibson make it clear that this was not an easy task. The general pattern of strategy and structure has been, as Chandler suggested, that structure follows strategy. In the early years, skilful identification and pursuit of market opportunities were key to building sustainable competitive advantage. Success was shown in impressive growth numbers, which in turn led to the need for organizational change. Yet once a new organizational form that remedied most of the ills had been found, that form of organization served as the new platform for growth. The ease of replicating operations in different locales enabled Scotiabank to pursue a strategy of horizontal diversification.

It is important to note that the organizational growth to new locations, which was essential for the bank's survival, had an impact on strategy by creating information resources on which strategy could be founded. Interestingly, geographic expansion generally preceded expansion of the product line. Market complexities created a fascinating dialectical connection between geographic and product line

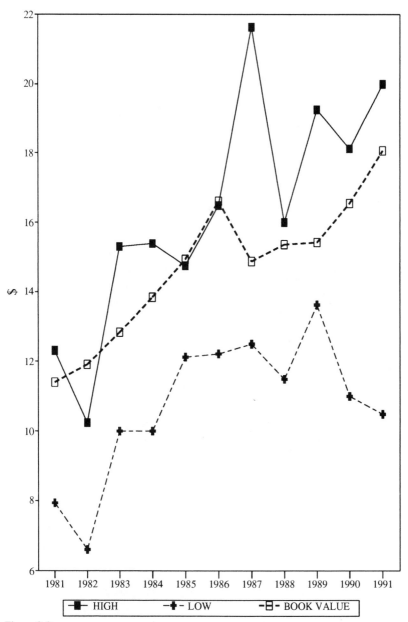

Figure 3.9
Stock-Price Performance

expansion. The costs associated with the location strategy demanded that new ways be found to lever the distribution system. This in turn created pressures to improve information technology, which then served to generate new products. The interplay of geography, products and information technology drive a fascinating process of strategic and organizational change.

Scotiabank has differentiated itself from other Canadian banks. Early strategic decisions led the bank to develop an international growth strategy with an entrepreneurial attention to market opportunities. As international competition increased and margins narrowed, Scotiabank has focused upon attaining a low-cost position and altering its market focus. Competitive market conditions have led to significant changes in recent years. Peter Godsoe, who was appointed president and chief operating officer in 1992 and became successor to Cedric Ritchie as CEO in 1993,[102] stands to inherit a profitable and interesting international bank. While some problems such as Olympia and York overhang the bank, the future looks bright. In many ways, the sour Olympia and York loan amounts to little more than a mortgage on their own head office. In fact, while many banks suffered in 1992, Mr. Ritchie retired on a high note, as Scotiabank's ROA of 0.72 placed it comfortably ahead of its nearest rival, the Bank of Montreal, which had an ROA of 0.62. Clearly, 1992 was the year of the nonconformist. The future is always uncertain, but Scotiabank has the strength to meet the unexpected, as it has done throughout its history.

CHAPTER FOUR

The Royal Bank of Canada

Our strong international presence and our position as Canada's leading bank over many decades have been significant contributing factors in achieving dominance at home.

1989 Annual Report, 4

The history of the Royal Bank of Canada reveals the successful pursuit of a growth strategy that sought to offer the broadest range of services to the greatest variety of customers.[1] This strategy was in place by the 1940s, as the 76th (1945) Annual Report made clear: "The details I have given you illustrate the policy and aim of the Bank to render banking services and assistance not to any narrow section, either in a business or a geographical sense, but to all classes of clients in the different communities served by our branches. We try to render this service and assistance in a spirit of friendly co-operation, and our doors are open to all who need a banking service."[2] As one might expect, such an aggressive strategic posture has placed great pressure on the organization to adapt to the tensions created by growth. Most recently, it has also had to adapt to the forces of globalization. Despite this, critics who see the Royal as retrenching should take care.[3] The international network will continue to be expanded. The ongoing process is one of *refocusing* to capitalize better upon core market strengths. This chapter traces the relationships between the markets pursued and their organizational implications.

The Royal is also interesting because, despite its relatively late start, it has grown to become the largest and arguably the most powerful bank in Canada. Achieving this position has meant not only adapting to organizational change, but accepting certain responsibilities associated with leadership. If the strategy and leadership of the

Royal is to be understood, its enterprise strategy, that is, its active involvement with public affairs, must be considered.

MERKEL, KINNEAR,
AND KENNY: FOUNDING
AND INITIAL EXPANSION:
1864–1908

The opening of the Royal Bank attested to the prosperity of Halifax in the 1860s. The Reciprocity Treaty with the United States and the American Civil War were responsible for a booming economy. Although there were other banks operating in Halifax such as the BBNA, the Bank of Nova Scotia, the Halifax Banking Company, the People's Bank of Halifax, and the Union Bank of Halifax, eight merchants decided that more banking services were needed, and announced the opening of the Merchants Bank on 26 April 1864. Unlike the other banks in this study, the Royal began its life as a private bank, not as a joint stock corporation. J.W. Merkel, a partner in De Blois and Mitchell, Auctioneers and Commission Merchants, became the first president, while other influential Haligonians on the board included T.C. Kinnear and John Duffus, who had both resigned directorships in the Union Bank to take part in the new venture.

There is not much known about its early operations as a private bank since no performance information was released; however, the prospectus issued in 1869 when the Royal decided to go public suggested that operations had been successful. Once again, it is worthwhile to consider the effect of location upon development. Clifford H. Ince in his chronology of the Royal made some interesting observations concerning Halifax's position in the world of the mid-nineteenth century. Communications with Quebec and Ontario were difficult because as those born since the construction of the Saint Lawrence Seaway may be surprised to learn, prior to the massive work on this waterway, the river represented a hazardous water route – in summer. In winter, the most accessible routes from Halifax to Quebec involved travelling via Portland, Boston, or New York. The result was, of course, a feeling of isolation in the Maritimes and a perspective that looked toward the Atlantic – Great Britain, New England, and the British West Indies rather than toward central Canada. The essential role of communications and its effect upon perceptions in commerce should never never be neglected.

The decision to go public in 1869 was the result of several political and economic changes. The end of the American Civil War, the failure of the fisheries in 1867–68, and the cancellation of the

Reciprocity Treaty heralded less benign economic conditions. Perhaps even more important, however, was the changing regulatory regime.[4] Confederation had created a new political reality and it seemed that the new Dominion Bank Act would restrict the scope for private banks. In order to retain its competitive scope, the Royal needed to go public. On 22 June 1869, it was chartered as the Merchants Bank of Halifax. Perhaps because of its four year history or some other causes for optimism, there was little trouble in finding subscribers to raise the authorized capital of $1 million.

The early years were marked by some other interesting differences. Under the first two presidents, Merkel (1864–69) and his successor T.C. Kinnear (1869–70), no branches were opened. The first branch was opened at Pictou in 1871 when Thomas E. Kenny (1870–78) was president.[5] Following this initial expansion, growth was fairly slow. By 1881, a network of only 13 Canadian branches was in place, with 10 in Nova Scotia and 3 in Prince Edward Island. The opening of 3 additional Nova Scotia branches and 5 New Brunswick branches in 1882 marked a significant change. In addition, 1882 saw the opening of the first foreign branch in Hamilton, Bermuda.[6]

Even more important for future development was the bank's entry into the Quebec market. The first branch opened at Paspebiac in 1885. This venture was not a success. The real entry into the Quebec market should be dated from the opening of the Montreal agency by E.L. Pease in 1887. Pease, who had been an accountant for the Royal in Halifax, played an important role in fostering a new perspective on "western" Canada.[7] By 1889, the Royal required larger premises that allowed the expansion of the services offered to include a new savings department. By 1900, the three Montreal offices indicated the importance of this area.

In 1895, the bank's geographic scope was extended in the Atlantic region when it opened an agency in St. John's, Newfoundland. In 1897, it made a further, and much more dramatic expansion when it commenced operations in British Columbia to service the developing Western gold rush. This came about because Pease had discussions with a friend, C.R. Homer, who had an interest in a large British Columbia property. Homer convinced Pease that the West was the land of opportunity, a view that was confirmed by the opening of the CPR in 1895. By 1899, the Royal had 39 Canadian branches, 10 of which were in British Columbia. Even more surprising was the expansion pattern: there were no other branches west of Quebec.

The year 1899 also saw an increase in international scope, as following personal investigations by Pease, the decision was taken to begin operations in New York and Havana. Both operations had some interesting features in their start-up phase. W.F. Brock and J.A. Springer were appointed joint agents for Havana. Springer brought valuable connections because he had been u.s. Vice-Consul in Havana and was fluent in Spanish. Later, Brock was moved to New York as second agent in 1899, which may suggest the emergence of a new career path in international operations. The New York agency developed with the approval and assistance of the Royal's correspondent, the Chase Manhattan Bank. The degree of cooperation promised by the Chase's president, H.W. Cannon, was delivered. S.H. Voorhees, an officer of the Chase, was appointed the first agent. These ventures suggested some of the complexities concerning competitive advantage that entered into the internationalization decision.

In 1899, the bank's network was further filled out when a branch in Ottawa was taken over from La Banque Jacques Cartier (later the Provincial Bank of Canada). This marked the beginning of operations in Ontario. The opening of an office in Republic, Washington added to the Royal's presence in both the West and the United States.

Such rapid expansion in scope and volume of business could not be managed without structural changes. In 1899, head office was reorganized to accommodate previous and future expansion. The cashier, David H. Duncan, became general manager for head office, the Maritimes, and Newfoundland, while Pease was appointed joint general manager with responsibility for Montreal, British Columbia, and the soon-to-be-opened Havana office. Interestingly, this organizational design treated international as simply another region. Personnel policies were also an area of ongoing concern, as benefit packages were reviewed.[8]

In 1900, a new name was sought that would better reflect the new status of the bank, and the Royal Bank of Canada was the choice. The bank also decided to increase its capital from $2 million to $3 million. By now, it was operating 37 Canadian and 3 international locations. Between 1869 and 1900, assets had grown from $729,000 to $17,844,000; net profits from a negligible amount ($18,000 in 1870, $42,000 in 1871) to $182,000; loans from $267,000 to $12,282,000; deposits from $285,000 to $12,016,000; and paid-up capital from $300,000 to $2,000,000.[9] This was clearly evidence of profitable growth. President Kenny believed that such success could be attributed to the work of Pease and the Montreal branch. In 1900, Duncan left the bank and Pease was promoted from joint general manager to general manager, a position that he held until 1916.

The passage of the new Bank Act in 1900 gave banks the right to issue bank notes in any British possession outside Canada. The Act simplified the mergers of banks as only the agreement of the banks and the approval of the governor-in-council upon receipt of the recommendation of the Treasury Board was required – not the previously required special act of Parliament. Banks were also now allowed to lend upon the security of standing timber and the right or license to cut it and to remove it. In addition, the Act made membership in the CBA compulsory. This did not affect the Royal, since it had joined the organization shortly after its founding in 1891. The opportunities created in international markets, natural resources, and domestic mergers were to have important strategic consequences as the Royal entered the new century.

The years prior to World War I were prosperous ones in Canada and the Royal easily thrived and expanded as the railways and immigration opened up the West. In order to maintain growth, new capital was raised in 1902. The capital issue was interesting because the purchasers' list demonstrated a widening international network. New shareholders included the Blairs of New York; G.F. Baker, president of the First National Bank of New York; John J. Mitchell, president of the Illinois Trust and Savings Bank, Chicago; and J. Ogden Armour, Norman P. Ream, and Marshall Field, all of Chicago. In addition to showing new connections with New York and the hub of the U.S. Midwest, the issue was also interesting because it sold at a premium. Investors clearly saw a bright future for the bank.

The Royal continued to follow commerce west as it opened branches in Toronto and Pembroke in 1903, although the Canadian network was not complete until 1906, when operations were commenced in Manitoba, Saskatchewan, and Alberta.[10] The branch network was further expanded via mergers and acquisitions, such as the securing the Yorkshire Guarantee and Securities Corporation, a private banking concern based in Chilliwack, British Columbia; the Banco de Oriente de Santiago de Cuba in 1903; and the Banco del Commercio, Havana, in 1904. The acquisition strategy was guided not only by standards on banking assets, including location, but on intangible assets, such as personnel. The Royal became the government agent in Havana for distribution of funds to the Army of the Liberation.

The role of staff in this expanding service industry was well recognized: without competent personnel, it would be impossible to retain the newly acquired clients. Enriqué Ros was as valuable an acquisition as the banking franchise in Cuba. The former manager of the Banco de Oriente de Santiago became the joint general manager for the Royal in Cuba. A similar case can be made for T.R. Whitley who joined the bank with the acquisition of the Yorkshire Guarantee and Securities Corporation. Whitley had a successful career in the bank as he became a supervisor at Winnipeg and later, a manager in London.

Such growth had its impact. By 1905, a clear shift of authority to Montreal could be detected as the two Montreal directors, Herbert S. Holt and James Richmond, met twice weekly to oversee operations. By 1907, the extent of the shift was recognized when Montreal became head office. The year was also significant because it was a year of general international financial problems which in the United States led to a panic following the failure of the Knickerbocker Trust Company and other New York banks. The Canadian banks had been more cautious and their financial stability allowed them to weather the storm. This demonstration of stability played an essential role in maintaining the flow of investment funds required for Canadian development. The Royal's new orientation was emphasized in 1908, when Herbert S. Holt succeeded Kenny as president and Pease became vice-president and general manager.

HERBERT S. HOLT: 1908-34

Until World War I, the Royal continued its expansion. Growth had increased the complexity of Canadian operations and a supervisory district was created for central western branches in Alberta, Saskatchewan, and Manitoba. T.R. Whitley was appointed the first supervisor. The bank also acquired an old competitor, the Union Bank of Halifax, which had offices in the Maritimes and Caribbean. Cost-conscious as always, the bank amalgamated at 10 locations in order to avoid costly duplication. In 1912 the Royal took over the Traders Bank, which had 90 branches in Ontario at a time when the Royal itself had only 36. This move provided needed depth to the national network, while in the same year, purchase of the Bank of British Honduras expanded international scope.

Perhaps even more important were some new initiatives. In 1910, James Mackie, who had been with the Bank of Scotland, was appointed to begin operations in London, England. In 1913, Globe Realty was created to manage certain real estate operations. Overall growth was steady and yet provided few reasons to make major changes; even the final revision of the Bank Act prior to the war altered little beyond implementing compulsory shareholders' audits and the management of central gold reserves under the CBA.

While all banks faced problems during the war, some of the Royal's practices were markedly different. After 1915, the bank expected those who desired to enlist to resign, although every effort was made to rehire all former employees after the war. But, more remarkable

Table 4.1
The Growing Branch Network in 1918

Location	No. of Branches
Alberta	34
British Columbia	40
Manitoba	29
New Brunswick	19
Newfoundland	6
Nova Scotia	54
Ontario	152
Prince Edward Island	6
Quebec	51
Saskatchewan	97
Yukon and North West Territories	0
Total Canadian	488
International	60
Total	548

than this policy was the expansion during the war. The Royal took advantage of the opportunity created by the war loans and improved commodity prices for Caribbean goods, and scanning for acquisition candidates continued. In 1915, the bank's attempt to acquire the Bank of Hamilton was rejected by the minister of finance, T.H. White, much to the surprise of both parties.[11] The specific reasons for the rejection are unclear, yet, it would not be unreasonable to suppose that the age old fear in some quarters of bank concentration played a role. However, the bank did not encounter any problems in 1917 when it acquired both the Bank of Nassau and the Quebec Bank (the latter increased the number of branches in Quebec by 26) or in 1918 when it took over the Northern Bank, which had extensive operations in the Prairies, especially in Saskatchewan. Between 1914 and 1918, a total of 61 new branches were opened and 48 were closed, a fact that bears testimony to the unsettled conditions of the time. However, it is important to realize the extent of operations by 1918 (see table 4.1).

Increased international operations, including new offices in Venezuela and Barcelona, created pressures for organizational adaptation. In 1915 the bank had an office under Voorhees in New York to supervise the Puerto Rico operations, but this arrangement proved insufficient to maintain administrative control. The bank later shifted headquarters to San Juan in 1917 under the management of W.A. McKinlay. Increasing regional differentiation was the response to pressures that resulted from expansion in the Caribbean and Latin America. In 1916, another important change occurred when Pease resigned. His successor as general manager was C.E. Neil, who had been elected to the board in a surprising move two years previously.[12]

Following the war, the bank revealed an even more ambitious expansion plan as 100 new Canadian branches and 14 new foreign offices were opened. The Royal was now represented in Paris, Buenos Aires, Rio de Janeiro, Montevideo, and even briefly, Vladisvostok. Such international growth was supported by the creation of a Foreign Trade department in 1919 and bolstered in 1920 when Graham F. Towers became the supervisor of this department and published a booklet on foreign trade. The following year marked the introduction of a monthly letter by Towers on trade conditions.[13] In addition, an association with London County Westminster and Parrs Bank Ltd. (later Westminster Bank Ltd.) was forged in 1919, and a new London branch was added in 1926. Another change – and an important one marking the need for increasing cooperation between international operations and domestic operations – was the decision to discontinue the practice of having a supervisor in New York and instead to have this office supervised by an assistant general manager at head office. During the 1930s, the addition of assistant general managers at head office was a key coordinating device.

Despite some economic problems created by the postwar adjustment period, which were made manifest in the failure of the Home Bank in 1923, the Royal prospered. An indication of this was the decision to add a 2 per cent bonus to the normal 12 per cent dividend payment.[14] New acquisitions in Latin America led to further regional differentiation as supervisory posts were created for the West Indies, Brazil, and Bogota. However, a phase of domestic growth ended in 1925 with the acquisition of the Union Bank. This was the Royal's last Canadian bank takeover. By 1929, the Royal, with its 838 Canadian and 106 international branches, managed the largest volume of Canadian assets.

The Depression augured a new era of banking, because both assets and branches were reduced.[15] The importance of reputation in the industry was made clear when rumours concerning the failure of McDougall and Cowan, a firm associated with the Royal, led to a short-lived panic. The Royal was not only able to weather the storm, but identified an emerging industry to help profitability during these difficult years: mining, especially gold mining.

In 1934, Herbert S. Holt retired as president and became chairman of the board. His successor, Morris W. Wilson, who had been general manager and vice-president, had the distinction of being the first president to have worked his way up from the bottom solely on merit. He also had the distinction of being the first president who would spend all his time at the bank.

MORRIS W. WILSON: 1934-46

Falling loan demand (at least from those with the ability to service their debt) created difficult conditions for the bank, although it was able to maintain a reasonable level of prosperity. Slack loan demand led to a new focus on the cost of individual services and the branch system itself.[16] In these new tight conditions, services had to profitable.[17] It should be noted that one of the problems was not controllable costs, but interest costs. Loans, deposits, and total assets had all reached a high in 1929. By 1933, deposits fell to their lowest level and did not surpass 1929 levels until 1938. Loans on the other hand followed a more erratic trend: the peak levels of 1929 were not reached again until 1948. This imbalance between deposits and loans created severe problems, and led to funds being placed in lower-yielding assets, such as government securities. Eventually deposit rates were cut. The result of such a situation where depositors were paid less and certain sectors, such as farmers, felt cut off from funds, was a ripe breeding ground for both public complaints and profitless growth. Moreover, this experience demonstrated certain disadvantages to a deposit-centred growth strategy and may serve to explain the broad preferences for loan-led strategies.

The importance of reputation was made clear as the Royal and its industry association, the CBA, sought to answer critics, especially in the West.[18] General Manager Sydney G. Dobson reported in the 68th Annual Report that there had been no foreclosures in Alberta over the last five years and that dedication to the small borrower could be seen in the fact that the Royal had 61,000 loans not exceeding $500. The attacks from the Social Credit party in Alberta were labelled unfair. In any event, whether due to public pressure or some other reason, the world of Canadian banking was dramatically changed in 1934 when the Bank of Canada was created. Perhaps any hostility from the Royal was tempered when a former employee, Graham F. Towers, was appointed as its first governor.[19] This appointment was yet another indicator of the Royal's ascendancy over other Canadian banks.

This is an appropriate time to explore a theme that emerged in the annual reports of the 1930s: business-government relations. The spectres of Social Credit in the West and the New Deal in the United States caused genuine concern. The proverbial banker's conservatism was shown in Wilson's anxiety over what he perceived as too many social experiments under way in the United States.[20] Even more distressing was the deterioration of relations between business and government in that country.[21] In this vein, the initial response to earlier criticism that the profit incentive was the only spur needed to encourage bankers to prefer loans to investments in lower-yielding securities was especially interesting. Not only banks but the basic social values of individualism and capitalism were again under attack.[22]

The Royal began to urge business to speak up by the early 1940s.[23] Earlier during the Depression, in response to critics, the annual reports had stressed the role of banks in the community, and a program of branch rationalization that maintained appropriate levels of service. Now, clearly, the need for social legitimacy had been recognized, but there was no suggestion in these earlier reports that the legitimacy of private business was being challenged. The astuteness of the Royal in recognizing the need to respond to the attacks that would arise as the economy readjusted to peacetime led to a focus on a proactive, enterprise strategy. The result was a tradition of statesmanlike positions taken by CEOs of the Royal. Even domestically, the environment demanded that the economic and political imperatives voiced federally and provincially be carefully weighed.

A new attitude was made clear with the advent of World War II. While all the chartered banks had employed their assets, including the branch system and financing skills, to further the Allied cause in World War I, it was noted that the position taken toward servicemen by the Royal in the early years of World War I had seemed somewhat less patriotic than that taken by others. At the same time, its attitude to costs had been business-like. There was a change by World War II. Servicemen were granted a leave of absence with benefits maintained and payments to cover the difference between army pay and three-quarters of their bank pay for married men, and two-thirds for single men.[24] No bank was now going to appear more patriotic than the Royal! The Royal also did a fine job of adjusting to the new role of women in banking, as roughly 70 per cent of the staff were now female. This was a marked change from 1939 when 79 per cent of the employees had been male. The 73rd (1942) Annual Report featured the inevitable discussion of how the wartime personnel situation strained the supervisors, but the 74th (1943) Annual Report highlighted the improved quality of service. This was said to be the result of the women's ability to learn new tasks quickly. Such praise shows that the Royal had a real feel for internal marketing in addition to enterprise strategy.

On the other hand, it is striking that the annual reports of this period project a "business as usual" tone. Canadians were urged to take advantage of opportunities created by the war, not only in the obvious commodity and manufacturing sectors, but also in the service sector of tourism.[25] The reports also paid attention to areas of traditional concern, such as the pulp and paper industry. It was clear that the bank had special expertise in this area as well as in mining. Earlier moves into Latin America had also led to an emphasis upon the potential opportunities to the south. The war had a positive effect on these commodity-producing countries too.[26]

Wilson left behind him a bank that was well-positioned to pursue the new financing opportunities of the postwar reconstruction period. Perhaps even more important, however, was his contribution to the development of strategy at the enterprise level. It was interesting that a person who had worked his way through all levels of the system and might be expected to remain focused only on operating details should be instrumental in causing the bank to reach new strategic heights. There could be a connection between challenges to legitimacy and the strategy to provide the broadest possible range of services to the greatest variety of customers. Broad scope not only closed strategic beachheads to competitors, but demonstrated the commitment to service demanded by diverse groups in the community. To be effective, enterprise strategy had to be linked to business strategy, as Wilson's successors also recognized.

SYDNEY G. DOBSON AND JAMES MUIR: 1946–60

Sydney G. Dobson was president from 1946 until he became chairman of the board in 1949, a position he held until 1954. James Muir was general manager from 1945–49, president from 1949–54 and chairman and president from 1954–60. These men faced the challenging task of giving leadership to Canada during its adjustment to postwar reality, as well as returning the Royal to international prominence. As stated at the beginning of this chapter, the 76th Annual Report summarized the Royal's market strategy, which was to serve the broadest possible range of clients. It also made remarks concerning how its foreign branches acted as local banks.[27] A strategy of national responsiveness was deemed appropriate, and the organization adapted to strong forces for decentralization. The Royal believed that it could act as a representative for Canada and enhance Canada's reputation abroad by functioning in this manner. It should be recognized, however, that such a strategy was in keeping with general perceptions of Canada as a neutral power. And it could also be profitable to expand with the local communities. The image projected was that of a socially responsible company that provided complete servicing in all dimensions. The strategic question was whether or not it was possible to be all things to all people and what were the costs of failing to carry out such a broad mandate.

The Royal also gave a clear picture that it was aware of the complex new global realities, as the annual reports for the years 1948–56 reveal. While Canada had once been in a position to moderate between two global powers, the United States and Great Britain, the devastation of the war had changed this. The 79th (1948) Annual Report acknowledged that Canada's future economic development was linked much more closely to the United States. Perhaps even more important than this realization was the further recognition of the ties between international and domestic business because of the role of foreign investment in fostering Canadian growth. If Americans were taking over the economy, Canadians had themselves to blame for not investing in the projects.[28] In fact, one of the roles of the bank's branch system was to facilitate the flow of foreign capital into Canada. Foreign branches of the Royal demonstrated the advantages of Canada to foreign investors, while local business development officers assisted investors in establishing in Canada.[29] In discussing the development of Canada's natural resource heritage, particularly the Blind River project, the 87th (1956) Annual Report stressed the importance of foreign risk capital. This strategy linking international and domestic activities required direct representation in foreign markets. Correspondent relations would not do, as the 82nd (1951) Annual Report stated: "[there is] no really adequate substitute in any business for direct representation by the organization itself."[30] In the transfer of both technology and information, especially confidential information, personal contact was critical for the creation of the mutual understanding and possibly the trust necessary for ongoing relationships.[31]

Given such an attitude concerning the importance of direct representation, the decision criteria for foreign investment merits consideration. The general manager, T.H. Atkinson, discussed these in the 83rd (1952) Annual Report: "By and large our growth in the foreign field has followed actual or potential channels for Canadian trade development." While at first glance this affirms the follower hypothesis and conforms to the bank's long-standing interest in trade financing, two other factors must be considered. First, that very year, despite trade opportunities, a branch was not opened in the Orient because adequate banking facilities were already there. Obviously, the potential for profit made under- rather than over-banked markets attractive. In the same vein, emphasis was placed on "potential channels." The Royal led as well as followed.

An especially interesting tie between international and domestic business was the opportunity to establish relations with companies of British and American origin in foreign countries. The 81st (1950) Annual Report revealed 3,000 accounts with such firms and it was held that the relations established worked to the Royal's advantage when the companies decided to locate in Canada. Such were the advantages of international representation and protected domestic capital markets.

On the other hand, the same annual report commented that the "flow" of u.s. capital had become a "flood" and discussed some of the associated problems. In particular, and not surprisingly, a massive inflow of funds had created upward pressure on the Canadian dollar. The Royal was an active advocate of a free float and urged the government to pursue this path. Yet, the 85th (1954) Annual Report had begun to show an awareness of the difficulties created for Canadian exporters and domestic producers by the high dollar as Canadian exports became more expensive and imported goods cheaper. There was a particular concern over the export of capital goods since Canadians were competing against firms that could offer better financing terms because of government assistance.[32]

Domestically, the Royal continued on the paths staked out earlier. One new wrinkle again illustrated the ties between international and domestic: the increasing use of international expertise as a marketing tool for domestic clients.[33] This was especially true because of new export opportunities created by the devastation of the war. The bank recognized the opportunity and decided to capitalize upon its competitive advantage in trade financing.

Muir also made efforts to take a leading position in the Canadian community. The importance of legitimacy and the danger of maintaining an attitudes such as "Let government do it" frequently appeared in the annual reports.[34] There was also greater leadership in issues strictly related to banking. Muir led the creation of a domestic money market and became outspoken on the behaviour of the Bank of Canada, the need for fair competition among deposit-taking institutions, and the need to promote policies ensuring that Canada was perceived internationally as a safe haven for funds.[35] Muir spoke for Canada and wished to be heard in Ottawa.

Organizationally, there was little change because the "decentralized branch system" was well suited for expansion in terms of both geography and product scope. The nature of such decentralization bears some discussion. Decentralization meant that the bank was able to respond to local issues and to ensure a level of local decision making. However, pressures for centralization were also created by the bank's the role in intermediating between savers and lenders at both a national and international level. Certain aspects of risk-management in intermediation demanded this. The bank's organizational design had to be sensitive to balancing such opposing forces. In reality, levels of decentralization are unlikely ever to be completely homogeneous throughout any bank. More experienced managers in larger markets need, and generally have, a broader range of discretion. The key therefore is to match the level of decentralized decision making to market needs and opportunities.

There were some changes. By 1955, the importance of international received organizational recognition, as A.F. Mayne was appointed associate general manager in charge of non-domestic operations, an emerging division within the bank. Further specialization occurred when the need to contain internal costs became apparent and a comptroller was appointed to oversee this area. A central credit information department was also created. Interestingly, while the need for maintaining trained staff in this service industry was discussed, the annual reports also made increasing mention of international as a career path.[36] International operations were being recognized as critical for the future.

W. EARLE McLAUGHLIN: 1960–78

What stands out about McLaughlin's tenure is not so much the new growth initiatives, whether domestic or international, but the changes in fundamental operating strategies that led to restructuring within the Royal. While the bank adopted some major new initiatives during this period, they were of less importance than were the organizational changes. Consider the 1967 reorganization and the events leading up to it. The Royal was reorganized into four areas of responsibility, each with a general manager:

Canadian District Division: Rowland C. Frazee
International Division: Jock K. Finlayson
Administrative Division: J.H. Cornish
Loans and Investments Division: W. Moodie

In essence, this divided the institution along two lines. Canadian District and International were based on geography, while Administrative and Loans and Investments were based on staff or functional tasks. The Administrative Division was charged with personnel, organizational planning, central administration, and secretariat. The Loans and Investments Division was responsible for credits, investments, economic resources, and inspection. In addition, C.L. Walker was appointed deputy general manager for marketing and public relations.

The key to the new organization was "management by plan." In the decentralized structure, authority was clearly delegated and managers were expected to achieve planned objectives. However, the role of the two staff divisions and the deputy general manager for marketing also revealed the presence of strong centralizing forces. The balancing of assets and liabilities and the management of overall risks both essential to strategic management in banking, demanded strong, centralized decision making and formalized procedures.

It is reasonable to suggest that organizations do not undergo the trauma of reorganization without good reason. Consequently we need to ask: Why did the Royal reorganize? Clarification on this point was apparent in the 1967 Annual Report: "'Reorganization' is in no way a reflection on past efforts of the staff. It is, rather, an attempt to adjust the structure to give the staff the best possible framework in which to realize their highest potential and to provide an organization even better fitted to serve the public."[37] The change was not meant to signal winners or losers, but to reveal that the organization had to adapt to the new environment in which it found itself.

The 1967 reorganization signalled a response to the impact of previous moves. In the international arena, new conditions in Latin America had emerged. Although the Royal and the Bank of Nova Scotia were the only two foreign banks not to be nationalized following the Cuban Revolution, exit from the market was negotiated.[38] Other countries were showing a similar desire for local control of their financial institutions. This increased the complexity of international banking not only because of the need for greater sensitivity to information concerning socio-political events, but because of the complications that arose in managing joint ventures. While joint ventures offered an attractive way of gaining expertise concerning new products and/or markets, they also demanded an organizational structure that could respond to problems.

A further example of the need to stay close to markets was the orientation toward Toronto in the early 1960s. This was a significant change.[39] Yet the new organization also recognized the need for coordination from head office. In 1961, a special electronics officer was added to computerize operations. By 1966, the Royal spoke quite confidently about the improvements in information flow made possible by electronic technology. Successful implementation of the changes was probably facilitated by an internal environment that encouraged and praised staff for their suggestions.[40] A divisionalized structure maintained a strategic balance through increasing the level of centralization.

The addition of a marketing division at head office provided an impetus both for the creation of products desired by the market and for ensuring their proper delivery.[41] The service organization had to be designed so that the staff could deliver the new products. A level of standardization and control at head office was the only manner to ensure uniform delivery and proper information flow through the system.

The Royal did not stay still. Internationally, in the 1960s, it joined forces with the Bank of America in Brazil, acquired an established bank in Belgium, founded an international merchant bank, Orion, as a consortium with three foreign banks, and strengthened its position in the Pacific Rim. Changes in international operations were dramatic. Finlayson stated in the 1970 Annual Report that while trade had been the original motive behind internationalization, providing international services such as multicurrency loans was now the *raison d'être*. In order to develop such services, a new emphasis on teams as a coordinating device was being stressed by 1970. The teams pulled together the best experts from many departments to create the innovative products required by the new realities of international business. Perhaps the best example of this was the teams of experts required to put together project-financing deals.

The new blurring of lines between international and domestic was recognized in the 1972 Annual Report: "While the division between domestic and international banking is becoming less distinct, Canadian style banking is not the way of the future abroad."[42] Retail banking would not play the role in international strategies that it did in Canada and had once in international. Rapid international expansion in 1973 with a new emphasis on achieving a global network in the wholesale market made this clear.

In 1968, 25 bankettes, or automated banking machines (ABMS) were added to domestic operations. But more importantly, the bank was developing a strategy for the new information-processing technology. The 1971 Annual Report provided an interesting account of how automated back-room transactions improved both the cost and quality of operations, presumably because of economies of scale and learning-curve effects. This also helped to free up front-line people to deliver the services that required a personal touch. New possibilities for specialization were directed toward improving service to the customer. Such an attitude, which essentially promised job security also created a less threatening atmosphere for the introduction of new technology. Successful implementation was thus the critical component of the strategy.

In 1973, this and other goals were made clear in a statement of "corporate philosophy" that had been developed in response to Frazee's question: "What kind of bank are we – and what kind of bank are we striving to become?"

Our overall purpose is to ensure survival as a progressive enterprise through short- and long-term profitability and by fulfilling our responsibilities to society:
• to provide potential and existing clients, throughout the world, with the broadest possible range and highest quality of banking and financial services;
• to provide employees with opportunities for personal development and achievement, and equitable compensation;
• to provide investors with an attractive and continuing return on their capital; and
• to act as a responsible corporate citizen, whose activities benefit the community, nation and society.

In order to achieve this impressive mission, a leaner organization that was better focused on the marketplace was required by 1974. The new organization would help the Royal to capitalize upon its advantages: an "outward orientation" and an international presence. Three new banking divisions were created in order to move decision making closer to the customer: Canadian, International, and Corporate. In addition, the number of Canadian districts was increased from eight to nine in order to sharpen the focus of the divisions.

It is interesting to note the creation of divisions based upon the type of client, rather than upon geography. The inclusion of a corporate division suggests the blurring of international and domestic lines alluded to earlier. While domestic retail banking was clearly different from international wholesale banking, Corporate drew upon aspects of both. Dealing with such corporate clients was one of the difficult problems facing bankers in the changing world of the 1970s.

The full extent of restructuring and renewal in the Royal cannot be appreciated without understanding that the organizational changes were not limited to drawing new organizational charts, but also included devising new processes. Frazee's discussion in the 1975 Annual Report held that it was not possible to have a unified management system in which complex interrelationships were managed to achieve corporate goals unless proper management processes were in harmony with the system. The Royal made an effort to avoid the distorted communication endemic to bureaucratic organization through such devices as the RSVP program. This program was developed so that employees could request and receive answers to their questions directly from top management. The effort here was to design the best possible communication system and then to make it work: sound strategy formulation had to be supported by optimal implementation.

The Royal continued to behave in a statesmanlike manner as it sought to right some social ills, such as improving the promotion opportunities for women and extending banking services to less affluent people via storefront branches. There was every reason to be concerned with general perceptions because of the important public policy issues that confronted the banking industry. First, prior to passage of the 1967 Bank Act, there was still competition for deposits from the near banks. But even more important was the presence of foreign banks. Although the latter could not act as banks in Canada, they could solicit business and book it abroad. The Royal urged the government to allow entry of foreign banks in order to ensure that they had no unfair advantages.[43] Once the reality, or inevitability, of foreign competition was accepted, then it became imperative to ensure a level playing field.

However, the greatest challenge facing the Royal and its survival in Montreal was the passage in 1977 of Bill 101, which required the use of the French language in the province of Quebec. The 1977 Annual Report discussed the possible impact of this legislation and urged careful consideration by the government of Quebec, while insisting that the bank intended to keep its head office in the province. Given the tense situation, such a statesmanlike posture was difficult to maintain. Perhaps the skills that had been developed in dealing with various foreign host governments were beneficial in helping the organization confront this threat in the home country.

The annual reports from the McLaughlin years bristled with an energy and a commitment to quality and growth. The new corporate emblem of the lion and the globe and the "dynamic visual presence" of the Place Ville Marie were not hollow attempts to create enthusiasm, but rather the natural outcome of a vigorous institution.

ROWLAND FRAZEE: 1978–86

The annual reports during the years 1978–86 discussed important relationships between strategy and structure as the Royal was reasonably explicit concerning its product market-scope and the organizational changes implemented in order to compete successfully in selected markets. The point was illustrated by a series of incremental changes made between 1978 and 1980, and by broader changes made in 1980.

In 1978, the Royal recognized that increasing competition, especially in the international sphere, required an addition to the organization. The major problem was that the financing needs of Canada's largest and most complex enterprises utilized resources from different areas of the bank. In addition, the increasing sophistication of the treasurers or chief financial officers (CFOs) of the larger corporations meant that prime clients increasingly turned to the Euromarkets and direct financial instruments as sources of their funds. The Royal responded to the increasing sophistication of its clients and the erosion of the barriers between international and domestic operations by creating a new unit designed to meet the needs of Canada's largest and most complex organizations: the National Accounts Division.[44] Customer rather than geographic focus had to be the base for this division.

However, increasing international competition had another effect that inevitably spilled over into domestic markets because of the ability of firms to fund their operations in markets such as New York, London, or Hong Kong: this was the need for increased efficiency. Competition in the unregulated Euromarkets drove down the price, or spreads, between deposit and loan rates, so that survival in these markets was threatened if non-interest costs were too high. Attention was directed to improving the productivity of its employees, or as it was more eloquently put, unleashing the "potential of the people in the organization." Since funding costs were also critical, it was emphasized that size was important in the Euromarkets. Only the large and strong would be able to compete.[45]

During these two years, there was also comment concerning the competitive domain. In 1978, it was made clear that, increasingly, the focus of international operations was wholesale banking.[46] Moreover, it was stressed that trade should be centred on the areas where Canada had a competitive edge: energy, communications, forestry, agriculture, mining, engineering, and transportation. Given the Royal's traditional strength in trade financing, it was probable that such industries were either already clients or were targets for the National Accounts division.

In 1979, there was a significant organizational change concerning U.S. operations as $100 million of additional capital was injected into the New York subsidiary and 10 senior managers were transferred to New York. This action served to strengthen an already strong position in the United States, since research had shown that the Royal was used by more U.S. MNEs than any other non-U.S. bank. At the same time, operations in London were furthered with the creation of a wholly owned merchant bank, Royal Bank of Canada (London), which was to complement the Orion consortium bank in assisting Canadian firms, especially those in the oil and gas industries, to enter the Euromarkets. The bank's leading position in lending to Latin American governments was also noted.[47]

Prior to 1980, the Royal had made an ongoing effort to respond as an institution to changes in the market place. However, in 1980, it underwent a much more radical restructuring. It is important to highlight the implications of these changes. The Royal chose to do so by its presentation in a special three-page section of the annual report entitled "Corporate Strategy." The challenge was to create a structure that would respond to the environment of the 1980s, which was described as "turbulent." Six key external factors for the decade ahead were identified: inflation, energy requirements, global redistribution of economic and political power, an unstable world monetary system, increasing political tension, and the impact of new technology. The new organization was to be two-tiered: one for corporate strategy and one for operations. The first level included the following:

Chairman and CEO: Rowland C. Frazee
Vice-chairman, Western Canada: Hal E. Wyatt (Calgary)
President: Jock K. Finlayson (Toronto)
Vice-chairman: Robert A. Utting (Montreal)

Their efforts were assisted by five executive vice presidents:

Executive Vice-president Canada: A.H. (Mike) Mitchell (Montreal)
Executive Vice-president National Accounts: John C. McMillan (Toronto)
Executive Vice-president International: Allan R. Taylor (Montreal)
Executive Vice-president World Trade and Merchant Banking: R.G.P. (Geoff) Styles (Toronto)
Executive Vice-president Finance and Investments: Brian D. Gregson (Montreal)

The executive vice presidents were described as "the new chief operating officers of their respective 'banks,' and the top level advocates of their designated businesses."[48] The design of this structure increased the responsibility of personnel at lower levels and placed emphasis on their role as "local and regional sensing agents of market conditions." The importance of location, or geography, to the organizational design was also evident in the location of the offices of the vice-chairmen and the president.

The new structure also paid witness to the increasing importance of Toronto. Finlayson, the president, was situated in Toronto in order "to direct and integrate [the] international corporate banking activities world-wide, including Canada. The Bank's recently created World Trade and Merchant Banking Division, as well as the International Division and the National Accounts Division [reported] directly to him."[49] Clearly, Toronto was displacing Montreal as the centre of operations. Such changes do not show the bank neglecting the West or Montreal, but rather increasing centralization to mirror the increasing interdependence of international and domestic markets. The need for integration led to the development of a global organization.

Following these moves, there were ongoing adjustments to market dynamics. The Royal continued to focus on cost control and to invest in new technology with the aim of creating and sustaining a position of leadership.[50] In 1983, it was announced that Allan R. Taylor's role had been expanded and his title changed to include chief operating officer. This not only signalled the rise of Taylor's fortunes within the corporate hierarchy, but shifted more responsibilities to an officer situated in Toronto.

Rather than comment upon numerous minor adjustments to the organization, it is more important to note the philosophy guiding these changes. The Royal continued to stress how the organizational design must unleash the potential of the individuals within the institution. For example, the strategy guiding further automation was to improve service to the clients by increasing back room support for the front-line people.[51] The bank recognized the need to assist and empower such staff as the complexity and variety of the product line was expanded. In this context, the effort to develop a service philosophy, which was seen as essential for fulfilling the bank's goal to be a socially responsible corporation,[52] was also essential if it was to respond to changes in the marketplace.

The Royal characteristically struck out in both directions. It was already well positioned for investment banking with subsidiaries, such as Orion in London. The Orion venture was also interesting for two other reasons. First, in 1981, the Royal decided to go it alone and bought out its partners in the venture. This move was in keeping with the basic forces operating in this information-based industry. At first, the Royal had lacked certain expertise in international markets and had required partners. However, over time it acquired greater technical skills and customer knowledge, and thus had less of an incentive to share intangible assets with partners. Further, with increasing sophistication of the loan syndication market, the bank may have had less of a need for the Orion-type consortium. Second, while the trends discussed above created opportunities, investment banking was a different business. Typically, investment bankers were more highly paid and perhaps more free-wheeling than were the traditional bankers who were used to assessing the credit worthiness of borrowers. Merging two such different types of businesses with their different cultures was a significant organizational challenge. The Royal posted some good performance numbers, but there were clashes requiring management attention.[53] The role of Orion in attracting Canadian business serves to further underline the internationalization of banking.

The extent of the breakdown of barriers between international and domestic can be seen in the effects on retail banking. An important and seemingly profitable segment of retail banking was the one populated by High Net Worth Individuals. In order to compete in this segment in which financial services organizations such as the Swiss banks and American Express compete, the capacity to coordinate products with both domestic and international features was essential. It should be noted that this type of business was also valuable in establishing contacts for corporate loans.

A further result of the interdependence of international and domestic markets could be seen in the role of the Treasury department, described in the 1983 Annual Report as "banker to the bank." This department managed the bank's funding and developed new international products vital for assisting Canadian firms dealing in international markets. By 1985, it operated seven units across the country featuring one stop shopping. Moreover, the Treasury department continued to market its expertise by offering new products, such as currency swaps and advanced cash management products.[54] Being competitive in the international arena was essential for the domestic competitive strategy.

Project financing was another force that demanded the coordination of diverse services.[55] This was accomplished by project managers. The use of such managers meant that specialized services could be extended to smaller corporate clients. The ability to centralize information and to develop new products required changes in the manner in which clients interacted with financial services firms. The client would benefit from improved service while the bank positioned itself to sell more of its services to the client. The complexities of the emerging financial services market led to the development of relationship managers.

As discussed previously, the Royal had always aimed to provide a broad scope of operations in terms of both geography and product lines. During the 1980s, it continued to utilize certain traditional tactics, such as the creation of a Japan desk to try and use subsidiaries of Japanese companies operating in Canada as a springboard into their home market, or the marketing of Treasury expertise to attract clients.[56] However, international operations revealed a much more interesting trend: rationalization. The 1985 Annual Report announced that operations had been streamlined in some areas, principally in the Caribbean, while efforts were made to strengthen operations in Europe and Asia Pacific, including China. Despite the pursuit of some profitable opportunities in retail, the streamlined operations were meant to enhance and maintain competitive advantage in the corporate sector.[57]

In 1983, prior to these moves toward rationalization, the Royal had announced its intentions to focus on the United States, as well as on other specific markets such as the Euro-Australian market.[58] The Royal needed to maintain an extensive international network in order to obtain the information and funds to compete, but increasingly, narrower market niches were being targeted.

ALLAN R. TAYLOR: 1986 –

Allan R. Taylor has taken a strategic position emphasizing differentiation via superior service *as perceived by the customer*, a human resource strategy to support such differentiation, and aggressive moves to win market share. The period since 1986 has been one of fundamental importance to Canadian banking as the banks have adjusted to new forms of global competition and re-recognized the importance of their retail franchise. Perhaps even more fundamental has been the recognition of the importance of people. Strategic implementation has become even more vital than strategic formulation. All major competitors can quickly identify attractive market segments, but which ones have the ability to execute the strategies in turbulent markets?

Changes in international markets, with their inevitable spillover into domestic markets, were summarized in the 1986 Annual Report:

Considerable management attention was also devoted to the challenges presented by external market forces. The most dominant of these is the securitization of credit, which now involves the creation of tradeable financial instruments out of almost everything from corporate loans to consumer mortgages. Closely linked to securitization is the internationalization of world capital markets. Many of our customers now have global access to the capital markets, due to the breakdown of tradition local market barriers, the removal of foreign exchange controls and gains in communications technology. A third key trend is disinter-mediation, the by-product of securitization and the linkage of the international capital markets. Conventional corporate loans are less in demand as borrowers seek – and find – finer pricing via securitized loans.[59]

The new international environment forced organizational changes. The new CEO, Allan R. Taylor, announced the following internal changes:

While stability is a widely noted strength at The Royal Bank, the capacity to adapt rapidly and smoothly to change is also a critical attribute. With this in mind, responsibilities of the most senior management team were realigned last June to reflect the changing needs of clients in our diversified markets. An important change was to replace the traditional division of The Bank between International and Domestic groups with Bank-wide mandates for the manage-ment of each of our principal businesses.

J.E. Cleghorn, president, manages our banking network worldwide. A.H. Mitchell, Vice-Chairman, oversees corporate resource management, including finance and the technological underpinnings of electronic banking systems. R.G.P. Styles, Vice-Chairman, oversees our Global/Corporate Investment Banking and Treasury Group. R.C. Paterson, Senior Executive Vice-President, is responsible for Investment Banking in North America and Treasury. M.J. Regan, Senior Executive Vice-President, manages marketing and product development for our retail and commercial banking business. B.D. Gregson, Senior Executive Vice-President, has Bank-wide responsibility for credit risk management.

The central goal of the management team is to build on our track record for top-flight customer service. By serving customers well, we aim over time to substantially improve profitability – specifically to attain a return on assets of .75 per cent and a return on equity of 16 per cent.[60]

Over the following years, the global orientation and marketing focus of the organizational divisions were strengthened as the profitability targets were raised, until by 1991, the target had become .90 per cent.

Canadian retail has regained centre-stage. In Taylor's first annual report as CEO, he stated two goals: excellence in financial services across Canada, and vigorous participation in selected international markets.[61] It is important to recognize that the two goals worked together. In an environment where international cannot be separated from domestic, a strong retail base was essential for international competitiveness. The reorganization plan had important consequences for the manner in which the retail market, which included independent business, would be served. Parallel to the path of succession in the Bank of Montreal, John E. Cleghorn, the person once in charge of retail, has been promoted to president and is positioned to be Taylor's successor.

During the period since 1986, the Royal has sought and made significant gains in major retail markets. Its consumer deposits rose from 49 per cent to 61 per cent of the deposit base over five years, while its market share climbed to 25.6 per cent.[62] Market share has typically hovered around a market-leading figure of 25 per cent in key markets, including tax sheltered deposits, such as registered retirement plans, consumer loans, and in independent business.[63] Even more important has been the lead taken in new products. By 1989, the Royal had captured 50 per cent of the market share in mutual funds offered through banks.[64]

The thrust into new product areas was especially important because it represented the future of retail banking. The Royal was no longer content with providing traditional services; rather, it along with the other Canadian majors, wanted to be in the position to provide the complete services that their product scope made possible in their private banking activities in Switzerland and other global centres. Critically, expansion in private banking was at the expense of rivals: one third of the customers came from other banks.[65] Private banking also offered entry into a very interesting market. In the turbulent world of the 1980s and 1990s, people and capital were mobile. Presence in Hong Kong and other centres provided an important position in capital and information flows.

The Royal built the largest retail investment dealer network through its acquisition of Canada's largest investment dealer, Dominion Securities and its subsequent acquisitions of Vancouver-based Pemberton Securities Inc., as well as Montreal-based Neil Mantha Inc. to increase presence in the West and Quebec. The product line was completed with the addition of Action Direct, the discount brokerage arm of Royal Bank Investor Trading Company. The creation of Royal Bank Investment Management and the binding agreement to purchase International Trustco were further strategic moves in this direction. The 1990 acquisition of 70 per cent of Marcil Trust Company, specialists in real estate, strengthened its base in the trust industry. Complaints concerning regulatory restrictions on car leasing and insurance demonstrated the damaging effects on firms of outdated legislation striving to meet the changing financial needs of Canada's population. Market-share received increased attention during the period because it was viewed both as a condition and a measure of success: size was important.[66] The Royal did not intend to participate in domestic markets that it could not dominate.

As had been apparent in corporate banking for several years, technology was an important driver in changing banking. The Royal positioned itself on the forefront of technological change as it developed a strategy of improved back-room processing to free time to improve service at the front lines. The rapid expansion of ABMS allowed the Royal to develop the largest service-delivery network in North America.[67] But the advent of the machines also forced changes on the service strategy by raising the question: What was the appropriate level of service? The vast number of routine transactions, including cash withdrawal, bill payments, and even deposits, could be accomplished electronically. The ABMS did not need to be located in a branch. Electronics destroyed traditional physical limitations on distribution and created a significant source of fee income because customers of other banks who were members of the Interac system used Royal machines. Nothing made this point more dramatically than the creation of virtually global electronic retail banking networks, such as the Plus system that linked the United States, Canada, Japan, Puerto Rico, and the United Kingdom by 1987.[68] Key aspects of global retail banking, which had once been the preserve of exclusive private bankers, were moving downmarket. This repeated trends in other markets where technology had destroyed profits.

The importance of technological drivers meant that traditional banking organizations had to be redesigned. The extent of the redesign went far beyond rationalizing back-room activities to designing the branches in order to provide appropriate levels of service. The layout of the branches had to be such that customers were directed on a path that took them from ABMS to customer services representatives and finally to personal bankers. The more complex the transaction, the greater the customer's need for human contact and counselling. Such complexity demanded that personal bankers have increased information on client accounts via service reference files that documented the details of each customer's dealings with the bank.[69] Technology both improved the service capability and unleashed the potential for cross-selling. New branches such as that in Toronto's exclusive Hazelton Lanes or the Super Branch in Burlington showed the way of the future.

The effects of technology are oddly contradictory in that they create a global village à la McLuhan and simultaneously generate the information base that allows for increasingly narrow target markets. Centrally created and managed product development and monitoring permitted the bank to focus on local markets as well as on different target markets. At the same time as the Royal segmented the market for VISA users with Gold Cards and developed other credit products for younger borrowers, it also used retired Royal Bankers, the "Grey Panthers," to meet the needs of Canada's aging population. Given this last initiative, it was not surprising that in the fall of 1992, the Royal was the first to offer group retirement products. The thrust was to develop relationships with different target markets by offering products and delivery mechanisms that made customers feel comfortable as they discussed their personal financial affairs. Transactions at a teller's wicket were no longer the model. Now bankers had to listen.[70]

The new attitudes toward employees and customers meant that rather than merely lamenting a number of poor loans to independent business or to the agricultural sector, both of which made up a large portion of the loan portfolio, attempts were made to save the loans through improving the quality of the management advice provided. In an era of relationship management and fee based services, this was a socially responsible and potentially profitable strategy.

As discussed above, from a retail perspective, the Royal entered investment banking in a significant way. In a world buffeted by deregulation and disintermediation, a significant presence in new product areas supported by technology was developed. Success in the market meant having a broad array of computer-based financial services products and computer support for both account managers and customers. At the core of the Royal's strength was the size of its Canadian book and international operations, which was matched by few North American banks.

In the sweeping changes made in 1987, the bank streamlined corporate operations. Following reviews of the "value added" created by individuals at all levels, it was announced that there would be a 10 per cent cut in employees at the Canadian head office and regional headquarters by 1988. Geoffrey Styles, vice-chairman in charge of investment and corporate banks, and three other senior officers took early retirement.[71] John Cleghorn was put in charge of the corporate banking function as well as new product development and computer systems. Investment banking was strengthened with three new executive vice-presidents, John Sanders, Paul Taylor, and Bruce Galloway (World Treasury). Organizational changes were guided by market segmentation principles.[72] The bank developed the following divisions:

1 Commercial: mid-size and public organizations
2 International Banking Network: mid-market outside Canada

3 National Accounts: large Canadian
4 Corporate and Government: global services to MNES
5 Correspondent: other financial institutions

Key to the organization, however, was that all five units were placed under a common umbrella. This allowed greater flexibility to each unit while promoting a global outlook.

In aligning the organization with the environment, it was recognized that while the specific needs of different companies would vary with the degree of sophistication of their financial management, the same forces of globalization and technological change affected all segments.[73] This gave rise to a policy whereby the bank stressed electronic connections that provided their customers with both global and domestic services, such as cash management or payroll. The complexity of banking relationships in the 1980s and 1990s demanded that banks use account managers who would work with product specialists in the bank so that the customer received their desired package.

Treasury products in three key areas are major components in modern financial services. These are foreign exchange, money markets, and rate risk management products.

The strength of the Royal can be demonstrated in various ways. It has a world class reputation for rate risk management products.[74] Volatile interest rates and foreign-exchange rates have shown corporate treasurers the merits of managing positions sensitive to such movements. In foreign exchange, the Royal with its trading volumes of $13 billion per day has developed such expertise that treasurers have ranked it first in Canada and fifth globally.[75] It was also the leading Canadian dollar-trading bank in Tokyo.[76] Perhaps even more telling were its satisfied customers and market penetration. Surveys of customer satisfaction reported that 98 per cent of Canadian customers and 94 per cent of U.S. customers would recommend the Royal.[77] The U.S. data is significant, because among all banks dealing with U.S. *Fortune 500* companies in treasury products, the Royal ranked third in market penetration.[78] Clearly, the Royal was succeeding in its prime target market.

Response to new cross-border opportunities created by the FTA was quick. An office in Buffalo was added to a network that already included offices in Dallas, Houston, Los Angeles, San Francisco, Chicago, Pittsburgh, Miami, and Portland. This was only one initiative. As always, the Royal looked to technology to develop and support its competitive position. In 1991, an agreement was struck with PNC Financial Corporation to facilitate cross-border EDI. GM's

Canadian suppliers were the first users of this new joint system. Integration of North American markets demanded closer, and faster information flow. The incident also attested to close ties with GM. Earlier in 1987, the Royal had developed for GM an innovative money-market program call SNAP which was a form of special short term note.[79]

Closer integration between commercial and investment banking was key to meeting the demands of corporate clients. In this context, the efforts of the Royal in London were interesting. In 1986, activities in London were expanded via the acquisition of Kitcat and Aitken, a London stockbroker, and the creation of RBC Gilts as a primary dealer in U.K. government securities. By 1987, there was a retrenchment as Orion decided to focus on 12 core products and the different parts of the Royal began to share premises. The hope was that physical integration would mirror and hopefully assist market integration. By 1990 Kitcat and Aitken was closed as the Royal limited its competitive focus in Europe. While the episode was not a success, the integration of previously diverse skills and fiefdoms should be noted. The same challenge was met far more successfully in Canada where Royal's account managers were rated the best in the business in an independent survey.[80]

The Royal has developed significant skills and market power since 1986. Key to its growth was its human-resource strategy. A new emphasis on training and compensation packages designed to promote service and profitability succeeded: earnings improved and the Royal was named as one of the 100 best companies for which to work.[81] The bank was "listening" to both its customers and its employees. Efforts went beyond rhetoric. By 1991, programs such as the Employee Share Ownership Program meant the 80 per cent of the employees were shareholders. Moreover, the bank made efforts to respond to the changing environment by recognizing the needs imposed by modern family life and the difficulties faced by women, visible minorities, and the handicapped. The service organization learned to service its own. Perhaps nothing made this more clear than the rationalization of the organization. To improve productivity and responsiveness, in 1987 the Royal added 930 positions at the branch level, while 659 were cut at head office, and 733 in international. Actions spoke loudly.

The bank offered a fine example of an organization changing with the market place in order to be able to identify and to service the needs of its clients. It continued its tradition of being the most international of the Canadian banks, but focused its network on selected profitable markets. Leadership has also been taken on important public issues.[82] Most important have been Taylor's speeches promoting Canadian unity (the 1991 annual meeting was the occasion of an important speech on this topic). The bank has also made clear that it objected to the excessively slow pace of financial services reform. On a more positive note, however, the promotion of community giving via the "Imagine" received strong support, as Taylor was the volunteer chairman of the organization. "Imagine" was an initiative of the Canadian Centre for Philanthropy to stimulate personal and corporate giving and volunteering. On the international front, the donation of roughly $880,000 to World Wildlife to finance a new centre for rain forest studies in Guyana channelled funds in a blocked account to productive uses. The spirit in which the bank sought to improve the communities in which it operated expanded upon its previous leadership position in public affairs.

STRATEGY AND FINANCIAL PERFORMANCE

The Royal underwent significant asset growth during the period 1981–91, as can be seen in figure 4.1.[83] The dynamics of the growth were somewhat understated by the use of a logarithmic scale, but this was done in order to focus upon the significant capital growth during the period. Virtually constant capital growth led to a bank with the muscle to compete for market share. Generally superior credit ratings and the implied lower funding costs were a key source of competitive advantage.

Figure 4.2 provides a different perspective upon growth. Despite the rapidly expanding ABM, growth of service delivery units has not kept pace with employee growth. To keep this in perspective, it is important to consider the changing nature of service delivery. Electronic connections to customers, so vital to the Royal's strategy, were not included in the figures. It is also interesting to note that employee growth was slow or even negative until 1987. The effect of the "little bang" and the opportunity to enter into new fee generating activities led to the need for both new and better trained employees. As will be discussed later, the rise of the number of employees combined with the restriction of physical outlets in part attests to the new imperatives for relationship managers and product specialists as well as to a highly developed delivery system.

Figure 4.3 examines growth in geographic terms.[84] Here a dramatic shift can be seen. Since 1985, the Royal has expanded the role of its Canadian operations. There was a general retrenchment from other markets, although there were efforts to maintain a certain presence.

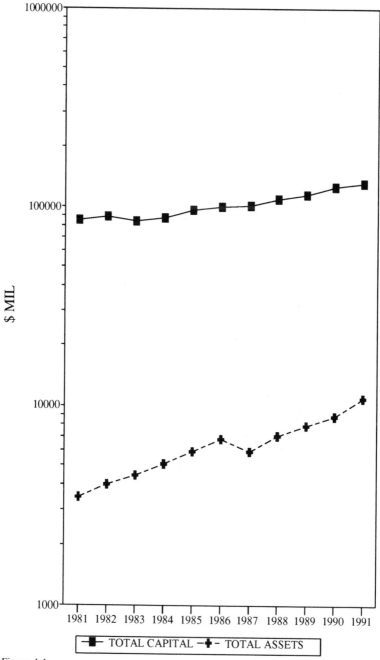

Figure 4.1
Royal Bank of Canada Asset and Capital Growth

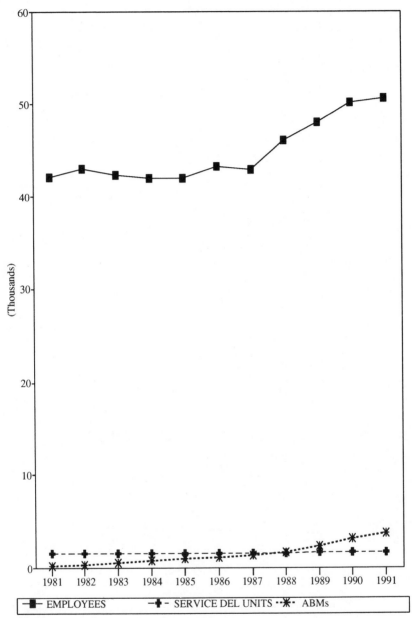

Figure 4.2
Employee and Branch Growth

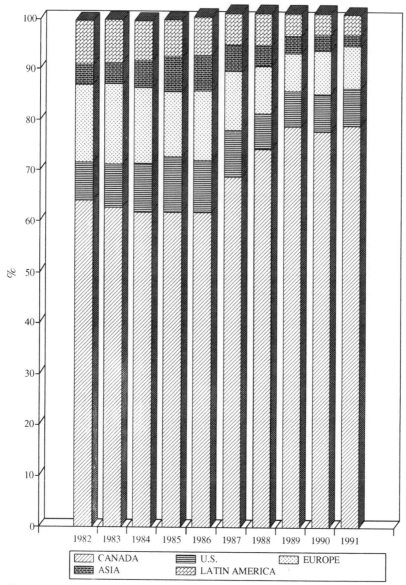

Figure 4.3
Location of Assets

When comparing the Royal to the other Canadian banks, the difference in size must be taken into account. Movements in the U.S. portfolio were somewhat surprising. Despite several public statements by the bank and commentaries by experts, U.S. expansion has not been obvious or rapid. However, activities among Fortune 100 companies in the United States is substantial and provide a strong base – especially in certain key markets, as discussed earlier. The question is whether future expansion will occur through a dramatic move, such as the Bank of Montreal's acquisition of the Harris or the CIBC's acquisition of communication loans from the Bank of New England, or through slow and steady growth. Despite attention to renewing retail and commercial links in Latin America, memories of times past may restrict growth in these markets.

Figures 4.4A and 4.4B reveal changes to the asset portfolio. The two figures are generally consistent and are different only because of changed presentation by the bank. The striking trend from figure 4.4A was the dramatic increase in mortgages. Retail played a more important role. Figure 4.4B makes clear a sharp increase in loans at the expense of bank deposits. Again this probably reflected a shift in asset portfolio construction away from international and toward domestic. It would also be consistent with creating a higher-yielding asset portfolio, as was discussed in the Bank of Montreal chapter.

Individuals played a far more important role in the deposit base, as figures 4.5A and 4.5B show. The 1993 acquisition of assets from Royal Trust was a consistent yet major move in this direction. The Royal greatly enhanced its ability to service high net worth individuals both domestically and internationally with this strategic move. Consistent with the move to retail and commercial lending was the performance of deposits from other banks which declined in both figures. Movement away from unprofitable international business such as syndicated sovereign loans decreased the need to recycle dollars from interbank and certain segments of wholesale banking. Simultaneous efforts to alter the composition of asset-and-liability portfolios were made to enhance both quality and profitability.

The strategic moves led to generally higher net income, as figure 4.6A reveals. The gains occurred as other income was steadily increasing and there was a general, although gradual, improvement in loan losses, excepting the 1987 blip. Net-interest income was interesting. The series seems generally steady, although the level is higher in 1991 than in 1981, which could attest to benefits from repositioning. Perhaps most surprising was the virtually steady growth of non-interest expenses, despite the focus on streamlining. Even though efforts were made at cost containment, expenses grew.

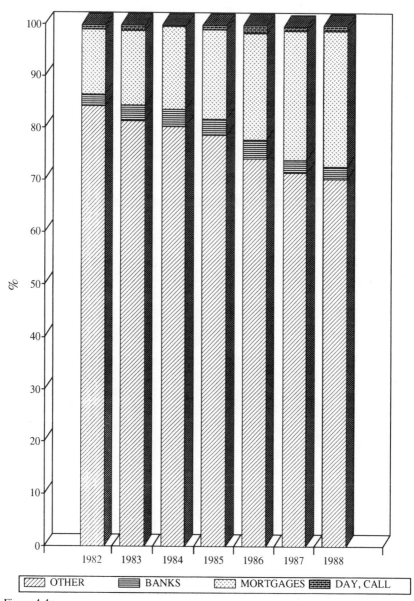

Figure 4.4A
Asset Portfolio: 1982–88

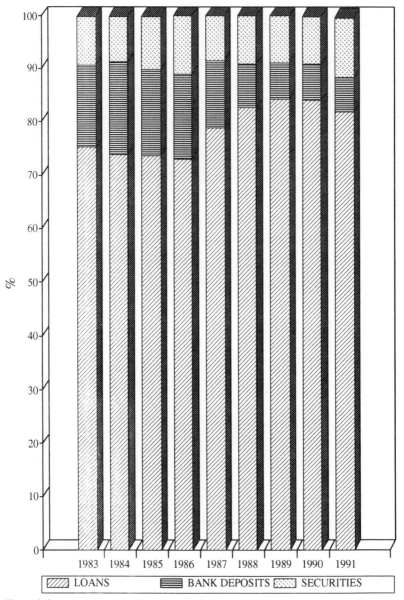

Figure 4.4B
Asset Portfolio: 1983–91

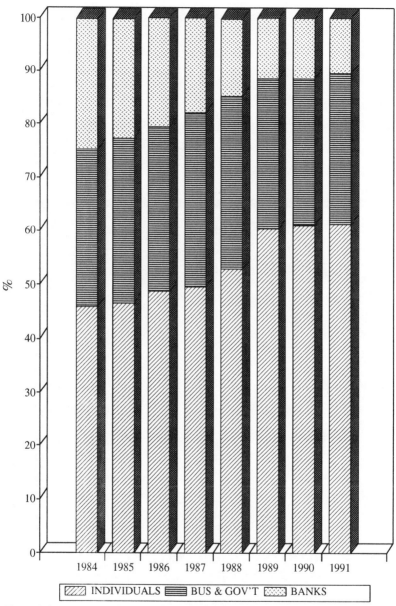

Figure 4.5A
Deposit Portfolio: 1982–88

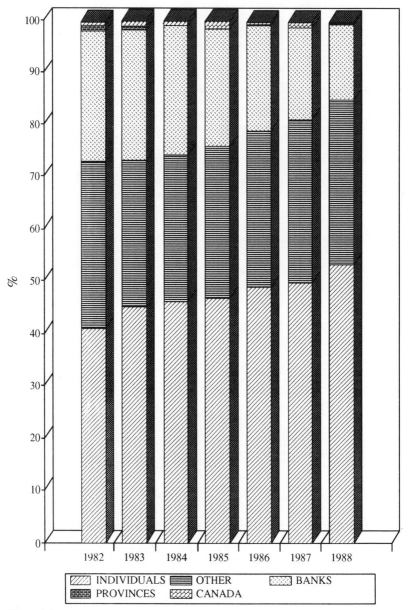

Figure 4.5ʙ
Deposit Portfolio: 1983–91

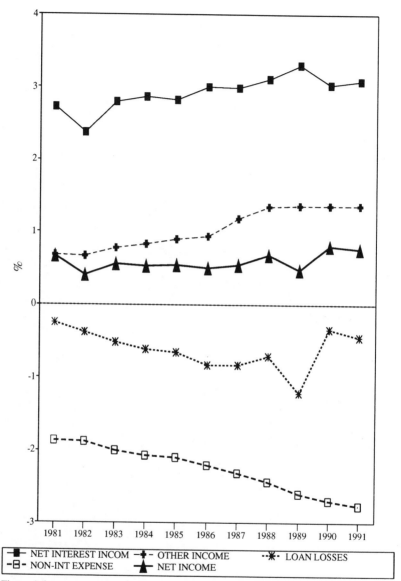

Figure 4.6A
Analysis of ROA

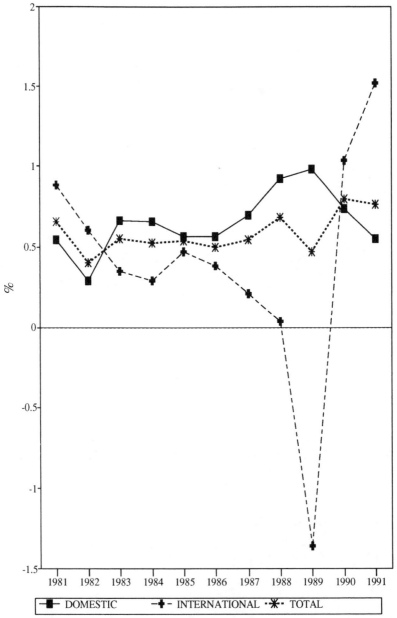

Figure 4.6B
Analysis of ROA

However, the improvement in net income could suggest that the increased expenses served to generate income – by attracting a better deposit-and-asset base as well as by developing the people to sell the new and sophisticated products at both the retail and corporate levels.

The importance of the domestic market for profitability can be seen from figure 4.6B. Only at the beginning and end of the period was international ROA positive for total ROA. International earnings problems were driven both by history in the form of loan losses and by the unfavourable business conditions created by the intense competition discussed earlier. Despite the obvious problems, the stabilizing effects on earnings from international diversification can be seen in the early 1980s and more importantly in the 1990s, the time of the "made-in-Canada" recession.

Figures 4.7A and 4.7B analyse the contribution of six major products to other income – an impressive growth area, as seen in figure 4.6. Examination of the two graphs attest to a strong and reasonably steady income stream that can be derived from a strong retail base. Service charges, credit cards, or as we see in a 4.7A, deposit and payment (DEP and PMT) services, and investment management are important revenue streams. At the other end of the spectrum, foreign exchange (FX) has played an important role, while capital market fees (CAP MKT) and off-balance (OFF B/S) sheet items have been a major growth area. Growth in this area and in bankers acceptances (BAS), letters of credit (LCS), and other commercial products in part reflect the increased use of direct financial instruments by corporate borrowers and may be related to the shift to retail in the asset portfolio.

Non-interest expense portrayed in figure 4.8, at least at the level of aggregation considered here, demonstrated few clear trends, other than a slight decline in the role played by salaries and benefits. In this context, the relatively steady computer expenses should be noted. Technology expenditures were a constant and ongoing expenditure in this information industry.

Stock-price performance was a key financial measure. Figure 4.9 shows consistent premiums paid over book, especially since 1988. The market believed that the Royal knew what it was doing with its assets. While expenses have climbed, there was clearly the expectation of increased revenues associated with the expenditures, not only in the minds of the bankers, but in those of investors. A bold move to increase loan-loss provisions for the 1992 year in light of the recession and problems such as the Olympia and York losses has been hailed as a welcome change to past reporting. Since the market deals in expectations and not just announced results, the new realism

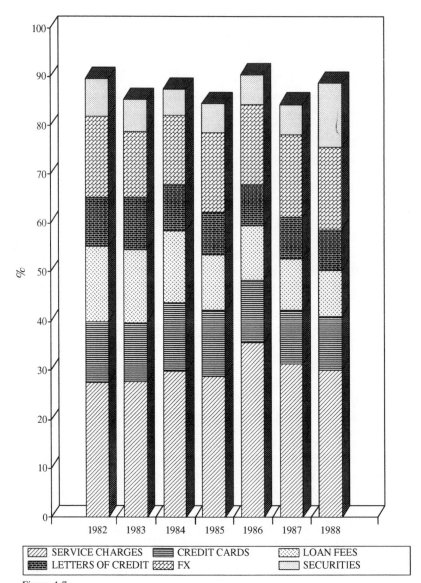

Figure 4.7A
Other Income: 1982–88

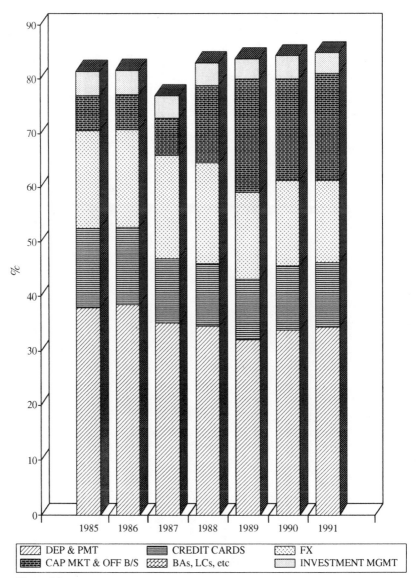

Figure 4.7B
Other Income: 1983–91

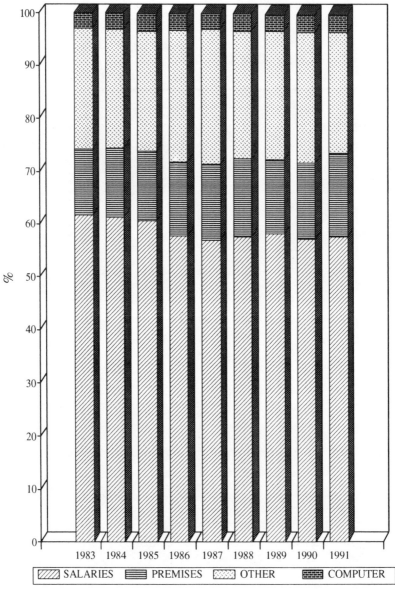

Figure 4.8
Non-Interest Expense

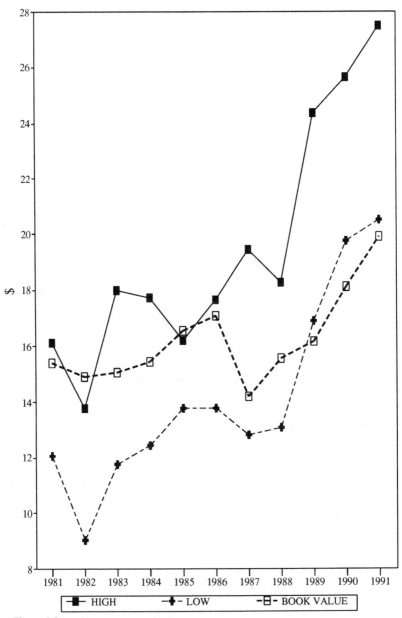

Figure 4.9
Stock-Price Performance

could be beneficial for the bank. It is also interesting to note that this move was taken by a bank whose 1991 annual report was judged the best in the world by Lafferty Business Research.

CONCLUSION

The Royal Bank provides us with an example of a bank that has aggressively sought growth in all directions when market conditions warranted it. By the 1930s it had succeeded in becoming the largest bank in Canada – a position it has not relinquished. A reading of the annual reports reveals a bank that was keenly conscious of the problems associated with growth and that was constantly striving to develop an organization that fit with the market structure of the industry. In this regard, it is fascinating to hear the repeated concerns concerning bureaucratization. The Royal made definite efforts to avoid becoming immobilized by its own structure, not only through shifting the boxes on an organization chart, but through monitoring the processes that go on within and between those boxes and lines. Such concern, clearly understood at the top and voiced to the organization as a whole could account for much of the Royal's success. This bank truly understood what organization meant.

On the other hand, while it seemed appropriate to see the Royal as a bank that wanted to be all things to all people, it is also apparent that it began to refocus and right-size its operations. By focusing on value added, the bank has decided to compete only where it can compete profitably. The Royal remains an international bank, but one that is far more selective in its market scope. This strategic theme has been reinforced in 1992. In a year made virtually profitless by hits from real estate and restructuring, the bank has announced plans to make itself leaner and more competitive. While the 1992 results cannot be pleasing, the decks are cleared.

The efforts made by the CEOs of the Royal to maintain a strong public posture also merit comment. In an industry that receives such public scrutiny, the successful firm must manage its public affairs. The Royal may have been successful because of a clearer appreciation of the role of enterprise strategy in strategic management. The Royal has made significant efforts to maintain legitimacy with both its employees and the broader public. Its report on the effects of Quebec separation released during the Charlottetown Accord referendum campaign demonstrated the risks that the bank was prepared to take to maintain its statesmanlike position. In an era when banks and their problem loans receive so much attention, such a position could be an important advantage. The new competitive spirit engendered in Taylor's 1987 reorganization has created a bank well suited to the new market realities. Ongoing efforts, such as the recent restructuring to attack the u.s. market from fewer centres, will serve to maintain the fit between the organization and its markets.

CHAPTER FIVE

The Canadian Imperial Bank of Commerce

The financial services industry of the 1990s will bear little resemblance to that of the past. World events, many unforeseen, are rapidly altering the environment in which financial institutions operate. By anticipating the new realities and forging ahead, CIBC has positioned itself to enhance its existing capabilities and seize new opportunities in North America and selected areas around the world.

1990 Annual Report, cover.

Just as Scotiabank and the Royal Bank reflected their Maritime origins and the Bank of Montreal its early government connections, so too did the Canadian Imperial Bank of Commerce (CIBC) develop according to its own unique pattern. More than the other banks previously studied, the CIBC was established to serve local interests.[1] It was less focused upon international trade than upon meeting the local banking needs of the community. Thus, while the nature of the Canadian economy demanded a certain degree of internationalization, the overall growth pattern of this bank revealed a stress on the early development of its Canadian branch system.

The choice of growth vectors apparent at the founding has had a major impact upon the development of the CIBC. Its historical legacy still exerts a lasting influence not only through bricks and mortar or the other physical assets acquired during its lengthy history, but also through a culture that affects the manner in which the decision-makers view the world. In the 1970s and 1980s when some banks seemed intent upon becoming international banks centred in Canada, the CIBC concentrated upon remaining a *Canadian* bank with global reach. Recently while the Royal and Scotiabank were refocusing their international networks, the CIBC was further developing its North American presence and its global network from its strong Canadian base.

WILLIAM McMASTER AND
THE FOUNDING OF THE CIBC:
1867–70

The CIBC's founding on the eve of Confederation provides a fascinating portrait of both the economics and politics of the time. The close interconnection between public policy and financial institutions was made quite clear by the struggles of William McMaster to establish much needed banking facilities in central or "western" Canada, as it was then known. McMaster recognized that the area was under-banked, a situation that resulted in part from the dominant position of the Bank of Montreal. As noted in chapter two, E.H. King directed the Bank of Montreal upon a very conservative policy in Canada West because he did not trust the "names" that provided the funda-mental security to the accommodation paper that was the heart of the business.[2] As a result, after 1862–63, the Bank of Montreal channelled deposit funds raised in Canada West to the importers of Montreal or to the gold market on Wall Street.[3]

The situation was exacerbated by the failure of the Bank of Upper Canada and the Commercial Bank of Canada in the 1860s. McMaster did not agree with King's appraisal and sought to fill the niche left vacant by the country's leading bank and the failure of other more speculative ventures. The opportunity and need was nicely expressed in a letter by Archibald Greer, the first cashier of the bank: "We do not oppose anyone, all we seek is the good of the country. We believe that the floating capital which some banks get hold of is loaned out of the country. Our policy is to benefit our respective localities by employing our own and the floating capital coming under our control, in the support of the trade and industry of the place."[3] Notwith-standing the charge that pursuit of regional preferences or interna-tional business was detrimental to the interests of western Canada, the desire to have financial institutions devoted to serving the interests of the community in which they were based seems both powerful and genuine. Such beliefs did then (and still do) form the basis for problems created by the public perception of the role of financial intermediaries.

However, it was one thing to recognize a need and another to pursue the opportunity created by the unfulfilled need – a situation that was especially true in the case of regulated industries. The government was reluctant to grant new banking charters either because of difficulties caused by some of the new banking practices, as revealed by the problems of the Bank of Upper Canada and the Gore Bank in Ontario, or simply because of its attention to other matters. Such a hurdle did not stop a man as resourceful as William McMaster and the influential business people supporting him. He sought out William Cayley who held the charter for the Bank of Canada and purchased it. Viscount Monck, the governor-general, assented to an amending act to change the name to The Canadian Bank of Commerce on 15 August 1866, and the bank that would become the CIBC was born.

Because of the uncertainties attendant upon the deliberations concerning Confederation, little was done to establish operations until February 1867, when the necessary committees were struck. Response to the stock issue was strong and the CIBC found little problem in raising the necessary investment capital in Ontario. Another indication of the public desire for banking services can be seen in the early branching of the CIBC. Almost immediately after opening in Toronto, branches were opened in London, St. Catharines, and Barrie. Inquiries from other communities requesting branches were turned down because the CIBC intended to pursue a strategy of limited branching with operations restricted to legitimate banking operations.[4] Complexity would be minimized by both restricting geographic and product line expansion. Conditions fostered such rapid growth that the organization soon felt the need for change. By November 1867, it was apparent that a new assistant to the cashier or an inspector should be appointed to ensure that the system was working smoothly and efficiently.

In 1868 the CIBC moved to expand its product offering to include a savings department in Hamilton and Guelph. The innovation was not designed to capture new clients so much as it was to maintain a solid deposit base during the time of crop movements. Survival meant adaptation and the development of a deposit strategy matched to the loan position.

Although the CIBC remained focused upon local interests, the economic realities of the time meant that it was impossible to serve Canadian interests without establishing some international connections. This was made clear by the activities of William McMaster himself. McMaster, an Irishman who had emigrated to Toronto in 1843, had business dealings not only in Canada, but also in Manchester. Through the firm of William McMaster and Nephews, he began dealings in trade financing in association with Caldwell Ashworth in New York. Later, McMaster's connections formed part of the CIBC's international network. In addition, an account was established with the London and County Bank in England. These links gave the CIBC a sufficiently broad network among Canada's principal trading partners to allow a proper servicing of the business interests of Upper Canada. There was a further agreement with the Merchants Bank of Canada (Montreal) and later the Molson Bank to facilitate exchanges between the two Canadas.

The charter was not the only early political hurdle facing the CIBC. The mid-1860s were a time of controversy concerning the type of banking that was appropriate for Canada. William Hamilton Merritt of Welland had introduced legislation in 1850 to establish a banking system in Upper Canada based upon the "free banking" system of New York. This model promoted independent local banks and prohibited branching. For a time there was a dual system in operation in Upper Canada: however, the "free" system was found lacking. This could have been the end of the matter had it not been for new and influential supporters of "free banking" who emerged in the post-Confederation parliament, including E.H. King. King's desire to maintain the pre-eminence of the Bank of Montreal led him to attempt to influence the minister of finance to pass legislation that would hamper the efforts of other banks to challenge the hegemony of the Bank of Montreal. John Rose, Galt's successor as minister of finance, seemed willing to follow King's advice.

The political manoeuvring that was created, or at least spurred on by King's actions had some interesting sidelights. From his seat in the Senate, McMaster fought Rose and King to obtain legislation that more closely followed the desires of Ontario bankers and would allow the development of branch banking in Ontario. Strangely enough, this meant that McMaster, a Liberal, was supporting the legislation of Sir Francis Hincks and the Conservative government. In doing so, McMaster opposed powerful interests in his own party and even persuaded some of his Liberal colleagues to support the opposition legislation.

This success cleared the way for some other important legislation being masterminded by McMaster. The CIBC needed royal assent to its proposed merger with the Gore Bank – a merger that had been approved by both sets of shareholders[5] – and to an increase in its share capital in order to allow further growth. Such legislation was also passed in the 1870 session of Parliament. The effect of this session on the development of banking in Canada was profound. After 1870, banks in Canada were placed upon equal competitive footing: moreover, the government had displayed a willingness to allow the banks to grow to meet the needs of the Canadian economy. It had been decided that a branch system was appropriate for Canadian conditions.

The acquisition of the Gore Bank by the CIBC offers insights into how the banking scene had changed during the 1860s. First, while the Gore basically found it impossible to continue operations because of problems created by the failure of other banks in Upper Canada and two successive correspondents in Montreal, it also became clear that the era of such small, local banks was coming to an end. The Gore had been established in 1836 under the difficult conditions that existed in a pioneer community. Throughout its life, it had served its community, but the volatility of local economic life now made it clear that banks would require a broad, diversified base in order to survive. The Gore was not in a position to pursue the growth needed to achieve a diversified base because of the manner in which the failure of other banks had impaired its capital. It hence became a takeover target.[6] Although as a bank the Gore was not a "success," it was sufficiently attractive to cause a bidding war between the Bank of Montreal and the CIBC. The success of the CIBC in acquiring the third-oldest bank in the province may have been instrumental in alerting King to the potential threat posed by the new bank and inspired his efforts to influence Parliament. The Gore incident provides a fascinating insight into banking competition at the time of Confederation.

EARLY EXPANSION UNDER
McMASTER, DARLING, AND
COX: 1870–1907

Initial expansion was guided by three presidents: the Honourable William McMaster, 1867–86; Henry W. Darling, 1886–90; and the Honourable George Albertus Cox, 1890–1907.

The year 1870 was an important year for the CIBC and once again revealed the importance of international operations for Canadian banks. In this year, the Bank of Montreal opened an office in London, England, which gave it a cost advantage over the CIBC. If the CIBC were to remain competitive, it would have to obtain more favourable terms from its London correspondent, including a decrease in the commission charged on acceptances and uncovered credit facilities. Both of these would be difficult to obtain because of the competitive environment in London at that time. However, McMaster was able to negotiate a most favourable deal with his old friend, David Davidson of the Bank of Scotland, Edinburgh.[7] The Scottish Bank had just opened a London branch and was anxious for the business, although the role of McMaster's personal connections should not be downplayed. Relationship management has always been part of financial services.

The opening of a New York agency in 1872 provides insight as to why Canadian banks have been successful south of the border. In general, U.S. banks resisted foreign operations. The extent of this early ethnocentrism could be seen when the CIBC acted for the U.S. government after the U.S. came into possession of the Philippines following the Spanish-American War. The CIBC had had a correspondent in Manila for many years, while by 1872 no U.S. bank had such a connection. Consequently U.S. banks were not equipped to carry out many of the foreign banking transactions required by American business and government. Typically, Canadian banks established connections to U.S. companies, not only in Canada, but in third markets.[8] Conditions such as these led the CIBC to expand into the United States with the opening of a Chicago branch in 1875.[9]

Under McMaster's guidance, the CIBC continued to adapt and to innovate. Growth necessitated the separation of the Toronto branch from head office, at least on the ledger. This was an important step in responding to pressures from previous growth as well as in fostering future growth. It was clear that McMaster recognized the importance of the timely exchange of information in banking when the CIBC responded to new opportunities created by technological change and connected its Hamilton and Dundee branches by telephone on 20 May 1879. Perhaps an even more important move directed by McMaster was the bank's focus on the West.

The year 1879 was a critical one for the bank because it was the year that Macdonald announced his new "National Policy." The industries of Ontario protected by the resulting tariff policies would provide a growing clientele for the CIBC. It was also the year that the impact of the CPR began to be felt by the CIBC not only because of the opening of the West, but because of the flow of new capital into Canada. Although the CIBC turned down requests from Winnipeg, Emerson, and Brandon for branches, it did begin to strengthen its Western ties through stronger bonds with the Ontario Bank and the Bank of British Columbia. While the West was seen as an emerging area, its full importance was not yet recognized by the bank and so no branch was opened until 1893.

In 1886, McMaster's failing health caused him to announce his retirement at the July annual meeting. Fourteenth months later, the veteran senator died. McMaster's successor, Darling inherited a reasonably strong bank. Runs on other banks in the late 1870s had shown the strength of the CIBC and left it in an improved position in the important Montreal market. However, some problems came to light as Byron Edmund Walker, the new general manager, investigated accounts in 1886. It was decided that the CIBC needed to institute tighter credit checks and be prepared to close down accounts that got into difficulties. Delinquent accounts demanded investigation, not simply further credit to carry them through difficult times (a lesson bankers often forget during times of rapid growth). In adopting such measures, Walker was instrumental in raising the professional standards of the CIBC.

It should also be recognized that the bank grew slowly during the 1880s; branch openings were roughly equal to closings. While Darling's tenure as president was short, it was notable for some innovations. Although there were few branch openings, there was an important change in the strategy of branching when in 1887 the CIBC decided to experiment by establishing branches in the retail centres of Toronto. Previously only the Dominion Bank and the City Bank (Montreal) had had multiple branches in one city. In addition, the bank moved to expand its international network. J.H. Plummer, the assistant general manager, was dispatched to Great Britain in 1889 and connections for letter-of-credit (LC) business with Europe, South America, and Australia were all improved. The relationship with the Union Bank of Australia proved to be one of long duration. There was also a change in personnel policies when the CIBC hired its first female employee, Joan Inglis, as a typist for head office in 1887.

When Cox ascended to the presidency of the CIBC in 1890, he was able to witness yet another important change in Canadian banking: the establishment of the CBA in 1891. This organization grew out of the cooperation developed among the banks in making their submissions to Parliament concerning changes to the Bank Act in 1890. The new era of cooperation among banks was a far cry from the attitudes of the 1860s. The CBA was also charged with improving the level of education among Canadian bankers in the same manner as the Institute of Bankers had done in England.[10] The participation of the CIBC was evidenced by the fact that out of twenty-five essay submissions to the CBA contest, twelve came from the CIBC.

There was rapid growth during the 1890s, as assets grew by 50 per cent between 1895 and 1898. As previously mentioned, a branch was opened in Winnipeg in 1893, and an agency was opened in New Orleans to service the cotton trade.[11] While the period saw a change as deposits began to grow, domestic loan demand left little available for foreign lending. In fact, in 1893, the CIBC was turning down requests from the United States for funds, an indication of its commitment to Canada.[12]

In 1898 the CIBC opened a branch in Dawson City in the Yukon. The first request for a branch there came from trading companies, but the CIBC refused because of the relatively undeveloped infrastructure of the territories. Poor communications and a shortage of police protection did not provide fertile ground for a bank. However, when the Canadian government requested that the CIBC open a branch and an assay office, the bank complied. The romance of the gold rush, as chronicled by the poet Robert Service, a one-time employee of the CIBC, cannot be doubted, but the activities of the bank attest to something different. There were great difficulties in operating a branch that required new skills in assaying in an area not serviced by telegraph until 1899, nor by regular mail service until 1900.[13] To overcome some of the inherent difficulties, the CIBC supported its gold-rush operations with new branches in Vancouver and Seattle (which were trade centres with the Yukon), as well as in Skagway, Whitehorse, and Atlin. Again, the requirement of being international to be competitive in Canada should be noted. The advent of these far-flung operations and their successful operation truly demonstrated the value of the annual inspections that the CIBC had initiated, and of its procedures and control systems. This episode also demonstrated that while the government did assist the banks, the banks in turn recognized their obligations.

The Yukon adventure also illustrated the important role that Canadian banks played in ensuring the orderly settling of the West. In order to understand the different settlement patterns between the U.S. and the Canadian West, the role of both the banks and the Royal Canadian Mounted Police must be taken into account.[14] Financial and economic stability were linked to political stability.

The CIBC's centre of gravity shifted further west with the acquisition of the Bank of British Columbia in 1900.[15] This was the first major amalgamation to take place among Canadian banks in several years and it had some interesting features. The Bank of British Columbia had been established in 1862 by interests in London, England to participate in profitable business on the West coast.[16] From its inception, the Bank of British Columbia had an international orientation, not only because of its British ownership and control, but because of the extent of its operations in the United States where it frequently did more business than it did in Canada. Moreover, the bank was not in trouble when it was taken over. However, the bank's shareholders had come to believe that it was time to end the experiment in controlling a bank from such a distance. The volatility attendant upon changes in the coast economy made old dangers even more apparent. Because the bank was sound, more time and attention could be devoted to the procedure of takeover. Plummer was able to make a careful appraisal of the assets of the Bank of British Columbia and the two banks were able to come to an amicable settlement.

With the acquisition of the Bank of British Columbia, the CIBC found itself in a new business: Hawaiian sugar. While the trade may not have been too brisk at the turn of the century, this new activity positioned the CIBC to participate in trans-Pacific trade as it developed. More importantly, the acquisition gave the CIBC its own branch in London, England and demonstrated an international organizational capability.

This Western move was somewhat tempered in 1903 when the Halifax Banking Company, the old rival of Scotiabank, amalgamated with the CIBC. The reason behind the amalgamation was the imminent retirement of the Halifax Banking Company's cashier and president. Perhaps due to the few organizational pressures created by the cautious growth policy of this bank, no successors had been trained. While sentiment at the Halifax Banking Company hoped to find an ally in a local institution, such as Scotiabank, when the CIBC made an offer, the directors preferred to take the offer than continue separate operations. The CIBC further extended its business in the Maritimes with its acquisition of the Merchants Bank of Prince Edward Island. The directors of the Merchants realized by 1906 that not only was their bank failing to grow, it was actually declining in size. The era of the small local bank was nearing its end in the Maritimes at the same time that the CIBC was on an aggressive policy of national expansion. Under such conditions, accommodation was soon reached by the two banks.

These three acquisitions gave the CIBC both a strong national network as well as new-found strength to pursue opportunities in both Atlantic and Pacific trade. Because it spanned the entire continent and was represented in both New York and London, the CIBC found itself in a position to reach beyond the seas. In addition to geographic expansion, it also expanded the range of service offerings by distributing stocks and bonds through its branch system. While the bank realized certain scope economies, it was clear that in many communities the CIBC was the only financial institution; hence, the task fell to it by default. However, by 1901, branch managers were being warned to ensure that their clients were informed that the CIBC would act only as distributors of stocks and bonds, and did not make any recommendations.[17] The use of bank money orders was being aggressively promoted by the CIBC in 1905 – in fact, the CIBC took the lead in Canada with this product.[18]

In 1894, a staff of 385 was adequate to run the CIBC; by 1904, however 840 people were required. While some of these were needed to staff new branches, the expanded operations also required changes at head office. The strain of administering and controlling branches at a distance led the CIBC to move toward a district organization with resident inspectors. An inspector for the Pacific Coast branches resident in Vancouver was appointed in 1901. By 1903, it was clear that further changes at head office were needed. The number of staff was increased and the organization was both broadened and more carefully delineated. Previously, it had been possible for a single individual to track all the details of a transaction, but now the scale and complexity of operations made that impossible.[19] It became necessary for head office to be broken down into different departments, each with its own specialties. Such differentiation also created the need for integration. This was accomplished through the formation of committees that met on a regular basis. For example on every Monday, Wednesday, and Friday, the general manager, the assistant general manager, the heads of departments and certain assistants met to discuss the affairs of the CIBC. A new executive structure had been developed to manage operations of a scope and complexity undreamt of by the founders.

A further example of organizational differentiation came with the bank's creation of the Dominion Realty Company Ltd, which was to own and erect bank buildings. The CIBC had come to realize the importance of location and control over the physical environment in its premises.

Along with expansion came the problem of staffing the new branches and positions. Measures such as the pension plan that was introduced in 1891 and the payment of fairly generous bonuses in 1899 may have been motivated in part by the need to maintain a highly trained staff.[20] Like any other service industry, a bank must make significant investment in human assets, which are far more mobile than physical assets. One solution was to recruit new personnel elsewhere, preferably from another country in order not to initiate an expensive recruiting war in Canada. As mentioned earlier, this tactic had been used by other banks such as the BBNA. By 1905 the CIBC began to recruit in Scotland. In due course, it broadened its recruiting area to include Ireland, an occurrence that would have pleased McMaster.

Under Cox's tenure, the CIBC had grown significantly, not only in size but in scope, since it now spanned the entire nation and reached far into foreign lands. Moreover, Cox had guided the institution through significant organizational change that included improving office technology and facilitating formation flows. Clearly the CIBC of 1907 was significantly different from the bank that he had inherited. Yet, the CIBC was still true to the tradition of serving local interests.

SIR EDMUND WALKER: 1907–24

When Sir Edmund assumed leadership of the CIBC in 1907, he found that the bank's expansion into the West had not been without its problems. The CIBC found itself with too many loans and in the embarrassing (although profitable) position of turning down new business through the simple device of raising rates. Interestingly, there was an exception. The CIBC did not desire that the rates for moderate loans to farmers be affected as the branches made efforts to return to their authorized credit limits. The CIBC continued to adapt to the pioneering conditions and the influx of immigrants so vital to the development of the West. As a service to immigrants from many lands, the CIBC was the first to give its branches the capability of remitting funds to any location in the world. Once again, the ties between domestic and international banking in Canada were apparent.

Competition for customers in the West was keen as several other banks were rushing to extend service to the new area. One result of this competition was a spate of bad loans. The reason for the bad loans may call to mind the "go go" banking of the 1970s and the borrowing patterns of many Third World countries and real estate magnates. Customers were borrowing from several different banks so that the banks did not realize the extent of the client's indebtedness. The head office of the CIBC warned its branches to scrutinize very carefully where borrowers resided in an effort to avoid making such loans. Problems such as these and the complexities of doing business in diverse locations may also have encouraged the CIBC to appoint Sir John Aird superintendent of the CIBC's business between Lake Superior and the Rockies in 1908.

Further differentiation in the bank's organization was apparent in 1909 when it brought into use the term "auditor" to designate the person assigned to ensure that the daily routine of the CIBC was being performed properly. The title of "inspector" was now reserved for those concerned with examining of the liabilities of borrowing customers. Growth both fostered and made economically rational this further specialization.

The increasing number of branches, both domestic and foreign, continued as the CIBC sought to establish a complete network. The extent of its operations can be seen in table 5.1, which compares the branch network in 1901 to that of 1911. As shown, the most glaring gap in the national network was the sparse representation in Quebec. This situation was remedied in the same manner as the gap in the Maritimes had been: by an acquisition. In 1911, the CIBC entered into negotiations with the Eastern Townships Bank headquartered in Sherbrooke. When the CIBC approached the Eastern Townships Bank, the latter was already considering expansion plans because it had come to realize that only large banks with extensive scope were likely to survive. Considering the advantages of allying with the CIBC as opposed to financing its own growth, the directors of the Eastern Townships Bank came to the conclusion that union was desirable. Through the merger in 1912, the CIBC acquired 84 branches in Quebec, as well as 15 others elsewhere.

Now, if anything, the CIBC was primarily concentrated in the East. In 1912, the Maritime network was further rounded out when the bank commenced operations in Newfoundland. That year also saw the CIBC extend its reach into the Orient as a direct account with The Chartered Bank of India, Australia, and China in Hong Kong, was opened by the Vancouver branch. This bank was the CIBC's oldest correspondent in Asia as ties dated back to 1889. Despite the fact that these markets were difficult because of communications and foreign-exchange problems, the CIBC began to develop business with China and Japan.

World War I created the same massive dislocation for the CIBC as it did for the other banks. The bank took an early opportunity to display its loyalty to the Empire when it was the only Canadian bank to participate in Great Britain's first war loan. It demonstrated patriotism to Canada by offering the use of its branch system to help the government. One of the more interesting projects in which the bank took part, especially given its strength in the West, was a program designed to improve farm production. The branches collected the names of farmers and sent them to the Extension and Publicity division of the Dominion Experimental Farm in order that the government could send these farmers the most up-to-date technical information. In addition, the CIBC instructed the branch managers to make every effort to impress upon farmers how serious was the need to improve farm production. In assuming such a role, the bank acted as an important and positive instrument of public policy.

During the war, the CIBC looked to Brazil and the West Indies because of interruptions in normal trade. After the war, the Foreign department of the CIBC began to compile a list of the manufacturing resources of Canadian firms in order to respond to the inquiries of

Table 5.1
CIBC Branch Network, 1901 and 1911

Location	1901	1911
Ontario	45	66
Quebec	1	3
Nova Scotia		13
New Brunswick		1
Prince Edward Island		5
Manitoba	1	21
Saskatchewan		52
Alberta		40
British Columbia	12	33
North West Territories and the Yukon	2	3
England	1	1
United States	5	5
Mexico		1
Total	67	244

companies desiring to export to new markets. Pamphlets were also issued to assist new exporters. The CIBC was doing everything it could to ensure that Canadian business got a fair share of the postwar market opportunities.

The CIBC made several changes to accommodate itself to the new international dimensions of the postwar world. Foreign exchange departments were added to the larger branches in recognition of the need to meet the revived international business. Accounts were opened with Federal Reserve Banks to respond to the increasing importance of the United States. As well, branches were opened in the West Indies to develop further the legacy of the Halifax Banking Company. China and Japan were investigated, but it was determined that the banking needs of these countries were already being met by their domestic banks. The existing correspondent relations established earlier would suffice for now.

Domestically, the CIBC felt that it had lost ground in Ontario, Manitoba and Saskatchewan. Some of this was made up when the bank acquired the Hamilton Bank in 1923, but while it kept an eye out for expansion, it generally believed that Canada was overbanked. There were already too many branches. In order to cut costs, all the major banks embarked on a program of rationalization in the 1920s. The competition that had produced bad Western loans and over-branching was replaced with a new spirit of common concerns for the overall health of the industry.[21] Destabilizing competition was not the Canadian way after the founding of the CBA.

The failure of the Home Bank in 1923 coupled with attacks by "Progressives" during that year's Bank Act hearings led to some internal changes.[22] The CIBC had previously added a second vice-president to the staff and had increased the level of decentralization, giving senior managers more authority. At the same time, it had instituted tighter controls which were made necessary by both the difficult postwar conditions and by the new decentralization. Some of the changes included grouping industries and financially related customers in order that the CIBC would have a more detailed understanding of the nature of its exposures. Given the increasing complexity of business, more knowledge of clients was needed to assess credit risk. In 1923, the CIBC moved from a semi-annual to a monthly evaluation of assets. Volatility meant more frequent inspection and centralization.

The CIBC continued to invest in information technology when it rented a private telegraph connection for its New York and Havana offices to improve the speed of communication. In 1920 it also made an effort to improve communications within the institution itself: in order to improve staff morale, it began issuing a new internal publication entitled *The Caduceus*. Sir Edmund did not miss the opportunity provided by this vehicle to promote a sense of the need for both exactness and initiative as a requisite for employees. The spirit displayed in the pioneer communities must not be lost.

Under Sir Edmund's leadership, the CIBC both became a truly national bank and expanded its international operations. An impressive series of mergers created an extensive branch system and allowed it to grow at a rate faster than the banking system. Between 1887 and 1924, the assets of the CIBC grew at 21.8 per cent, while the assets of all banks grew at only 11.4 per cent. The legacy, however, was not only one of growth, but also one of public service. Despite increasing international operations, Sir Edmund always placed Canada first.

SIR JOHN AIRD: 1924-36

Sir John Aird succeeded Sir Edmund in 1924. During the difficult years of the early 1920s, he ensured that there was a new emphasis on efficiency and economy. There was a major effort to lower the cost structure of all the Canadian banks through the rationalization of the branch system during the Depression.[23] Branch closings exceeded branch openings for many years in this period, as the bank and its rivals closed many unprofitable branches. At the same time, however, the CIBC went to great lengths to ensure that communities were supplied with banking services, even to the point of transferring accounts to competitors when they left the community. In turn, some of the CIBC's competitors closed branches where the CIBC was the stronger branch. A good example of this was the use of an airplane to establish a branch for a mine in northern Manitoba. Other cost-cutting moves were the formation of committees to simplify daily transactions and to standardize transactions. Greater concentration in the industry made it possible to achieve economies of scale which in turn improved the CIBC's profitability.

Naturally sluggish conditions also called for greater efforts to generate new business. To address this challenge, the CIBC developed some basic tactics. First, it placed increased emphasis on advertising, and second, on foreign markets. It also recognized the importance of the New York call market as an outlet for funds, and of new opportunities created by growing tourism in the West Indies.[24] Another signal of the increasing importance of foreign operations was the promotion to general manager of Sydney Henry Logan, a man with foreign experience.[25] A renewed effort to target certain industries was undertaken. From the 68th (1934) Annual Report on, increasing attention was paid to the role of the mining and forestry industries. Finally, the bank also became involved in the development of a new product: the personal loan. In 1936, the annual report broke down the loan portfolio as follows: agriculture, 21 per cent; manufacturers and other producers, 18 per cent; wholesalers/retailers, 7 per cent; private individuals: 15 per cent; government and municipalities, 14 per cent; brokers and bond dealers, 13 per cent; construction, 3 per cent.[26] The marketing of the new product was assigned to a personal loans department.

The Depression created strained public relations because the banks were perceived to be hoarding money. Aird and Logan went to great lengths in public statements to assure Canadians that simply for profit the CIBC would prefer to lend rather than to invest in securities and other low-yielding assets. However, it was no favour to a borrower to be encouraged to take on debt that could not be serviced.[27] The Western orientation of the CIBC may have made it particularly sensitive. It was interesting that in his final statement in the 70th (1936) Annual Report, Aird commented upon the unfairness that forced farmers to sell at world prices while they had to buy goods at higher prices because of protective tariffs.[28]

Upon his retirement in 1936, Aird left the CIBC housed in a magnificent new Toronto building. The towering structure was a visible assurance of the soundness of the CIBC and the Canadian banking system. A country dependent upon the inflow of foreign capital must have a system recognized as a safe haven for funds. Otherwise, in troubled times, funds would become both expensive and hard to find.[29] The CIBC believed that the tenants of the new building could be potential clients for the CIBC. A location strategy with an emphasis not only on convenience, but also upon symbolic reassurance via architecture was emerging.

THE McKINNON ERA

Although Alan E. Arscott, S.M. Wedd, and James Stewart managed the CIBC prior to the ascension of Neil J. McKinnon to the presidency in 1957, there was not the same sense of a dominant personality at the helm during these years. From the postwar period until his retirement in 1973, McKinnon guided the CIBC.

Domestically, there were adjustments, but few basic changes. The CIBC participated in the new types of lending to assist the rebuilding of Canadian industry,[30] and continued to focus on natural resources and agriculture. From 1949 on, Calgary became the centre for participation in Alberta's oil and gas boom.[31] The CIBC realized the importance of location and established the Petroleum and Natural Gas division in Calgary, rather than at head office in Toronto. This may have been in response to a certain hostility from the West to central Canada. A similar division was not opened in Toronto until 1962. To fortify its position, the CIBC continued to issue publications concerning the oil and gas industry.[32]

The dominant growth vector in the CIBC's strategy was still the development of the branch system. With the acquisition of the Imperial Bank in 1961, the newly named Canadian Imperial Bank of Commerce could proclaim that it had the largest branch network of any Canadian bank. The importance that the bank attached to the branch system could also be seen in its innovative efforts to reach new markets through opening branches in colleges. Flying banks were sent to service the North and banks on ships to visit isolated maritime areas. As an added convenience to its customers, the CIBC began promoting cash dispensers, a move made possible by the increasing use of computers.[33]

The development of the Kinross Mortgage subsidiary was fully in keeping with the branching strategy.[34] Meanwhile, the CIBC continued to seek larger customers and was able to boast in the 96th Annual Report, that it had the highest commercial loan total ever reported by a Canadian bank.[35] Efforts to expand the presence in this segment saw participation in Triarch, a company for equity investing, as well as in United Dominions Corporation which specialized in medium- and long-term lending.

The expansion into the United States begun earlier was now greatly strengthened. In 1949, a special representative for business development was appointed in New York and the New York operations were expanded with the development of the Canadian Bank of Commerce Trust Company in New York in 1951. Further attempts to penetrate the u.s. market followed with the appointment of officers for Chicago in 1956 and Dallas in 1958. These latter two sites were in keeping with the CIBC's focus on petroleum and agriculture. The CIBC also expanded in the West Indies and formed the Caribbean Trust Company in 1962.

The 1959 appointment of a special representative in Zurich marked a new stage in internationalization. The annual reports of the early 1960s began to place more emphasis on the international connections of the CIBC, as well as asserting that the CIBC was known worldwide as a specialist in natural resources, agriculture, and industrial development. Creation of a natural-resource division at head office in 1962 further attested to the CIBC's specialization.[36] The CIBC began to use officers abroad to make its expertise available to firms wishing to enter Canada.[37] Foreign branches not only followed trade, but served to promote foreign direct investment and to build client relations within the protected Canadian market. Protected capital markets made it possible to recruit business.

Entry into Hong Kong in 1968 further expanded international operations, and discussions in the 106th (1972) Annual Report demonstrated growing recognition of the importance of the Pacific Rim for Canada. With the development of larger projects, especially in the natural-resource sector, it became imperative to be represented in the growing Pacific capital markets. Participation in the new international banking involved the use of consortia or joint ventures. The 105th (1971) Annual Report discussed the CIBC's interest in Crédit Commercial de France, Banco Finasa de Investimento s.a. (Brazil), the Private Investment Corporation for Asia (Main Office, Tokyo), Adela Investment Corporation s.a. (based in Lima), and the Development Finance Corporation (based in Sydney).

Organizationally, there were few changes. The regional structure of the CIBC was well suited to the growth of the branch system, and the presence of an international department at head office provided adequate coordination. The growth of the institution contributed to its continuing need for qualified bankers. The CIBC supported its personnel in taking courses through the CBA and provided courses, including those on customer relations, at its own staff college. By 1972, it was placing increased emphasis on the recruitment of women – an obvious response to changing social conditions and staff shortages. As well, the CIBC, like others, found itself entering the electronic age. By 1968, planning for an on-line strategy emerged and by 1970 it was reported that most of the Toronto branches were on-line.

While the era was one of growth, the annual reports did not convey a dynamic spirit. Not all would agree with this statement. Robert MacIntosh saw McKinnon as the prime mover in ending the tyranny of a 6 per cent interest rate ceiling on the activities of banks.[38] But the annual reports of the period reveal a culture that seemed both conservative and secretive. Despite the changes taking place, it is difficult to detect any real sense of dynamism following the Imperial acquisition in the organization – instead the impression is one of consistent incremental growth with a new attention to international operations.

J . PAGE R . WADSWORTH AND RUSSELL E . HARRISON: 1973–81

Upon the retirement of McKinnon, J. Page R. Wadsworth was appointed CEO, Russell E. Harrison chief operating officer (COO) and Donald Fullerton, executive vice-president. Fullerton had international experience in New York. As with the other Canadian banks, the 1970s was a time of increasing internationalization because of the ceilings imposed by the Winnipeg Agreement of June 1972 and later Anti-Inflation Board (AIB) legislation that limited profits from domestic operations by restricting price increases on services. As the government sought to manage price increases domestically, the banks viewed the domestic market as inadequate to support the profit growth demanded by shareholders. A further factor promoting the growth of international operations was the era of megaprojects requiring syndicated lending and the interest of companies in the growing Euromarkets. Given that Euromarkets tended to have narrower spreads and to be less profitable, it was not surprising that the banks followed, rather than led, their clients into these markets.[39]

The first annual report issued in 1973 by the new executive team revealed the emerging interest in international operations. A vice-president was appointed to head European operations from London and the concept of area management was expanded with similar treatment for Nassau and the Bahamas. A new vigour was apparent from the discussion of full-service branches that had been opened in

Frankfurt and Paris, participation in international banking ventures in the medium-term Euromarket, and joint ventures, such as the International Energy Bank. The CIBC hoped to develop its international scope by leveraging its skills in natural resource projects now that many LDCs were borrowing to develop their natural resources.

The following year's annual report announced that the CIBC was formulating a strategic plan that would emphasize broadening its base. There was an interesting change in the format of the document. It contained a report from the executive management team, Wadsworth, Harrison, and Fullerton, which was followed by reports from the senior vice presidents: James G. Bickford for International Operations; Derek G. Keveney for Administration; Charles M. Laidley for Loans and Investments; Basil E. Langfeldt for Domestic Regions; and David A. Lewis for Deposit Business, Marketing, and Consumer Services. The report's prioritizing of contents with International Operations ahead of the other areas of responsibility symbolically attested to the new importance of such activities for the CIBC, as did the increase in profits and the 40-per-cent increase in assets for the year.

Later reports attested both to the increasing competitiveness and the growth of the Euromarkets. Competitive conditions meant that some years, such as 1975, saw a considerable contribution to profits from international operations while other years were less profitable. But even more significant was the growing scope and complexity of international operations. By 1974, the need for an international services department to coordinate the CIBC's product offerings was recognized.

Three strategic thrusts could be identified. There was increasing attention to the Euromarkets with the creation of specialized offices for Euroloans in Toronto and London, as well as a new association with Hambros Bank Ltd., U.K.[40] The same was true of the Far East, where Canadian Eastern Finance Ltd was set up in association with Cheung Kong Holdings. The importance of U.S. connections became apparent, with greater discussion of both the California operations and the opening of a new office in Atlanta.[41] The need for U.S. dollars and the effect of U.S. regulation had a major impact on the CIBC's international strategy, which was true for all the other banks as well.

Domestically, the CIBC hoped to build on its strengths in the fields of agriculture and oil and gas as well as to develop new expertise in the textile and garment industries by opening an office in Montreal.[42] As well, the traditional emphasis on the strength of the branch network and service to smaller retail accounts was maintained. On-line computerization continued to form an important part of the branch strategy, and by 1978 1,020 of 1,832 branches were on-line. However, despite the new emphasis and profits from international, there were real problems facing the bank, especially in the area of cost control. Moreover, cost-control problems were coming from several directions: the cost of funds, loan-loss provisions, and operating costs. The 1970s saw an increase in the use of high-cost deposits as customers became more aware of the role of using interest-bearing accounts to manage their funds. There was also increasing competition for funds, which may have contributed to an increase in the CIBC's use of hedged foreign-currency deposits.[43] Perhaps of even greater significance was the effect of increased loan-loss provisions discussed in the 112th (1978) Annual Report. Fullerton made it clear that the CIBC needed to pay increased attention to asset-quality control in the future. A bank that had problems with assessing credit had a fundamental operating problem that had to be rectified through some form of organizational change. The bank's difficulties were further compounded by the fact that, by 1976, domestic operations had become less attractive because inflation was driving up operating costs while AIB regulations were restricting prices.

The problems affecting profitability resulted in organizational change. The inability to manage costs suggested an organization that was out of control. In order to remedy this situation, the proper information had to be available and assessed centrally and in a timely manner. Clearly, it was impossible to recognize a mismatch between assets and liabilities if the information concerning such activities was not available in one place. Decentralization of operations demanded centralization of information. The CIBC restructured itself for the domestic market with the recognition that there were two fundamentally different market segments: consumer and general business, and corporate banking. The first step was to reorganize around these two segments at head office and then to establish their counterparts in the field. The head office move, however, was essential if proper control was to be exercised. The control structure over field operations needed development if profitability was to be attained. At the same time, consolidation of administrative functions was required in order to ensure that the information required to manage a complex and interdependent portfolio was available.

Thus as the CIBC entered the 1980s, it was clear that while increasing the international base was important for domestic operations, implementing centralized control over costs was even more important. Harrison continued to grapple with the giant enterprise and reorganized the CIBC. The 114th (1980) Annual Report announced the following changes. Fullerton was now in charge of strategic planning and international, John A.C. Hilliker of branch operations, and Laidley in charge of corporate clients. Besides the noteworthy addition of strategic planning, there was a basic split between corporate, retail, and international. Observers have also suggested that the CIBC's poor performance led to an attempt by Fullerton to become CEO in 1980. At the time, Fullerton's title was changed from COO to president and vice-chairman responsible for international operations – a seeming demotion. Ironically, the new position was an ideal one for training the future CEO.[44]

The annual reports convey the impression that Harrison's era was one of consolidation, not new initiatives. Efforts to expand in the United States were highlighted, but the CIBC seemed intent on maintaining its basic portfolio, which was dominated by energy and agriculture in Canada. This was made clear in the 115th (1981) Annual Report: "We are a Canadian bank and our priority is to serve Canadian customers." Such a portfolio was not one that was likely to produce high returns in the environment of the late 1970s and early 1980s, while the lack of diversification increased earnings volatility.

R. DONALD FULLERTON:
A STRATEGIC PLAN FOR THE
1980s

Although Harrison was still CEO for the 1983 Annual Report, the report was most notable for the first presentation of the strategic plan developed by Fullerton. In announcing his retirement as CEO, Harrison admitted that it was time for a new role: he had been too preoccupied with the internal operations of the CIBC and not attentive enough to the external role of the CEO.[45] While Fullerton took control of the day-to-day affairs of the bank, he also displayed a new concern with the future and the long-term strategy. In fairness to Harrison, a focus on the day to day could not have been avoided, since the major problem that had been revealed in the strategic analysis of operations was that the bank's cost structure was out of line. In order to improve this situation, reorganization that streamlined management and electronic technology to facilitate information flows had to be implemented. While such remedial measures addressed some of the problems that had been recognized earlier, there was also a new concern with the market strategy. Rather than simply focusing upon Canada, Canadian operations were leveraged into global operations centred upon North America, a policy stated on the cover of the

1990 Annual Report. The CIBC recognized the sweeping changes in the financial services industry of the 1990s and adjusted to the new competitive realities.

The strategic plan recognized that one tactic for improving loan losses was to attract a higher quality of client. This meant better marketing, both in the sense of designing the product desired by the market place and making the market place recognize the superiority of the product. Moreover, the new focus on designing product lines for the market offered the potential for reducing costs. A realistic approach to providing what different client groups desired could eliminate the costly proliferation of product lines and lead to more efficient operations. The new focus on the market interface could be beneficial in improving income and reducing costs.

Central to the re-examination of the market interface was the attempt to develop appropriate specialization within the institution. The first effort could be seen at the branch level, with the development of 100 commercial banking centres. The CIBC believed that this program would facilitate providing to commercial accounts the needed expertise, while also allowing for better retail service through a clearer focus of the retail branches. Further evidence of the new approach was the decision taken in 1984 to drop retail banking in California in order to concentrate on commercial. In the same vein, the use of ABMS was promoted because it freed tellers to provide the services that required the human touch.[46]

In 1986 there was further structural reorganization within the bank. The program was extended with the 1986 reorganization. Three strategic business units (SBUS) with the following missions and presidents were established:

1. Individual Bank: A. Warren Moysey
   "The mission of the Individual Bank is to profitably market a range of financial services primarily directed at individuals, independent businesses, automobile dealers, and farm customers in Canada, all customers in the West Indies and individuals elsewhere. The Individual Bank also develops and markets a selected range of products and services to meet the needs of Private Banking customers in selected worldwide locations."[47]
2. Corporate Bank: A.L. (Al) Flood
   "The mission of the Corporate Bank is to profitably market a competitive range of financial services to corporate, government and other financial institution customers and prospects on a worldwide basis. The development of business and markets will occur through implementing a Global Relationship Management approach which will be a fundamental component of the structure and identity of the Corporate Bank."[48]

3. Investment Bank: Paul G.S. Cantor

> The mission of the Investment Bank is to profitably market a competitive range of investment banking products and services to existing and prospective customers on a worldwide basis; and to engage in direct dealing for its own account in financial markets on a basis consistent with established performance objectives and risk parameters. The focus of the Investment Bank is to be transaction-driven and this will be the fundamental component of its structure and identity."[49]

The split between corporate and investment banks is interesting since the two units presumably serve a similar client base. The key difference is that one is "relationship"-driven, while the other is "transaction"-driven. This is not an uncommon split between the more relationship oriented commercial banks and the transaction-driven investment banks. Yet, the organization faces certain problems. Does the division preclude achieving synergies between the two arms of CIBC, and in the extreme promote internal competition rather than cooperation? Moreover, can two distinct cultures exist in one organization serving a similar customer base?

In the *Financial Post*, Sonita Horvitch stated that the extensive organizational changes at the CIBC far exceeded those made by the other Canadian banks. Especially interesting, given the CIBC's traditionally Canadian orientation, was its global focus. In part, this served to change the manner in which the bank viewed the world, but more importantly, it recognized that increasing worldwide integration was taking place in financial services. With the entry of the foreign-owned Schedule B banks, or Schedule 2s as they are known now, the new world of banking was obvious even in the Canadian market.[50]

The mission statements made clear the intention to broaden the customer base. Fullerton started in this direction in 1984 when industry specialists for telecommunications, financial services, and transportation were added. The loan portfolio needed new diversification to avoid the volatility that had plagued the bank. In addition, a tremendous effort to generate new fee-based services was evident. As corporate treasurers became more knowledgeable, loans became increasingly commodity-like. It was no longer possible to depend solely upon spreads for healthy earnings. Determining the total financial needs of the client provided opportunities to discover markets for new fee-based services, which was the key to future profitability. Product offerings were thus expanded as the CIBC moved from "simple banking" and entered the financial services industry.

Another interesting feature of the new organization was the centralization of management services in a new unit, the Management

Services Group, that essentially "serviced" the other sbus. Under
Executive Vice-President Marcel J.M. Cassavant the group had the
following mission assigned to it:

The mission of the Management Services Group is to effectively provide the
administrative, financial and support services required to sustain and co-ordinate
the activities of The Commerce's operating banks at the corporate level. This
includes developing corporate-wide policies and procedures and maintaining
data-gathering, reporting and control mechanisms which complement the
resources of the operating banks.[51]

This statement clearly highlights the cibc's need to coordinate the
diverse, yet highly interrelated activities that characterized a global
bank. In 1987, the importance of the group was further signalled in
an unusual move when an outsider, T. Iain Ronald was recruited from
the Hudson's Bay Company and appointed president of the group. The
new strategy and organization demanded a commitment to using state-
of-the-art information technology. The cibc of the 1980s was proud
to discuss how its computer terminals enabled it to provide better
information and service, both internally and to customers. By the
1986 Annual Report, the intent to become a leader in new information
technology was apparent. Technology could help the new structure
become integrated by facilitating teamwork, because teamwork
depended on knowledge of what the other players were doing. The
emphasis on teamwork not only required the cibc to acquire technology,
but to develop a new philosophy guiding information flows.[52]

The new strategic plan recognized that, in order to be effective,
the bank had to provide the services that the market desired and be
able to respond quickly to identified needs. This meant devising a
new structure that could withstand the stresses generated by the
conflicting forces of decentralization and interdependency. On the
one hand, the need for rapid decision-making and an accurate knowledge of the market demanded increased decentralization. On the other
hand, the increasing interdependencies within the financial world
demanded more coordination and centralization. Just as a relationship
manager in corporate banking was required to oversee the cibc's total
relation with that client, so the cibc as a corporate entity needed to
understand its relationship with the world. The new structure with
its global emphasis and the investment in information technology
showed that the cibc was attempting to come to grips with these
pressures.

Individual or retail banking had always been the core of the cibc,
which, until recently, had the largest branch network of the major
banks.[53] Throughout Fullerton's reign as ceo, the retail group was

responsible for consistent growth in mortgages, personal loans, and deposits. Such growth was fostered by unflagging attention to marketing, human resources, and technological support.[54] Improved marketing awareness was evident in programs such as gold cards, service packages for youths and seniors, branches in stores, alliances with travel groups, such as Aeroplan Gold, and helping to bring major league baseball to Toronto with the Blue Jays. CIBC also attempted to introduce sophisticated technology into retail banking with LinkUp, a product designed to bring retail banking into the home and office.[55] Yet all was not smooth. As in other areas, Fullerton created a certain management turmoil because of his complaints concerning the lack of support he received from his management team. In the case of retail, Warren Moysey, a CIBC banker for twenty-eight years, left the bank in 1990 and was shortly followed by his second in command, John Myers. Holger Kluge was appointed Moysey's successor as president of the retail bank.

Interestingly the bank revised the annual report so that a question-and-answer format was used to present results instead of the usual business unit presentation of results. This technique effectively demonstrated the diverse factors that were being brought together to provide service to customers. Rather than telling the reader – whether customer, employee, or shareholder – what the bank was doing, the bank was cast in a responsive mode. Moreover, the questions did address major concerns of the day such as the environment and charitable donations, as well as traditional business issues such as diversification and regulation.

Retail banking clearly demonstrated the important changes sweeping the industry. While the obvious linkage was between domestic and retail, segments such as private banking were clearly global. The high net-worth segment of retail banking could not be serviced with operations only in Canada. The burgeoning global private banking network included London, Frankfurt, Geneva, Tokyo, Bahrain, Hong Kong, Guernsey, Nassau and Grand Cayman and offered a full range of banking and trust services in an effort to capture a share in this important segment. While the CIBC offered private banking in Toronto and Vancouver, legislation limited product offerings such as trust services in those locales. Adopting a proactive strategy meant going to other markets to be prepared for the changes that would come to Canada. Specialized Asian banking centres in Vancouver, Toronto, and Calgary revealed a similar effort to target specific markets.[56]

As important as geographic expansion was product line expansion. In order to meet the demands of Canada's aging population, CIBC added retail stockbroking with the acquisition of Wood Gundy in 1988 and Merrill Lynch's Canadian retail network in 1990. The option on Morgan Trust Company in 1989 was an important move to position CIBC to provide trust services in Canada when regulation changed. Fullerton's strategy brought aggressive expansion to the bank on all fronts.

While investment dealers have been discussed in their retail context, the more important thrust for CIBC was the strengthening of investment banking as an SBU. The significance of this sector, which dealt with the direct financial instruments that had become more important in the prime segments, was addressed with the creation of a separate business unit in 1986. This was the same year that CIBC acquired the London stockbroking firm, Grenfell & Colegrave, once again engaging in activities outside Canada to gain experience. The international network was further strengthened in 1987 when CIBC acquired a 50 per cent interest in the Australian stockbroking firm D & D Tollhurst. This strategic move permitted the bank to have a worldwide network. Given the later alliance with Gordon Capital in 1987 and the acquisition of Wood Gundy in 1988, it was almost a case of structure leading strategy. The organizational form was put in place to accommodate future expansion when Canadian banks would be allowed entry into the securities industry: "By building rather than buying an integrated dealer in our initial phase, we have established Commerce Securities, Inc. as one of Canada's recognized investment banks."[57]

In this vein, it was interesting that CIBC integrated Wood Gundy into its organization much more closely than did the other banks their investment bank acquisitions. The 1988 Annual Report quoted an unnamed Canadian newspaper as describing the relationship between the CIBC and Wood Gundy as "making for one of the most integrated marriages on Bay Street." The complementary nature of the two firms demanded a close relationship if the potential synergies were to be realized. The ascension to CEO at Wood Gundy of CIBC banker John Hunkin signalled that this trend will continue. In the upper tier, Wood Gundy brought expertise as a leading issue house in Canada and the Euromarkets, while CIBC added swap capabilities. In the middle tier, a difficult market for investment banks to reach, CIBC's branch network brought marketing clout to Wood Gundy. The same was true for retail. However, if the marriage between products and distribution was to be a success, an organizational merger had to take place.

Investment banking capability was essential for being competitive as globalization of markets transformed the financial services industry. The CIBC focused upon London, New York, and Tokyo, but also developed strength in important adjacent markets such as Hong Kong, Australia, New Zealand, and emerging Asian economies.[58] Of particular interest was the 1986 joint venture with Li Ka-Shing's Cheung Kong Holdings to form CEF Capital, a regional investment bank, in Hong Kong. This venture provided an important window on the rapidly expanding economies of Southeast Asia and deepened the important relationship with Li Ka-Shing that dated back to 1974. It also served as an interesting basis for other relationships. In 1990, CEF New Asia and an alliance among Commerce Cheung Kong, GE Capital, Mitsubishi Corporation, and Nikko Securities was formed. Interestingly in the same year as these relationships were developing, Wood Gundy became the first investment dealer to receive its investment banking license to operate in Japan.[59]

The investment-banking strength that CIBC developed in the 1980s gave it the financial muscle to develop its corporate business. The extent of the changes taking place in the world of corporate finance were exemplified in two important deals reported in the 1987 Annual Report. First, CIBC described as a "milestone" its participation in the purchase of Husky Oil, of which it assumed a 5-per-cent ownership position. There was a new policy of "assuming small, minority interests in Canadian companies offering excellent long-term potential.[60] Second, the new nature of relationship banking was demonstrated by the manner in which the investment and the corporate banks cooperated on both sides of the Atlantic in the 1987 acquisition of Maple Leaf Mills by Hillsdown Holdings of the United Kingdom. The kinds of products and expertise needed to maintain relationships with evermore sophisticated clients demanded relationship managers who could tap into and coordinate all areas of the CIBC's expertise. The mergers and acquisition market exemplified this.

Despite increased attention to international deals such as the financing of a petrochemical firm in the People's Republic of China or the participation in the "Chunnel" between England and France, the importance of the U.S. market increased over the period. By 1986, the corporate bank with 104 centres had a solid base for international expansion,[61] especially in the United States with distribution of capital market products in New York, Chicago and Los Angeles.[62] By 1989, the importance of the United States was reiterated:

We are a North American bank and are working aggressively to strengthen our business base on this continent. Being the fifth largest bank in North America in terms of assets and the fourth largest in terms of deposits, we are uniquely positioned to serve corporate customers in the United States as well as Canada.

Our u.s. Corporate Bank, for example, was recently reorganized as a merchant bank with global capabilities to better meet the critical financing need of American clients like York International. This means that Commerce is now well equipped to advise, structure and provide for all layers of a client's capital.[63]

In the 1990 Annual Report, the u.s. focus continued to sharpen as approximately $750 million of loans to the communications industry were acquired from the Bank of New England. The CIBC presented itself as the full service provider to the communications and entertainment sector, which included cable, broadcasting, publishing, and cellular industries. Relationship managers operating out of New York and Chicago could draw from experience gained in building one of the largest global portfolios (over $3 billion) in this sector. The CIBC was building upon strength, as it declared in 1991: "Commerce has a strong corporate presence in the United States and is striving to become North America's leading relationship bank."[64]

Relationship has become the dominant marketing theme, not only in corporate, but in all segments. The cost of developing relationships, both in terms of time and money, make them a strategic resource to be leveraged. Forays into leasing, such as Commcorp, alliances with the accounting firm KPMG Peat Marwick, selling of Home insurance products, the decision to enter other forms of insurance and the trust industry, as well as the lobbying to open the field of car leasing were all efforts to expand the product base in order to cement relationships. But while the CIBC clearly signalled its commitment to being a full-service provider, the question of how to build relationship remained. Where profits or potential profits generated by the overall relationship warranted, relationship managers were the route, as corporate and private banking revealed. However, using managers was too expensive for general retail banking. There efforts had to be focused upon forging relationships with "communities" or with the 1,570 neighbourhoods in 13 countries that CIBC operated in 1987. The efforts and resources that were devoted to improving front-line service and to investigating technological links at the retail level all attest to the importance of cementing bonds.

The creation of the Administrative Services Group as a separate entity was especially interesting in this context. The signal given by this was that the bank was striving to create a unit designed to service its front-line people who would in turn service the customer. In the annual reports, training efforts and technological expenditures as support mechanisms received considerable attention.

To ensure that Commerce people maximize the advantages technology offers, a renewed emphasis was placed on training and education. In 1987, the Training and Education Department set up a world-wide corporate video network, linking Commerce's Canadian and foreign branches and offices through 1,700 video units. The network reflects the bank's commitment to effective communications and open new ways for the bank to deliver on-site training and up-to-the-minute information on products, policies, programs, and bank developments.[65]

Investment in technology was required to ensure that internal information flows could keep pace with financial flows and that the effects of turbulent markets on the bank and its clients could be monitored. Just as he had realigned the bank with market sectors, Fullerton strove to ensure that the administrative side of the bank promoted information flows that made cooperation possible. The task of the administrative services personnel was to remove back-room functions from the point of delivery, so that service rather than administrative details could be the basis of meetings with customers. The technological transformation of the bank during the 1980s was essential for its competitiveness in the markets it entered.

By 1988 the change in format had enabled Fullerton to establish a formal fit between strategy and structure.[66] In the following years, the effort was to promote forces that would bind the bank into one cohesive whole able to benefit from the possible synergies in the financial services markets. The shift to emphasizing "vision," "mission," and "values" recognized that until the bank's strategic plan was internalized by every employee, the task of implementation was not complete. This prompted the bank to employ further initiatives to expand professional development for staff, such as turning the King Ranch, a former luxury resort just north of Toronto, into a training centre. It is clear that the CIBC realizes that its battles are far from over. When Fullerton announced his retirement in 1990, he could look back upon an era that had seen significant changes. Fullerton had sought to shake up the institution, as an article in the *Globe and Mail* chronicled.[67] However, the changes were not without problems.[68] There was some upheaval within the executive ranks, including as already stated, the departure of Warren Moysey. Fullerton's successor Al Flood has inherited a bank that is far better organized, although significant problems remain, such as the effect of the projected Olympia and York loan losses,[69] the departure of Paul Cantor, CEO of the investment bank, and the perception of the CIBC in some quarters as a lumbering institution. Flood's organizational changes may help to alter that perception. The merging of the investment bank and the corporate bank under John Hunkin is a positive move in coordinating all the considerable forces of the CIBC upon the corporate market. Further, phasing out the administrative bank now that its mission has been accomplished in the eyes of the bank should not only lower overhead, but may improve performance by pushing the administrative functions to become more directly responsive to markets. It will be interesting to see if the leaner organization is able to be more nimble.

STRATEGY AND FINANCIAL PERFORMANCE

As with the other banks, there has been a steady asset growth since 1981 which has been supported by a far more rapidly growing capital base, as figure 5.1 shows.[70] Once again, a logarithmic scale has been employed in order to reveal the very real efforts devoted to raising capital during the decade. Capital bases, which are far stronger now than they were during the era of troubled LDC loans, provide reasonable security against current problems, such as the Reichmanns. The periodic near-catastrophes that seem to plague the banking industry may or may not be avoidable, but strong capital bases and prudential caps on exposures to clients and industries allow banks to survive. There would be far greater cause for concern if asset growth had outstripped capital growth during the era.

There is no clear trend to employee growth in figure 5.2 as it declined, then grew, and now is again in a period of decline. The most interesting aspect of the figure is the change in service delivery strategy. The branch network has been a traditional strength of the CIBC but, unlike the Royal, there has been relatively little branch growth during the era. There also appears to be no obvious relation between changes in employee numbers and service delivery units. The steady growth of ABMS indicates once again the effects of technological change upon delivery channels in the banking industry. While there is a complementarity between retail branches and ABMS, at some point the development of electronic channels will lead to significant redesign of the delivery system, as is taking place at a greater pace in some U.S. jurisdictions.

Figure 5.3 portrays the geographic strategy of the CIBC by charting the location of assets by location of ultimate risk.[71] Despite some efforts in the early and mid-1980s to decrease reliance upon Canada, by 1991, the portfolio is slightly more Canadian than it was in 1982. Curiously, in spite of the acquisition of loans from the Bank of New England, the overall amount of U.S. assets peaked around 1985 and has fallen since. This could be due to the vagaries of how loans are booked. As is the case with the other major banks, the significance of Africa, the Middle East and Latin America has declined. It will

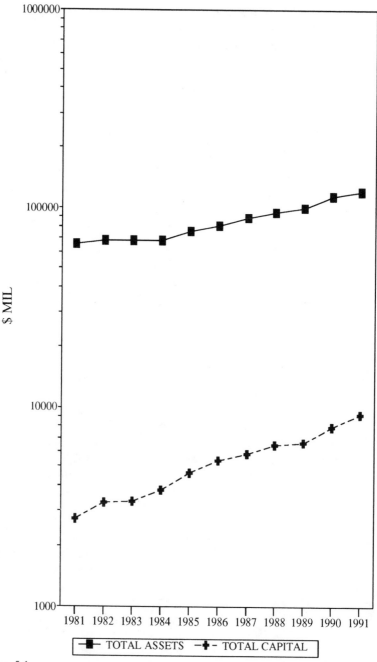

Figure 5.1
CIBC Asset and Capital Growth

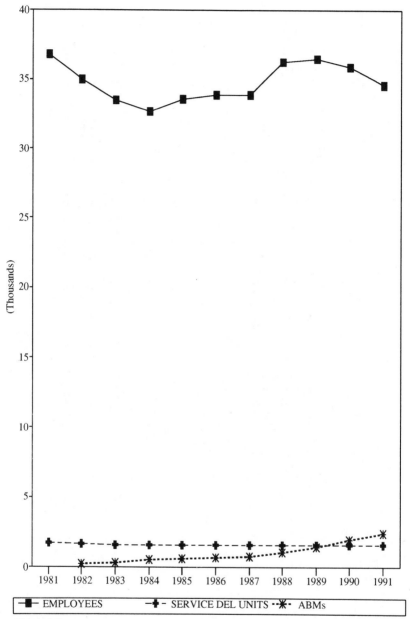

Figure 5.2
Employee and Branch Growth

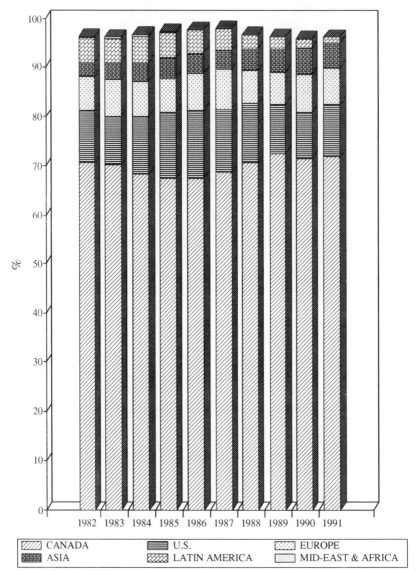

Figure 5.3
Location of Assets

be interesting to see if there is a change in the Latin American figures following the ratification of NAFTA. Asia has been one of the few growth areas, although the percentage contribution is relatively light. The CIBC has expressed the intention of becoming a North American bank, but at this time, it remains clearly Canadian.[72]

The asset breakdown shown in figure 5.4 reveals clearly the general trend to retail banking that was chronicled in the 1991 annual *Euromoney* rankings of the world's best banks. There has been a dramatic growth in mortgages against a decline in other assets. Deposits with other banks suggests that the relatively small international operations have diminished almost to the point of disappearance. Interestingly, while the geographic portrait was relatively stable in its emphasis on Canada, the breakdown by product reveals the growing importance of retail banking.

Figure 5.5 with the shifts in deposit structure further attests to the growing importance of retail banking. Deposits by individuals have shown reasonably constant and considerable growth. In comparison to figure 5.4, deposits by banks played a far greater role than vice versa at the CIBC. However, despite certain fluctuations, the diminishing role of other banks as depositors is relatively clear. The overall impression created by figures 5.4 and 5.5 is that the CIBC's business is overwhelmingly with Canadian individuals and corporations with a strong base in retail banking.

The composition of income shown in figure 5.6 leads to some important observations. First, as we have seen before, during the period, there has been a constant increase in other income that, combined with general improvement in the level of net-interest margins, has yielded higher levels of net income. The changes in the asset-and-deposit portfolios seem to have borne fruit not only with improved net-interest margins, but also with links that have been forged to a client base that requires fee-based services. The ability to provide such services was, of course, greatly enhanced by the acquisition of Wood Gundy in 1987. Since 1985, with the exception of 1989, the quality of the asset portfolio, as indicated by loan losses, has improved. Unfortunately, with the recent disclosure of provisions of $1 billion in the second quarter of 1992 primarily because of Olympia and York losses, expectations for the near future are not bright. The behaviour of non-interest expenses raises concerns. In the mid-1980s, non-interest expenses grew more slowly than fee-based income, however, since 1987, expense growth appears more rapid than income growth. If earnings do not materialize, this is an area of concern.

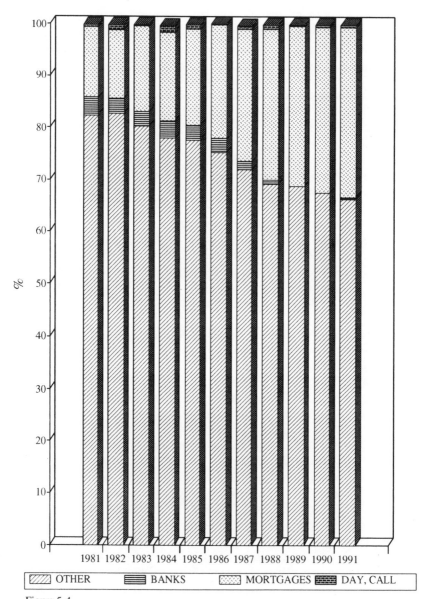

Figure 5.4
Asset Portfolio

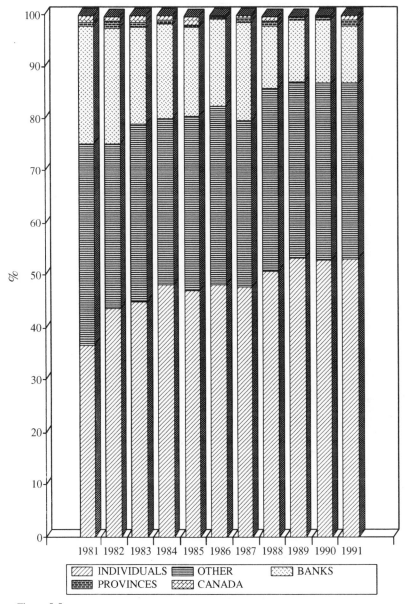

Figure 5.5
Deposit Portfolio

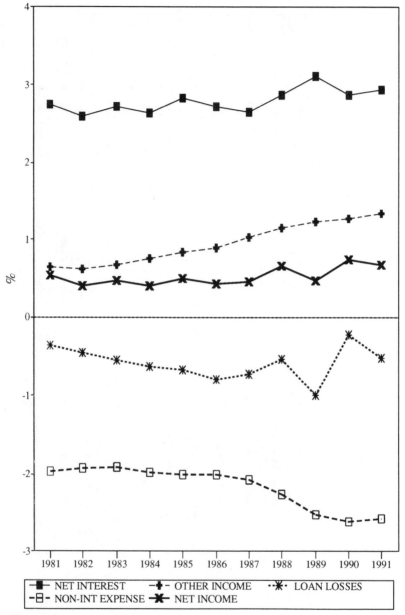

Figure 5.6A
Analysis of ROA

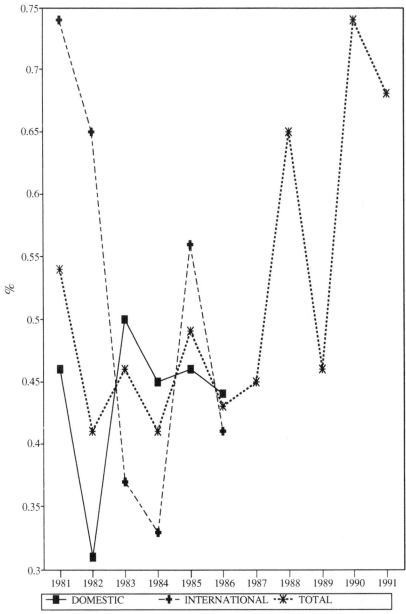

Figure 5.6B
Analysis of ROA

Figure 5.6B demonstrates the patterns of ROA for the total bank as well as for international and domestic. In the early part of the decade, international made positive contributions to income. In general, benefits of portfolio diversification can be seen as returns were often moving in different directions. However, with the weighting of the domestic portfolio, it was difficult to obtain truly significant offsets to domestic problems from international. Perhaps this was why the bank ceased reporting segmented results in 1987.

The significance of the addition of securities dealings can be seen in figure 5.7, where the major shifts in the pattern of income is accounted for by the addition of securities in 1987. Interestingly, despite renewed commitment to retail, there was no major gains in credit cards. On the corporate side, changes in practices and accounting methods account for diminished loan fees, but the generally expanded role of foreign exchange is interesting. This is especially so because of diminished international operations. The most likely explanation for the change is the expanded international operations of the bank's customers. Despite retrenchment, the refocused international operations provide a base for managing significant flows and earning significant revenues.

In spite of the importance of non-interest expenses, no strong trends for change can be seen in figure 5.8. In general, salaries appear to be in slight decline and expenses linked to computers are marginally increasing. Unfortunately, no obvious explanation for increasing costs leap out at this level of aggregation.

The above paints a fairly bright picture of the CIBC, which is supported by an examination of the performance of its stock price shown in figure 5.9. Prior to 1985, there was a significant gap between market and book value, with the low of 1982 being particularly glaring. Yet, by 1986, the bank had begun to trade increasingly at a premium to book. While the low price has never exceeded the book value, the management team must be reasonably pleased with the dramatic improvement in performance since 1982. In the eyes of the market, the CIBC has made significant gains.

CONCLUSION

Our examination of the CIBC concludes at an important juncture in the bank's history: the ascension of a new CEO, Al Flood. Donald Fullerton ably directed the bank to a sound strategic position by making the bank global in orientation while continuing to emphasize Canada and the retail franchise. He also raised the CIBC's public profile by entering into the constitutional debate.[73] In terms of shareholder

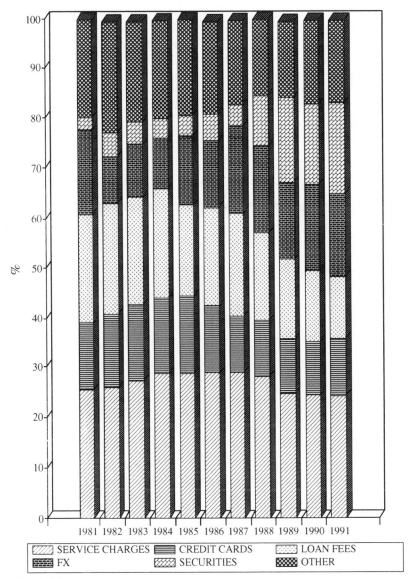

Figure 5.7
Other Income

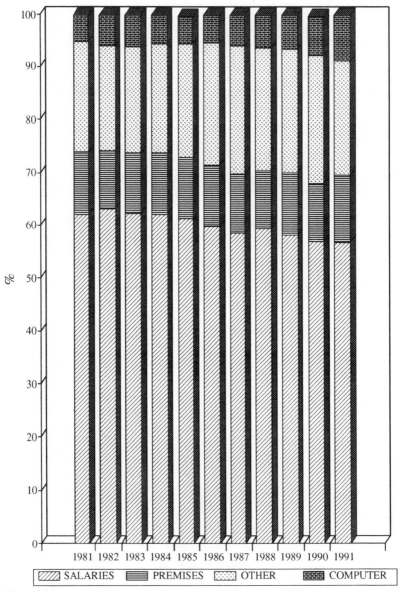

Figure 5.8
Non-Interest Expense

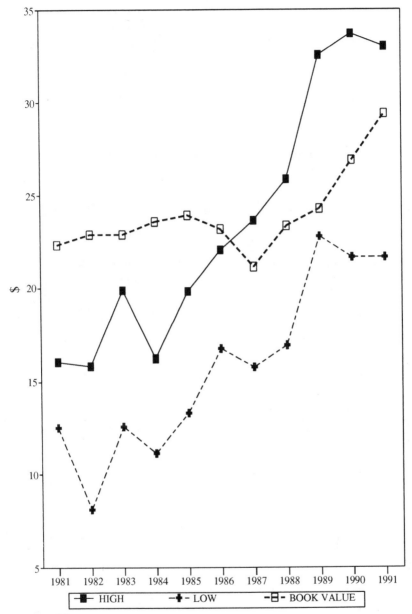

Figure 5.9
Stock-Price Performance

value, the achievement since 1982 is significant. Fullerton has passed on a bank that should continue to show renewed vigour. However, incidents such as the dramatic problems at Olympia and York haunt the bank. While there is little question in the minds of regulators and market watchers that the CIBC can survive and prosper, can company morale survive many more hits? There have been improvements at the CIBC, but how strong is the momentum?

In this vein, recently announced commitments to insurance and trust businesses will continue to strengthen the retail franchise. As the bank has shown with the integration of Wood Gundy, it will create one bank that is able to leverage its diverse assets in multiple markets. The 1992 purchase of Comcheq, which will make CIBC the largest payroll firm in Canada, further demonstrates the commitment to increase fee-based income. The new CEO has been given the opportunity to forge his own management team and the promotion of John Hunkin and the associated changes in corporate and investment banking augur well for the future. However, continuity would have some advantages with the difficult Olympia and York negotiations hanging over the bank. Fullerton has created a reasonable platform for the CIBC's continued improvement, but the challenges facing Flood are not insignificant. Flood is accepting the challenge. His response to a virtually profitless 1992 was dramatic: 2,500 jobs will be cut in 1993. The CIBC will continue to change.

CHAPTER SIX

Financial Performance and Strategic Change

The era ushered in by the 1980 Bank Act saw significant strategic change by the four banks. In order to understand such changes, it is important to add to our study a fifth bank, the Toronto-Dominion (TD). In the 1980s, the TD was generally ranked as the outstanding Canadian bank by both financial analysts and industry experts.[1] TD's rank in table 6.1, which combines rankings from *Euromoney*'s 500 and 100 Best, attests to its strength. Ranking by shareholders' equity as opposed to assets produces interesting differences from the ranking presented in table 1.1. While TD is the smallest of the Big Five in terms of assets, it is not in terms of capital. In strategic terms, this means that TD has the capacity for considerable asset growth and other strategic assets related to capital strength. Thus adding the profile of the TD is essential for understanding the changes that occurred in the Canadian industry during the 1980s.

Table 6.2 puts into perspective the relative size of Canadian and other North American banks compared to large Japanese and European banks. While the Royal is Canada's largest bank, it is not even half the size of Sumitomo, which is the largest in both Japan and the world. On a more promising vein, however, are the "best" rankings. J.P. Morgan, Banc One, and TD are all ranked among the top 10, followed closely by the Royal in twelfth place. There is no obvious correlation between size and performance rankings as only Deutsche Bank and Sanwa among the top 10 in size are ranked among the 25 best banks.

Given the broad geographic and product scope of the Canadian banks and the teething problems associated with adjustments to their mergers with investment banks,[2] their performance is impressive. It is interesting that the highest-ranked bank, the TD, was the only one that chose to build its own investment bank rather than acquire an

Table 6.1
North America's Largest and Best Banks in 1992

NA Rank	Bank	Shareholders' Equity $ Mil (us)[1]	Euromoney 100 Best Ranking[2]
1	Citicorp	9,489.00	Not Ranked
2	BankAmerica Corp.	8,063.00	39
3	Chemical Banking Corp.	7,281.00	Not Ranked
4	Royal Bank of Canada	6,912.11	12
5	NationsBank Corp.	6,518.00	81
6	J.P. Morgan	6,068.00	2
7	CIBC	5,969.59	34
8	Chase Manhattan Corp.	5,324.00	Not Ranked
9	TD	4,344.32	7
10	Scotiabank	4,125.64	71
11	Bank of Montreal	4,052.10	33
12	Banc One	3,814.10	5
13	Security Pacific	3,470.00	Not Ranked
14	Bankers Trust New York	3,412.00	25
15	Wells Fargo & Co.	3,359.80	61

Sources:
1 *Euromoney*, "Euromoney 500: Meltdown? What Meltdown."
2 *Euromoney*, "The World's 100 Best Banks: Horses for Courses."

Table 6.2
The World's Largest and Best Banks in 1992

World Rank	NA Rank	Bank	Shareholders' Equity $ Mil (us)	Euromoney 100 Best Ranking
1		Sumitomo Bank	15,217.33	48
2		Dai-Ichi Kangyo Band	13,599.58	55
3		Fuji Bank	13,527.15	92
4		Sanwa Bank	13,019.83	27
5		UBS Group	12,858.07	17
6		Mitsubishi Bank	12,010.69	30
7		Barclay's Bank	11,676.91	41
8		Sakura Bank	11,550.57	Not Ranked
9		Deutsche Bank	11,230.44	8
10		Compagnie Financière de Paribas	11,067.17	69
11		Industrial and Commercial Bank of China	10,593.23	Not Ranked
12		National Westminster Bank	10,371.16	84
13		Crédit Lyonnais	9,651.54	95

Table 6.2 continued

World Rank	NA Rank	Bank	Shareholders' Equity $ Mil (US)	Euromoney 100 Best Ranking
14	1	Citicorp	9,489.00	Not Ranked
15		Industrial Bank of Japan	9,431.02	83
16		Swiss Bank Corp	9,183.40	22
17		Caisses d'Epargne Ecureuil (CENCEP)	9,121.48	Not Ranked
18		ABN-AMRO	8,973.36	36
19		Bank of China	8,190.19	Not Ranked
20		Caisse des Dépôts et Consignations	8,091.26	14
21	2	BankAmerica Corp.	8,063.00	39
22		Rabobank	7,612.86	18
23		Tokai Bank	7,442.35	Not Ranked
24		Long-Term Credit Bank of Japan	7,379.88	Not Ranked
25	3	Chemical Banking Corp.	7,281.00	Not Ranked
26		Hongkong & Shanghai Banking Corp.	7,215.87	97
27	4	Royal Bank of Canada	6,912.11	12
28		Société Générale	6,873.55	12
29		Bank of Tokyo	6,742.19	74
30		Banque Nationale de Paris	6,692.36	91
31	5	NationsBank Corp.	6,518.00	81
37	6	J.P. Morgan	6,068.00	2
40	7	CIBC	5,969.59	34
47	8	Chase Manhattan Corp.	5,324.00	Not Ranked
58	9	TD	4,344.32	7
61	10	Scotiabank	4,125.64	71
62	11	Bank of Montreal	4,052.10	33
64	12	Banc One	3,814.10	5
72	13	Security Pacific	3,470.00	Not Ranked
75	14	Bankers Trust New York	3,412.00	25
76	15	Wells Fargo & Co.	3,359.80	61

Sources:
1. Euromoney, "Euromoney 500: Meltdown? What Meltdown?"
2. Euromoney, "The World's 100 Best Banks: Horses for Courses."

established investment dealer. While size does have advantages and the rankings of the North American banks do seem to point to a changing world order, it is still questionable what this means for the competitiveness of Canadian banks and the resulting effects upon the funding of Canadian corporations.

From the outset, it should be noted that there has been a trend toward greater strategic homogeneity among the banks. While historical differences in product portfolios such as Scotiabank's bullion operations remain, the breakdown in barriers among different national capital and product markets within and among nations has altered the range of viable strategic niches or positions. An interesting indication of this has been the Bank of Montreal's lead in cutting prime. As we have seen, virtually all Canadian banks altered their product market scope to focus upon Canadian retail banking. There have been similar moves on the commercial front, although for commercial, it would be even more appropriate to see the banks as developing North American strategies. Under the FTA, the "home" market is North America.

COMPARING THE BIG FIVE

Figure 6.1 portrays key components of the economic environment of the 1980s: volatility of exchange and interest rates. What is not as apparent but cannot be forgotten by battle-scarred veterans was the tremendous shock to the capital markets of 1987, which emphasized the tremendous volatility of globally linked capital markets. Fortunately, the basic strength of the system was also demonstrated. Following an initial decline of the Canadian dollar in terms of the U.S. dollar, we can see a general long-term strengthening in the second half of the decade. Another interesting feature is the frequency with which short interest rates were higher than long rates, that is, the yield curve was inverted. The combination of volatility and reversals in the yield curve emphasized the importance of interest rate strategies. In general, the volatility also created strong demand by corporate treasurers for risk management products and emphasized the importance of off-balance sheet, fee-based products. The emergence of clearer trends toward the end of the era, that is, the strengthening of the dollar and the decline in interest rates can be tied to the successful battle against inflation fought by John Crow of the Bank of Canada. In this context, it is important to note that while there was a decline in nominal interest rates, by the late 1980s and early 1990s low inflation led to relatively high real Canadian interest rates. These high rates ensured the inflow of foreign funds to finance the government deficit and to a rise in the value of the Canadian dollar, which became a relatively high-yield currency. All in all, this provided an interesting environment for Canadian multinational banks.

All banks enlarged their asset base, as figure 6.2 shows. However, there are different patterns. The Royal, CIBC and TD all show a pattern of consolidation in the early 1980s, followed by consistent growth. The theme of consolidation as a precursor to continued growth was an important strategic theme for the banks in the 1980s. It should also be noted that the growth trend for the Royal and the CIBC is steeper than the more moderate path pursued by the TD. Scotiabank's pattern approximates that of the Royal and CIBC, although the period of retrenchment is not as marked. The Bank of Montreal's path is different. During Mulholland's early years, asset growth was clearly the guiding strategy. The direction was changed in 1986 and a growth emphasis did not occur again until Barrett came into command. However, 1991 was a year of rapid growth. As we examine other performance measures, it is important to keep in mind this clear change in direction.

The recent severe recession has had its effects upon the banks. While most people would anticipate that the economic climate would lead to increased loan losses, many would not be as aware that the combination of asset growth and a slow-growth environment also leads to a lower earning portfolio because of an increase in lower earning liquid assets, such as cash and treasury bills.[3] The addition of these assets to the portfolio should lower the riskiness of the portfolio, but this is somewhat offset by the effects of the recession on other parts of the portfolio. Such excess liquidity also serves to explain some of the current battles over who is first to lower the prime rate. The most liquid bank has a greater incentive to attract higher-yielding corporate customers.

One beneficiary of tough times seems to be small business. The Bank of Montreal has been offering a special package to small business and agricultural clients since December of 1991. When the program was introduced, on floating rate loans of $100,000 or less customers were charged prime minus half a point plus a premium that varied with each client.[4] In June of 1992, the rate dropped another half point. Here again, the liquidity position of the bank may be an explanatory factor. Other banks have responded to these initiatives.

Asset growth must be supported by capital growth. The Canadian banks responded to concerns caused by LDC debt, a troubled energy sector, very troubled real estate and leveraged buyout loans (LBO), by increasing their capital ratios. Figures 6.3A and 6.3B which show capital as a percentage of total assets, display a considerable change by all banks. In part, such change was the result of increased attention by regulators to capital adequacy. The implementation of the rule of

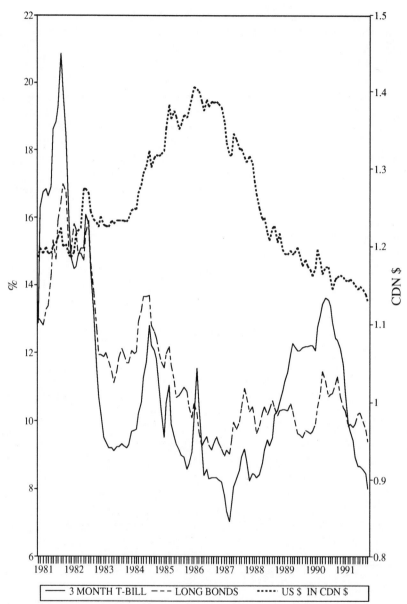

Figure 6.1
Interest and Foreign Exchange Rates

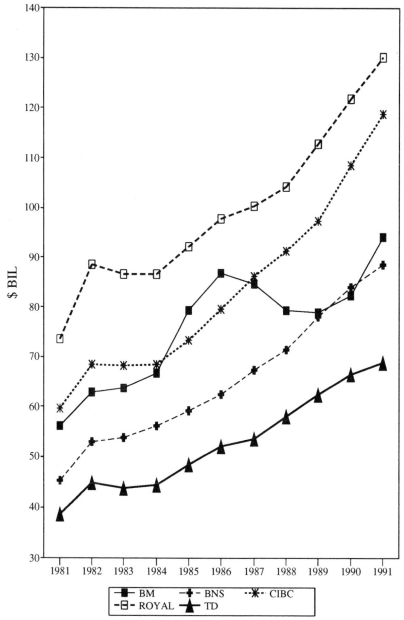

Figure 6.2
Asset Growth

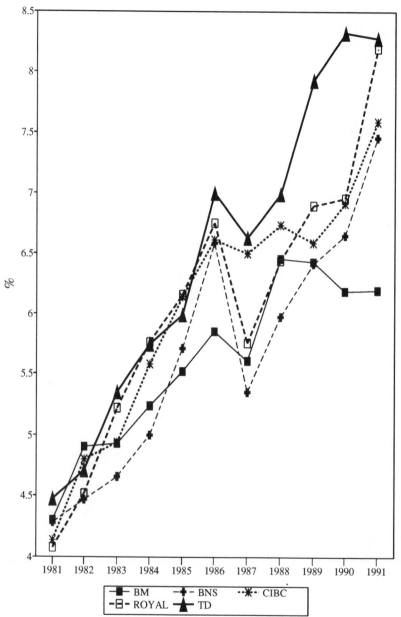

Figure 6.3A
Capital as a Percentage of Total Assets

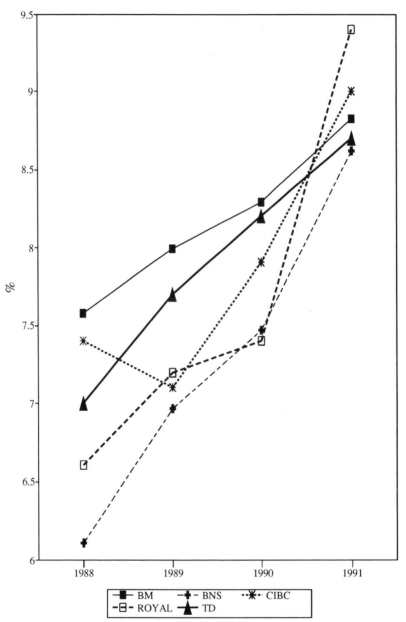

Figure 6.3ʙ
ʙɪꜱ Capital Ratios

the Bank for International Settlements' (BIS') standard of 8 per cent capital for risk-adjusted assets was an important step in levelling the playing field for all banks and establishing a base for confidence in the international financial system. Figure 6.3B shows that all the Canadian banks meet the guidelines by a comfortable margin. This is so even though Canadian definitions on capital are far more stringent than those of the United States or Japan. The conservative bias of Canadian policy-makers and regulators has been a constant theme in this study. It is to be hoped that markets recognize that 8 per cent does not always equal 8 per cent. If they fail to do so, our banks face a made-in-Canada competitive disadvantage in the international arena.[5]

An interesting offshoot of the push to raise capital is the role played by Employee Stock Ownership Plans (ESOPS). Participation helps to bind employees to the firm, promotes taking ownership of the mission or vision of the overall firm, as well as provides access to a source of retail investors.[6] In implementing such a plan in combination with dividend reinvestment plans, the Bank of Montreal raised $140 million, Scotiabank $95 million, the CIBC $129 million, and the Royal $176.5 million. The TD is the exception because it stopped its plan in 1988.[7] Another significant move has been to issue $US pay preferreds. In October of 1991, the Royal led the way, and was soon followed by the CIBC and then the Bank of Montreal.

In addition to capital, distribution channels and human resources were needed to support asset growth. Figures 6.4 and 6.5 show branch and employee growth. These growth lines are far more modest than those for asset growth. Of particular interest is the Royal's development of its branch network. During the era of the 1980 Bank Act, the Royal has created the largest Canadian branch network – it is, in fact, the largest in North America. The CIBC, Bank of Montreal, and TD have all reduced their branch networks. While some vagaries in definitions as to what constitutes a branch or a service delivery unit may reduce the accuracy of the numbers employed, the trends are relatively clear. The Royal and the TD define the two outlying trends, although the TD's 1992 acquisition of Central Guaranty will expand the branch network. The behaviour of Scotiabank is interesting. After a modest reduction in 1986, the network has been developed until it has surpassed that of the Bank of Montreal. The Bank of Montreal's strategy of reducing branches in the early 1980s would have supported the general move toward commercial banking, but their return to branch banking is not as aggressive as either that of the Royal or Scotiabank. It is interesting that the two steepest growth patterns are from Canada's most international banks.[8] After

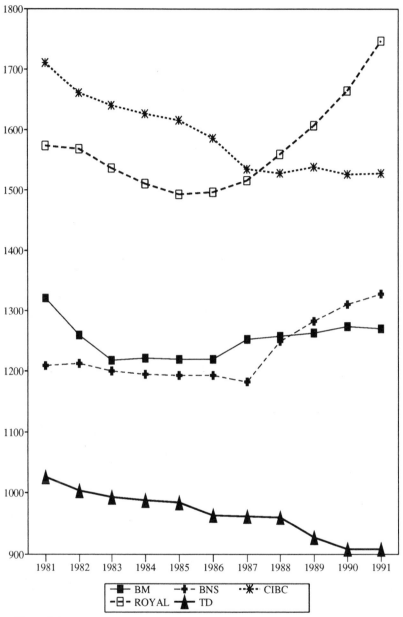

Figure 6.4
Branch Growth

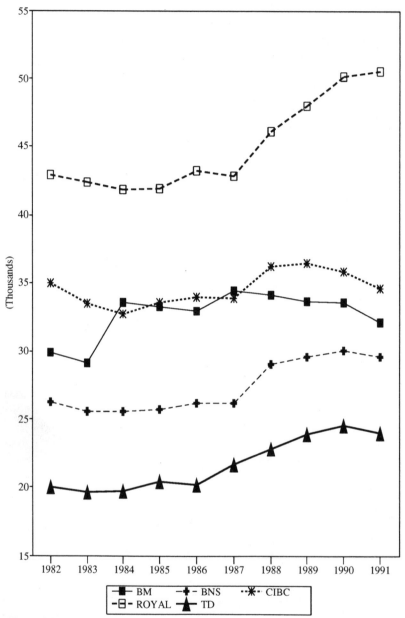

Figure 6.5
Employee Growth

some rationalization in the early 1980s as all banks responded to pressures to lower costs, the Royal and Scotiabank have developed a platform to enter the retail fray with a new vengeance.

In the modern electronic world, branches are only one distribution channel, even for retail. The 1980s witnessed tremendous growth in Automated Teller Machines (ATMS) which became known as Automated Banking Machines (ABMS) as their capabilities expanded. While all banks have developed this channel, once again, the Royal led the way, as figure 6.6 shows. However, the TD's activities in this channel are far different than in branching. Scotiabank's intentions are somewhat more difficult to determine, although there seems to have been a push in recent years to catch up with the others. Numbers do not tell the whole story, however, because unlike branches, ABMS are not proprietary but linked to one another via domestic and international systems such as Interac and Plus. While Scotiabank followed its traditional late-adopter strategy, with the development of Interac it could provide its customers with the convenience of ABMS, without incurring all the capital costs by providing a gateway to the network. This strategy also seems to have been explicitly recognized by the Bank of Montreal. The annual reports of the Bank of Montreal have been the least consistent in reporting its ABM installations but have been very consistent in emphasizing the number of machines available. At the other extreme, the Royal has emphasized its ABM network as a generator of fees. While customers of other banks *may* use Royal ABMS, this service is not provided *free* to the other banks. Thus, despite the proliferation of ABMS, their total effect on service strategies and locational rivalries remain unsettled. While ABMS are clearly a component of managing relationships, it is less certain if they are a cornerstone for building relationships. If so, the Royal is in a powerful position. On the other hand, Interac may simply be a utility. Will the development of this utility reduce customer loyalty and promote a more transactional approach in retail and provide a gateway for new competitors? Answers to such questions will determine the winning retail strategy for the 1990s. In this context, it is important to note that the telecomputational revolution was an important force in disintermediation in the commercial market.[9] Technological change will continue to transform banking in all markets.[10]

Discussion of retail banking leads to consideration of another remarkable strategic change: the move to North American banks, as figure 6.7 reveals. The five major Canadian banks all increased the percentage of North-American based assets in their portfolios, with the TD leading the way. The ranking of the TD, Bank of Montreal, Royal, CIBC, and Scotiabank merits comment. First, in terms of

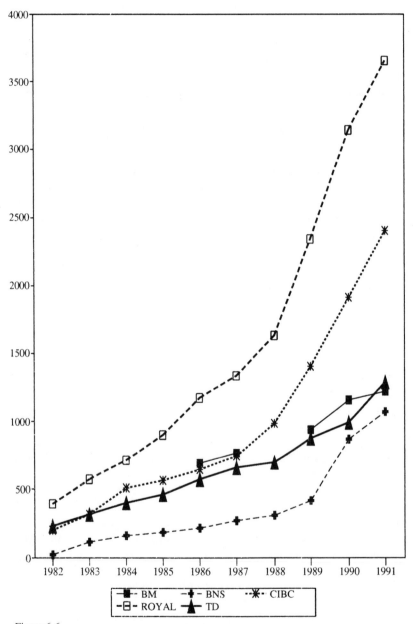

Figure 6.6
ABM Growth

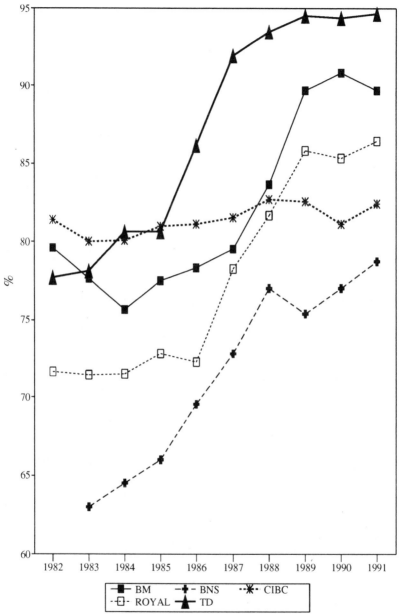

Figure 6.7
North American Assets as a Percentage of Assets

market share, the considerable difference in size must be remembered, especially when comparing the Royal to the smaller Bank of Montreal and the TD. Second, the extent of the portfolio change exhibited by the TD, Royal, and Scotiabank is rather startling. This is especially true when it has been accomplished without such dramatic moves as the Bank of Montreal's acquisition of Harris.

The movement to a North American base has been accomplished via different strategic routes at the various banks. Canadian assets have markedly increased for the TD, Royal, Bank of Montreal, and Scotiabank, as can be seen in figure 6.8. While the CIBC's position has not changed dramatically, it is interesting that it mirrored moves away from Canada by the Royal, the Bank of Montreal, and Scotiabank to some degree in the early 1980s. However, these three banks resumed their Canadian growth in the mid-1980s. Of particular interest is the changing order of the banks. Given relative asset size, the order of the TD, Royal, CIBC, Bank of Montreal, and Scotiabank reveals the dramatic increase of Canada as the Royal's base. The Royal, if any bank can, either dominates the Canadian market or is clearly positioning to do so. This has been accomplished while the international network has been refocused. The CIBC has fallen in relative terms in its domestic market. Scotiabank has retained its position as the nonconformist. While it has augmented its Canadian base in percentage terms, its operation is still considerably more internationally oriented. This is especially the case when it is noted that Bank of Montreal has a larger North American base.

Despite the Canadian banks strategic attempts to enter aggressively the u.s. market,[11] changes in the percentage of u.s. assets, with the exception of the Bank of Montreal, have not been dramatic, as figure 6.9 shows. However, over the period there has been net growth by Scotiabank and the TD. The Royal seemed to be making a move in the early 1980s and then backed off. This pattern must be placed in the context of the overall strategic moves made by the Royal and the others to focus global networks upon North America. Intense competitive pressures within the United States may have led to a pruning and focusing of the portfolios that will provide a solid base for future expansion. Focus as well as size is key, as the Bank of Montreal is showing in the u.s. Midwest, the CIBC in the communications industry, or the TD in the cable TV industry. Vagaries in booking practices probably mean that the numbers are understated. Given the prime target market in the u.s., it is quite possible that u.s. assets will appear to be non-u.s. because they will be booked in other jurisdictions for tax or other reasons. Discussions with bankers suggest that the u.s. numbers understate the case for the

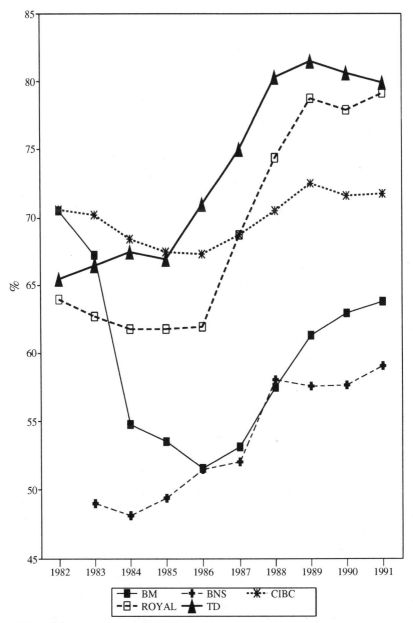

Figure 6.8
Canadian Assets as a Percentage of Assets

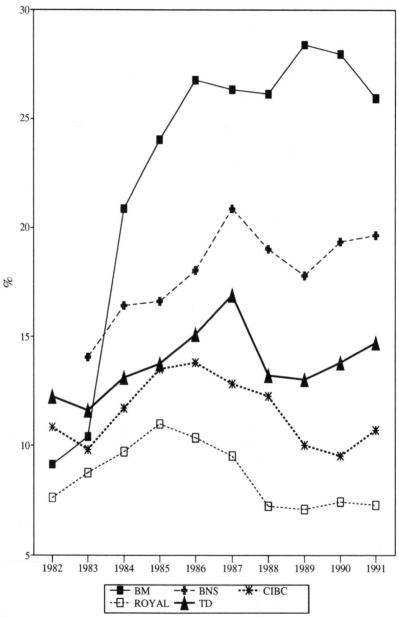

Figure 6.9
U.S. Assets as a Percentage of Assets

involvement of the Canadian banks in the United States, especially for Scotiabank. It should also be noted that the Canadian banks rank second only to the Japanese in U.S. market share, although it is a distant second with 8 per cent compared to 56 per cent.[12]

Figure 6.10 shows the steady retreat, or more properly, the write-down of activities in Latin America. Banks are not keen to return to their earlier levels and types of activities even if many believe that the LDC crisis is over. However, the emergence of NAFTA makes it appropriate to consider the role of Mexico, especially since Scotiabank has taken a 5 per cent stake in Grupo Inverlat. Greater economic integration will increase the activities of all Canadian banks in Mexico. At the moment, it seems most likely that there will be heightened involvement with firms entering into Mexico and with Mexican financial institutions, now that they are returning to the private sector. Business opportunities in Mexico and with Mexican firms will provide new opportunities in the coming years. As the guidelines of NAFTA lead to agreements with other countries in the region, activities will also pick up elsewhere, probably with Chile leading the way. The question is how quickly the other Latin American countries will put their houses in order and be perceived as having a sound business climate.

Figures 6.11 and 6.12 show the changes in the European and Asian portfolios. Virtually all the banks have reduced their participation in European and Asian markets. In fact, only the Royal remains committed to a full business development program in the European Community (EC). Despite the hopes of many, there is also no rush into Eastern Europe.[13] Hard-earned lessons with LDCs have not been forgotten. It is important to note that the degree of participation has not been that great by some participants, especially in Asia. However, the use of asset base may be misleading. Support for this comes from the TD – the leader in exiting from foreign markets, including LDC debt.

The market opportunity may be the traditional one of bringing clients into Canada. The TD, which has limited both its national and international expansion, found that its lean operations were the model for operations in the 1980s and 1990s.[14] Yet the core of its successful Japanese strategy was based upon superior knowledge of the Canadian market, rather than upon competitiveness in the Japanese market. Henry Schindele, TD vice-president and regional treasurer for Asia, gave the following explanation as to why the TD was the top profit maker among 83 foreign banks in Japan for fiscal 1990: "This was no fluke. If you go back to 1982, our strategy was entirely different from most foreign banks at the time. Other banks were

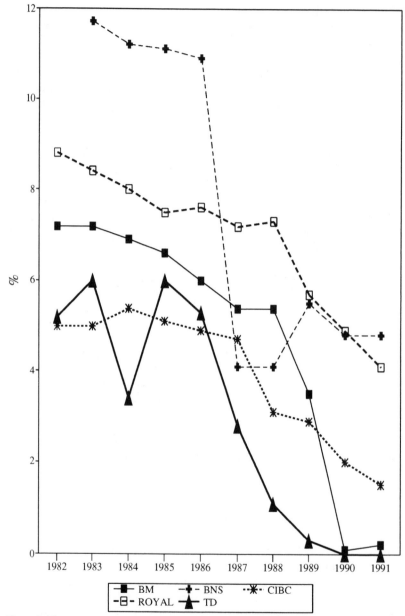

Figure 6.10
Latin American Assets as a Percentage of Assets

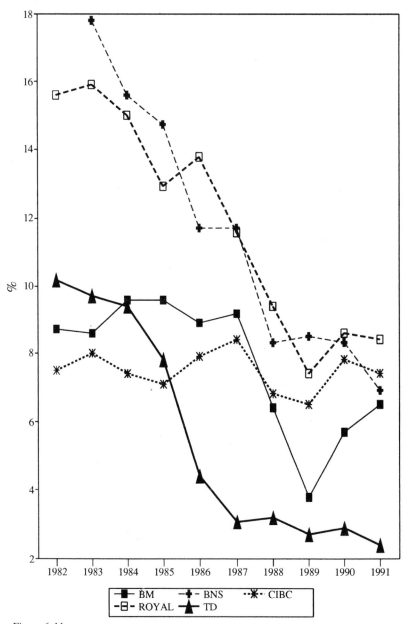

Figure 6.11
European Assets as a Percentage of Assets

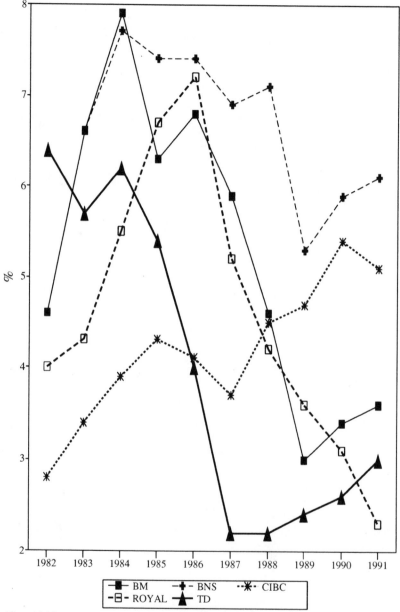

Figure 6.12
Asian Assets as a Percentage of Assets

lending at very low margins. We felt that Japan was a capital exporting country and that it would be like bringing coals to New-castle if we were to try to lend money to Japanese companies. Our strategy was to assist the outflow of capital from Japan to Canada and other countries."[15] As Nicks of Scotiabank demonstrated in the 1950s, successful Canadian banks seek to capture flows into Canada to exploit the advantages of their domestic market dominance. Consequently the increase percentage of Canadian assets combined with asset growth may be an indication of increased internationalization on the part of the banks. Many loans classified by ultimate risk as Canadian may be the result of American, European, or Japanese decision making. The importance of flows in generating stocks in this industry must not be forgotten.

The changing geographic composition of the portfolios does not suggest a retreat from internationalization. It does suggest, as has been emphasized in the individual bank histories, the need for increased focus in the intensely competitive financial services world of the late-1980s and 1990s. Regulatory changes in Canada combined with weaknesses in other sectors, such as smaller trusts in Ontario and elsewhere, created new market opportunities in Canada. The banks have been seizing these opportunities. Growth has limits and growth vectors must represent the best strategic path. In this context, the limitations imposed upon growth by regulators and new or pro-posed regulations upon capital adequacy must be recognized. Rationing or allocating capital to different activities or products is a key strategic decision in the 1990s. This is particularly true when capital is expensive or when banks from different jurisdictions face different costs of capital and equity. As figure 6.2 showed, efforts by the Canadian banks to improve their capital base has ideally positioned them to take advantage of new opportunities. The tre-mendous capital funding in recent years can no longer be seen as essentially a defensive move. The safety of the banks is regarded as a non-issue by informed observers, even in the light of troubles at Olympia and York and Bramalea.[16] Consequently, the efforts are to prepare for future initiatives. Given the size of the strategic slack, this is especially so if Canadian standards fall in line with her major trading partners' guidelines. However, it is possible that the banks wish to further improve credit ratings as a protection against disin-termediation by lower-rated industrial and service firms or to improve their position in the market for more exotic financial instruments where superior credit ratings play a role.

The fundamental question remains: What has been the effect of these strategic moves upon profitability? The key profitability measure for the banking industry is return on assets because it is the result of all revenues and expenses. Figure 6.13 shows the return on assets as percentage per $100 of assets for the five banks over the period. By far the most obvious trend is the performance of the TD bank: its performance figures virtually soar above the others until they start to decline and converge toward the others in the late 1980s and early 1990s. The shift in the TD's portfolio to Canada and in particular its heavy concentration in Ontario has left it particularly vulnerable to the recession and the post-FTA industrial restructuring that has ravaged the Ontario economy. It will be interesting to see whether the TD's performance will soar again when the Ontario economy revives, or whether there are other factors in the declining performance.

The convergence toward the end of the series and the ascendance of the Royal to the top also merit consideration. The convergence in terms of profitability should not be surprising, given some of the strategic convergence noted earlier. However, some caution should be exercised with respect to the Royal. It is quite probable that its recent gains are only beginning to demonstrate the effects of some bolder strategic moves. It is also interesting that the more international banks, the Royal and Scotiabank, have generally outperformed the other two major banks in this study. The ROA for the Bank of Montreal may not be as exciting as its press coverage would suggest, but its ability to maintain its ROA when others, excepting Scotiabank, were falling, certainly supports hopes for the future.

The anomaly of Scotiabank can be identified and in part explained by looking at the performance in figure 6.14 of net interest margins on an ROA basis. Net interest margins are a measure of success in the traditional banking business of matching savers and borrowers. Because all players increasingly play in the same or at least very similar interest-rate environments, depending upon their geographic and product market choices, there should be similar movements. The soaring success of the TD throughout most of the period attests to its skill in the core business. An examination of the patterns also suggests that the Royal is steadily emerging from the pack. One obvious explanation for this would be the bank's shift to Canadian retail banking where spreads between deposits and loans are higher.[17]

The pattern of Scotiabank is particularly interesting. From the earlier discussion of Scotiabank, two trends could be expected. First, interest margins should be narrower than that of other banks because of the weaker deposit base combined with asset growth. An aggressive asset-growth strategy will typically produce mismatches in maturities between loans and deposits as the bank must respond to

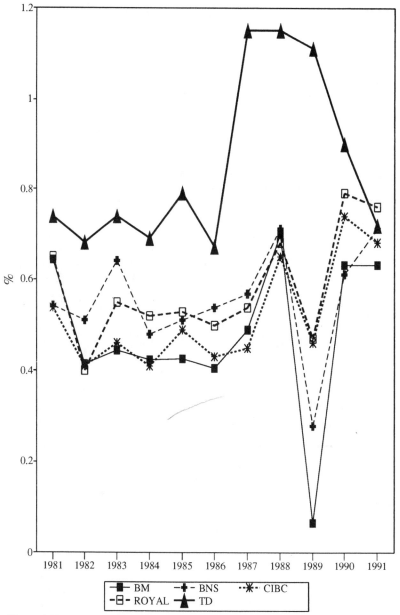

Figure 6.13
Return on Assets

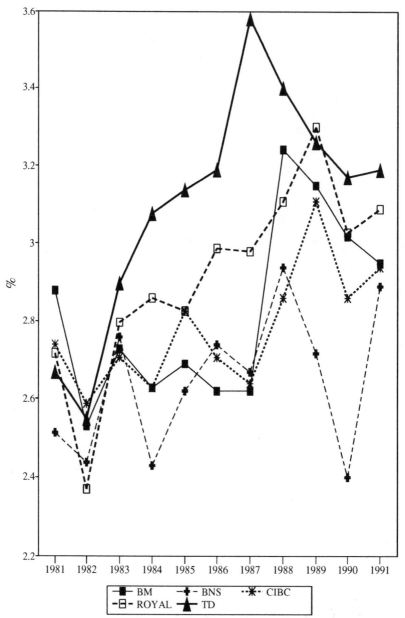

Figure 6.14
Net Interest Margins

the depositors' preferences to fund the loan. In Cedric Ritchie's address to the shareholders and in recent studies,[18] the bank's sensitivity to interest rate movements has been noted. The sharp rise in Scotiabank's net interest margins clearly reveals the benefits of funding longer-term loans with shorter-term deposits in times of falling interest rates. The rise by all others, excepting the Bank of Montreal, combined with statements by the Royal, suggests that others are willing to play the interest rate game, at least when the trends are believed to be relatively clear. The ongoing decline of the Bank of Montreal in this dimension differentiates it from the others. These changes could be the result of the successful wooing of corporate clients, the reverse of the Royal, or it could be the result of the price-cutting to gain share. It is far easier to lead loan rates down than it is deposit rates. There are also possible links to the asset portfolio. Superior asset quality could and should be tied to a lower earning, less risky asset portfolio.

Discussion of asset growth and loan diversification policies leads to a consideration of asset quality. The historical experience of loan losses on an ROA basis, as shown in figure 6.15, provides insights into the behaviour of the different banks. At both the beginning and the end of the period, there is a reasonable grouping of all the banks. They also move more or less together, except for the TD in 1986 and 1987. In 1981, the rank was Scotiabank, the TD, Royal, CIBC, and Bank of Montreal, while in 1991, the order went Bank of Montreal, Scotiabank, Royal, CIBC, and TD. No graph could make clearer the recent problems of the TD and Ontario than the sharp trend line from 1986.

Figure 6.15 provides grounds for some interesting speculation. Superior performance on this graph is not tightly tied to high overall performance – either in the global rankings provided earlier in table 6.1 nor in ROA.[19] While the recent problems of the TD did result in a downgrading of its creditworthiness, it must be emphasized that the fall was from the AAA ranks – the highest possible. Further, despite generally being closer to the bottom than to the top, the only Canadian bank that can match TD's credit ratings is the Royal. Despite some poor numbers, the Royal's credit rankings have improved. The seeming dilemma posed by these reflections may be resolved via different possibilities. First, loan losses could be too low. It is not obvious that the profit-maximizing behaviour would result in the lowest loan losses. Alternatively, it is possible that there are differences in accounting policies and/or market expectations concerning the different loan portfolios. In this scenario, the TD and the Royal may have earned greater credibility through earlier reporting of

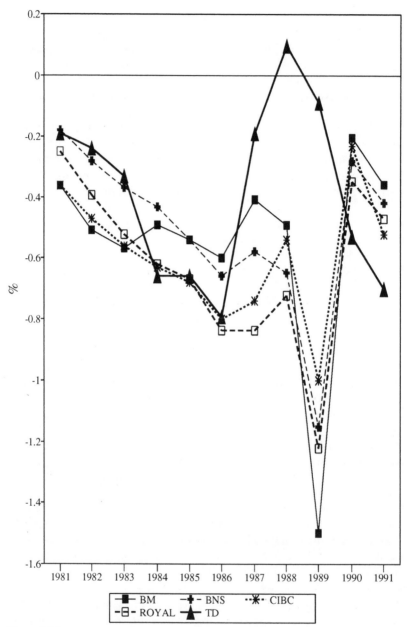

Figure 6.15
Loan Losses

difficulties. Whatever the answer, the relationships among asset quality, growth, and revenue generation are fundamental to an understanding of overall performance.

Given the importance of real estate to loan losses in the era, it is appropriate to discuss some other effects of troubles in this sector. We have frequently discussed the importance of disintermediation, that is, companies going directly to the market. The failure of Olympia and York may have dramatic consequences for the Canadian commercial paper market. Many investors were surprised to find that Canadian corporate paper was not as sound as they had believed. It will be interesting to see how Canadian markets respond in the future to the bright new products of investment bankers.

The other source of revenue for banks is fee-based. Figure 6.16A shows the almost uninterrupted rise in dollar terms of other income. In 1991, Statistics Canada reported that since 1987 the banks made their biggest revenue gains through service charges.[20] That was the year in which the banks began to buy investment companies. The trend lines for the Royal and the CIBC seem particularly impressive. It should be noted that in recent years, the rankings virtually replicate the rankings by assets size except for the positions of the TD and Scotiabank. The similarity between the TD and Scotiabank would seem to attest to earlier observations of Scotiabank's relatively weaker position in market segments demanding highly profitable services and TD's success in the corporate banking world. The slight tailing off of TD in 1991 was another factor in bringing it closer to the pack.

The increasing importance of fee-based products as a source of income is made clear by the role played by other income in the composition of total revenues shown in figure 6.16B. For all the banks, there has been a dramatic change. This will continue as banks continue their expansion into the trust business, mutual funds, and eventually, insurance products. Moreover, if one compares the spreads between the banks in 1981 to the later periods, a strong convergence can be noted. This is particularly true if Scotiabank's 1991 performance is not an indicator of any trend. This seems likely. There was a growth in absolute dollar terms in 1991 and the true income statement anomaly was the sharp change in net interest margins discussed previously. The bank's acumen in playing interest rates should not be used to downplay its success in developing its sources of other income.

Increases in other income also force us to re-examine the North American base of the bank. In a world where traditional credit products are less profitable, as disintermediation clearly demonstrates, fee-based products have become key strategic markets. It is

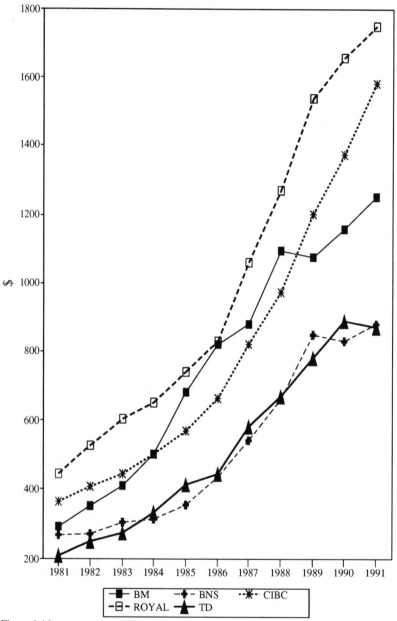

Figure 6.16A
Other Income

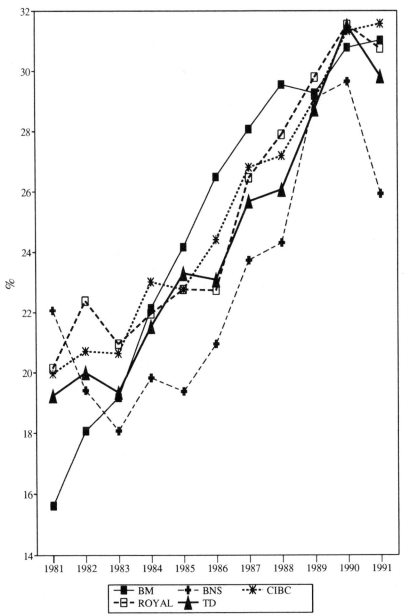

Figure 6.16B
Other Income as a Percentage of Total Revenues

unfortunate that it is not possible to break out the United States as a source of fee-based revenues. The current credit crunch in that country has created a tremendous opportunity to deepen relationships with customers and sell more services. An interesting segment in this regard is financial services institutions. The limited operational presence in the United States leads to the opportunity to sell various sophisticated services to other banks. Changes in the u.s. market with the emergence of new powerhouses such as Banc One or NationsBank that have limited international networks is another source of market opportunity for Canadian and other strong foreign banks. In addition, the u.s. credit card market has been identified as a possible source of growth.[21]

The increase in service fees has drawn some criticism. Articles in the popular press with titles such as "Shopping around can trim outrageous bank charges,"[22] reveal a popular hostility toward the banks. The article found clear differences for providing basic services, but did not really take into account the advantages of various packages offered by the banks. Nonetheless, in the 1987 study by Coopers & Lybrand, the CIBC provided lower-cost service for accounts with balances of $199, $600, and $1,001.[23] For the two lower balances, the TD and the Bank of Montreal had higher fees than their competitors.

Success in banking depends upon cost control, and consequently, productivity measures are important. Figure 6.17 compares the productivity of the five banks by calculating the ratio of non-interest expenses to revenues. Consequently, this graph must be read differently from the others: in this case, as in expense numbers, the lower the number, the better. Not surprisingly, the TD again differentiates itself as does the Bank of Montreal. As in other aspects, the TD is a model of a tight ship, while the Bank of Montreal seems to be a luxury liner. Among the others, this is one of the few dimensions upon which the Royal has not made significant moves. Perhaps this reflects for the Royal and for others lags in revenue emerging to offset the costs that must be incurred earlier to generate such streams. Scotiabank's position also reaffirms its strategy of aiming for the low-cost position. The overall success of Scotiabank given its product market choices depends upon tight cost-control management.

Evaluation of performance also takes place in the market place. A fundamental measure of success is the ability of managers to create shareholder value. One way of examining the success of managers in creating shareholder value is to compare the differences between the book value of company's assets and the market price. Figures 6.18A and 6.18B present the high and low trading prices of the bank's

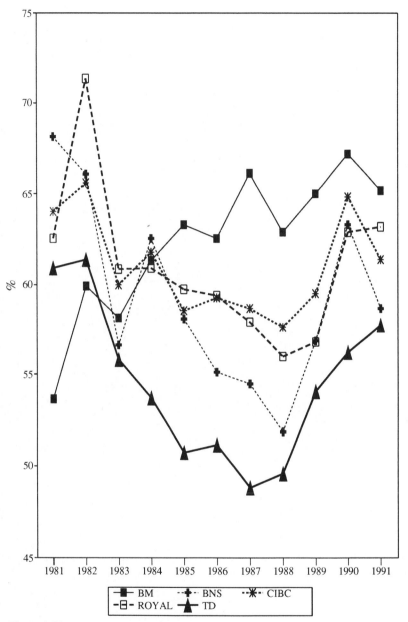

Figure 6.17
Productivity

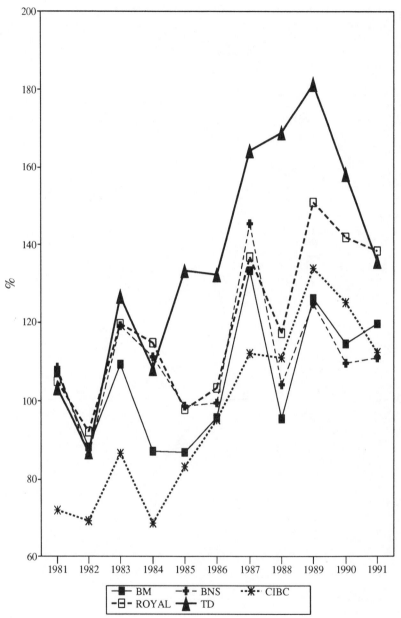

Figure 6.18B
Low Price as a Percentage of Book Value

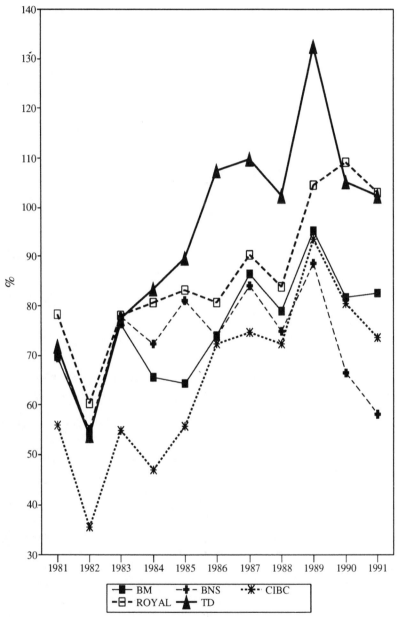

Figure 6.18A
High Price as a Percentage of Book Value

stock as a percentage of book value. The two patterns are quite similar and generally show the industry at higher levels than in 1981. The TD once again soars above the crowd in the 1980s, only to see a deterioration in the later 1980s and 1990s. On the other hand, steady gains in terms of comparative rankings can be seen by the Royal. Unlike some of the other numbers presented in this chapter, the dispersion is considerably greater. While at its low, the CIBC has traded at about 35 per cent of book value, at its high, TD traded at roughly 180 per cent of book. It is also interesting that, excepting the TD, there was a convergence of assessments in the mid-1980s, ruptured by a breakout by the Royal in the last two years. The grouping of BM, Scotiabank, and CIBC, especially in figure 6.18A, should not mask the very real recovery made by these banks. This recovery is more marked for the Bank of Montreal and the CIBC, while the volatility in Scotiabank's price is suggested by its lows. With an emerging strategic convergence, it is interesting to see how the market assesses the ability of the individual banks to be successful.

CONCLUSION

Strategy maps an organization on to a market environment. A key competitive arena is financial markets. The assessment of banks by depositors, bond-rating agencies, and stock analysts all affect the cost of doing business. While the numbers as presented are rosy, and often differences seem small, such differences can lead to major variations in external assessments of performance. These market assessments in turn influence current and future performance. The assessment of the effects of historical decisions upon future performance clearly demonstrates the value of understanding the historical decisions and forces that have shaped the present.

Despite some difficulties and differences in assessments of performance, it is also clear that most of the industry has emerged from the 1980s far stronger with a genuine strategic focus upon North America and increased abilities to earn fee-based income. The strategic transformation clearly shown in some of the graphs has been judged a success by the market. During the decade, there was a significant refocusing of the networks upon North America in order to generate flows. The strengthening of domestic operations must be seen in the context of an overall corporate strategy. Expansion of domestic product lines to compete with other financial services institutions seems to have raised rather than lowered costs. These costs should be expected in the context of a differentiation strategy. Moreover, it is clear that domestic strength allows Canadian banks to provide services such as payroll that differentiate them from their foreign-based competitors. Canadian operations may use Schedule 2 banks, but seldom as their lead bank. The question for the future is whether scope economies will dominate the economics of the industry. If they do, then some competitors can be both differentiated and low cost relative to other financial services competitors.

The year 1992 did usher in some dramatic changes, especially in the overall economic environment. The long term strengthening of the Canadian dollar abruptly ended as currency markets were troubled by political uncertainty in Canada and in the EC. Moreover, the hits from real estate, other bad loans, and restructuring generally lowered the reported ROA for 1992. Scotiabank led the pack with an ROA of .72, followed by the Bank of Montreal at .62, the TD at .58, the CIBC at .01, and last the Royal at nil. While the results caused some gloom in the banks, the ability of the banks to absorb such hits attested to the fundamental strength of the system. Moreover, aggressive moves by the Royal and CIBC to clear up their balance sheets should leave them well positioned for the future. It should also be added that the poor results were generally anticipated by the market. Competitive forces will continue to drive restructuring designed to secure the lower-cost structures necessary in this increasingly competitive environment. While no one can know the future, the stock market still seems to be telling us that not only has the past been good, but the future looks bright.

CHAPTER SEVEN

Changing Markets, Changing Strategies

It is impossible to understand *why* Canadian banks became major MNBS without understanding their strategies. By considering how the logic of intermediation demands the servicing of at least two distinct markets, growth strategies for intermediaries can be seen to be quite distinct from those of manufacturing firms. This was dramatically demonstrated in the 1970s with the recycling of petrodollars. OPEC countries had funds that far exceeded the ability of their capital markets to invest or more properly to absorb them. Consequently, they turned to foreign banks to "recycle" their funds by turning OPEC deposits into financial assets. The role of international growth in the strategy of an MNB must be understood in terms of maintaining a diversified balance among the three product lines of the bank: loans, deposits, and services.

Some readers might find the inclusion of services to be unusual. However, foreign-exchange swaps, one of the more important fee-based products, require knowledge of two partners with very distinct needs – for example, a small Canadian firm needing a yen loan and a small Japanese company needing a Canadian dollar loan. In order to internalize the market imperfections related to the identity of the two firms, financial services firms need a presence in the two markets. On the other hand, the desire to expand other fee-based services, such as payroll or information services, supports a different logic of horizontal international expansion. Yet access to increased information in international markets becomes a part of the service bundle sold in the home market. The study has shown that the rationale for internationalization of the Canadian banks and their success must be analysed in terms of differing strategic purposes assigned to international operations depending upon market structures.

Public policy with its emphasis on developing a secure Canadian-controlled banking system erected protective barriers that allowed the banks to pursue different strategies in Canada, especially prior to globalization of capital markets, the 1980 revision of the Bank Act, and "the little bang" of 1987. The same spirit that encouraged industry concentration further encouraged banks to seek complementary rather than directly competitive positions. A stable oligopolistic market structure demanded that different competitors seek differentiated positions in order to avoid direct competition and its inevitable consequence of price competition. The destabilizing effects of price competition had to be avoided.[1]

The results of the policies that promoted the development of banks based in Western Canada in the 1970s in an effort to support competition that would be more responsive to regional concerns was a clear demonstration of the inherent dangers of small, non-diversified institutions. The failure of the Edmonton-based Canadian Commercial bank and Calgary-based Northland Bank reminded policy-makers of the dangers for financial institutions of regionally concentrated deposit-and-asset portfolios. This lesson is still being learned with smaller deposit-taking institutions, such as Standard Trust or Central Guaranty. Governments with significant debt problems do not need turmoil that increases interest rates. Consequently, public policy fostered both the development of arbitrary comparative advantage for international markets and the promotion of differentiation in the Canadian domestic market. Size, international diversification, and limited competition were all components of a policy aimed at ensuring stability of the financial system that protects depositors.

The four banks displayed strikingly similar patterns of strategic development. First, virtually all developed a branch system and international connections quite early in their corporate history. Second, all recognized that improved centralized decision making was essential to impressive product line and geographic expansion. Corporate strategy was critical for designing and maintaining a balanced and diversified portfolio of deposit, loan, and other service products. Market conditions demanded reasonably similar responses. The effect of market environments was made clear in the 1980s as global integration influenced the competitive advantages protecting certain niche positions. This affected both small players as well as large combined commercial and retail financial services firms.

The need for delicate balancing at the corporate level was largely responsible for the major role played by the CEOs of the banks. In all the cases, eras were dominated to an uncommon extent by key decision-makers. Prior to the advent of computers and other information systems that facilitated centralized monitoring of the portfolios and decision making, the "computer" was the CEO and a fairly small executive committee. Considering the scope and complexity of the banks, the expertise and control of these small groups was surprising, yet inevitable. Customer service demands the coordination of a diverse number of specialists. But the forces of specialization could promote an imprudent level of global specialization in product areas, such as swaps, or in industries and customers, such as oil and gas, real estate, or sovereign lending. As economies become more interdependent, industry-level exposures become even more important, as past oil shocks and current real estate loans show. Geographic diversification will not offset industry focus. Only the view from the top provides the perspective that allows the forces of specialization to be shaped into a balanced, diversified portfolio.

Readers who know that the "great man" theory of history is out of vogue may find the emphasis on individuals surprising. However, the purpose of this study was to emphasize strategic differences among firms in a common industry. The different internationalization patterns were of especial interest. Structural features imposed a certain uniformity, but the strategic question became how to account for differences and variations among the organizations. Within this dimension, emphasis on decision making and the role of individual decision-makers became fundamental.

In the evolution of the Canadian banking industry, certain trends stand out. These can be identified by considering industry developments in six periods.

1 Strangled trade and the origins of Canadian MNBS: 1792–1871
2 New nation, new national policy, and new national banks: 1871–1900
3 Mergers and new internationalization: 1900–34
4 New corporate markets in Canada and abroad: 1934–67
5 The new international banking – the Euromarkets: 1967–80
6 Global competition in Canada and abroad: 1980–92

The year 1792 was a landmark because it was then that the first efforts to establish the Bank of Montreal surfaced. The other years all witnessed either the passage of or important reforms to the Bank Act.

The Bank Act served as a natural frame for the study of industry evolution because of its impact on the choices of market scope. The playing field established by the legislation was the common denominator that allowed the four competitors to select different positions.

It was in the light of these market conditions that the four banks developed their distinctive, yet highly interdependent competitive positions. The substantial changes in 1992 which moved Canada toward an omnibus financial services package from the previous pillar approach makes that year a natural end point.

STRANGLED TRADE AND THE
ORIGINS OF THE CANADIAN
MNBS: 1792–1871

Trade financing has always been essential to the rationale for the MNB. However, in the case of Canada, rather than simply following trade, merchants banded together to promote increased trade.[2] The needs of an economy based on exporting natural resources placed certain demands on the development of the economic infrastructure. To serve the trade needs upon which the local economy depended, banks were required to commence international operations. Consequently, the speed at which Canadian banks became MNBs should not be viewed with surprise. A second strategic aspect dictating the need for early internationalization was the small size of the Canadian market. As a colony, the different regions of Canada lacked highly developed capital markets. In order to manage asset and liability positions, banks needed access to capital markets that were better, deeper, and more liquid.

The history of banking prior to 1871 can best be seen by analysing the leading financial institution of the era – the Bank of Montreal. During this period, this bank established what became key success factors for the Canadian industry as well as certain proprietary distinctive competencies linked to the selection of market scope.

On the common front, branches were opened almost immediately and ties to New York and London were established. Second, there was the familiar pattern of growth creating pressures for organizational change. In the 1820s, the organization became more professional in order to correct problems with the loan portfolio. During this era, the president became a paid officer. The need for an inspector of branches was then recognized as basic to ensuring the proper management of the individual, dispersed branches. Later, further complexity was added through the extension of the product line to include savings accounts. This expansion was followed by the separation of head office from other branches to develop a capacity to cope with corporate level strategy, including monitoring.

Certain aspects of the early growth strategy merit comment. The Bank of Montreal feared by 1824 that it was losing effectiveness because of the changing commercial scene in Montreal. The response was to appoint John Molson, Jr. to the board of directors. The use of the board to establish and cement commercial ties was an important aspect of bank strategy and relationship marketing that deserves further study. In addition, the role of acquisitions must be analysed from both the strategic perspective of individual banks as well as from that of the overall financial system. When the Bank of Montreal entered a new market via acquisition of the Montreal Savings Bank, its superior control systems and corporate strategy allowed the incorporation of this different unit. Yet the ability to incorporate troubled banks into strong banks also served to maintain a stable banking system.

Certain unique features of the Bank of Montreal were also established. First, its basic conception of how banking should be carried out was strongly influenced by u.s. practices and thought. Second, the bank positioned itself as the leading financial institution in its role as as both the "bankers' bank" and the government's bank. This position demanded that locations necessary to service government demands be established, but locations had to be limited so as not to compete with the other banks who were customers for more sophisticated services, such as foreign exchange.

The leadership role further served to focus the bank on Canadian development. New York and especially London were needed, not so much for foreign-asset growth, but rather as a source of capital for Canadian development. The Bank of Montreal was valuable to the government because its access to foreign capital markets was frequently superior to that of the government. The relatively undeveloped Canadian financial markets could not supply the funds needed for large scale public or private projects, such as canals or railroads. The foreign offices were also needed to finance trade. Foreign connections were also marketed to smaller Canadian banks. International capabilities were the source of competitive advantage for targeted segments in Canada.

In this light, the response of King and the Bank of Montreal to the establishment of the cibc takes on added significance. To protect its position as the "bankers' bank," it was imperative that McMaster be prevented from using his connections in London and New York to challenge the primacy of the Bank of Montreal. Small banks that needed the services of the Bank of Montreal should be encouraged, but there was no need for a "bankers' bank" in Upper Canada to compete with that in Lower Canada. The success of the cibc's lobbying efforts essentially determined that Canada would become the home of a few large banks.

During this era, the viability of independent local banks also came into question. The difficulties of the Gore Bank revealed how the volatility of the developing economy made diversification a necessity. Moreover, it demonstrated the importance of acquisitions in growth strategies, as both the CIBC and the Bank of Montreal fought to acquire it. The CIBC's successful efforts helped to diversify its base while denying growth to its powerful rival. The pattern of competition among large institutions was reinforced.

During the pre-Confederation era, Scotiabank followed a similar pattern of growth and change as well as internationalization, but was largely content to serve its local market. The stamp of Scottish banking was placed upon the Canadian system as Scottish banker W.C. Menzies was hired to quell a crisis created by cashier James Forman's embezzlement. The importance of immigrants from the United States and Great Britain during the formative years of the banking system may have been instrumental in fostering an international perspective. An interesting change was the bank's reconciliation with its old rival, the Halifax Banking Company. Both banks realized that it was in their interests to form a common clearing house rather than persist in isolation. From such recognition concerning the importance of cooperation come later developments such as the Canadian Bankers Association and interbank markets. Given the danger created by excessive exposure to any one customer or industry, cooperation has become an essential feature of industry dynamics.

During this period, the Royal was in its infancy. The decision to go public in 1869 was interesting as a response to a changing political regime. This move was a necessity if the Royal was to be able to compete in the newly established Canadian market. It is also interesting that there was not the same rivalry between the Royal and Scotiabank as there was between the Bank of Montreal and the CIBC. Perhaps this was because both Maritime banks focused their growth plans on the Atlantic, while the CIBC was growing in the West where the Bank of Montreal was developing its expansion plans.

This era saw the emergence not only of the banking industry, but of a new nation, Canada, and of a new national policy. The creation of tariff barriers acted as a spur to foreign direct investment and made the international connections of the banks even more important. All the banks displayed a similar pattern of geographic and product line expansion, which was followed by the need for new mechanisms to ensure proper management. This was the familiar pattern, detected by Chandler, of structure following strategy. By the end of this era, it was reasonably clear, at least in the West, that only large diversified banks could survive.

NEW NATION, NEW NATIONAL
POLICY, AND NEW NATIONAL
BANKS: 1871–1900

The nation builders of Canada left a lasting imprint upon the Canadian banking industry. The first Bank Act made it clear that banks would be allowed, if not expected, to operate nationally.[3] The legislators recognized the value of the branch system for Canadian conditions after McMaster's battles in 1870. The new National Policy coupled with a desire to keep the strategic financial sector Canadian created a market environment where the Canadian banks would have exposure to MNES that were investing in Canada, but where they would not face foreign competition for these customers in the home market. The encouragement given to non-financial firms to enter Canada combined with the discouragement of financial MNES created a tremendous opportunity for Canadian banks to service foreign MNES.

The era saw a continuation of basic trends. The Bank of Montreal used its international network to consolidate its position as the "bankers' bank," a position made possible by King's earlier efforts. Scotiabank and the Royal began to develop their Caribbean network. In this region, the Commonwealth connection was clearly important. In addition, since Canada was not perceived as an imperialist power, Canadian banks may have been seen as more likely to implement a strategy of responsiveness to the host governments.

Scotiabank had a very interesting growth pattern, as it also commenced operations in Winnipeg, and later opened offices in Minnesota and Chicago. The bank made both of these moves prior to opening an office in Montreal. The entrepreneurial spirit of Fyshe was shown in the search for profitable opportunities while avoiding direct competition for large clients with the other majors. The bank recognized the westward shift in the country and moved its general manager to Toronto in 1898 to coordinate better its developing far-flung network. During this period, Fyshe placed his stamp on the bank by holding that large businesses would become self-financing.

Fyshe's successor, H.C. McLeod, also helped to establish an important tradition that international experience was critical for the CEO. McLeod's career had previously taken him both to Minneapolis and Chicago. Interestingly, this experience also signalled that the Maritime bank was recognizing the importance of the West for a national bank.

The CIBC first broadened its international activities with operations in New York and Chicago. Later, it seized opportunities in Toronto by opening multiple branches. The Winnipeg office served to direct attention westward, a move that was furthered when the Gold Rush led to expansion on the West Coast and in the Yukon. The bank developed strong ties to the mining industry very early in its history.

The Royal established its platform for later growth with its entry into Bermuda and even more importantly with the entry by Pease into the Quebec market. While Quebec served as the bank's centre, perhaps its most striking move was into British Columbia in 1897. Pease decided to go West where gold was developing the economy even though the bank had no other offices west of Quebec.

The period also evidenced the growth of cooperation among the banks with the creation of the CBA. The banks came to realize that it was in their common interest to shape public policy so that it would benefit the industry. This philosophy meant that the different expansion paths could be undertaken in a spirit of cooperation. As one might expect, the exception was Scotiabank, which had been accused of improper competitive behaviour in Winnipeg. However, the differences were resolved as the majors learned to live with one another.

MERGERS AND NEW
INTERNATIONALIZATION:
1900–34

The passage of the Bank Act in 1900 had important consequences. Changes to the Act encouraged loans to the timber industry, expansion to other areas of the Commonwealth, and mergers. The approval process for mergers was simplified. It was during this era that the banks established the base for substantial international operations.[4] Canadian policy displayed no hostility toward financial institutions. Rather, policy promoted the development of a few large internationally oriented banks. Domestic restrictions were placed on international operations if such restrictions limited the competitive position of the banks.[5]

The increasing stature of the Merchants Bank of Halifax demanded a new name: the Royal Bank of Canada. Montreal became head office in 1908, and under the leadership of Herbert Holt, the Royal grew to be the largest bank in Canada. Aggressive mergers allowed the bank to follow the westward growth of the Canadian economy and to expand its international networks. With Richardson at the helm, Scotiabank also embarked on an ambitious path of growth via acquisition. The CIBC under Sir Edmund Walker and Sir John Aird followed suit. During this era, the basic banking landscape for Canada was set.

The different roles of expanding international capabilities are of interest. While Scotiabank continued to focus upon trade, the CIBC's growth in Western Canada led to the growth of foreign-exchange capabilities to assist the new immigrant settlers. There was more than one link between domestic and international activities. The CIBC selected those most in keeping with a focus on its existing domestic clients.

The Bank of Montreal's merger with the British Bank of North America was another sign of the times. The public, rather than fearing industry consolidation, saw the merits of large institutions that could provide links to national and international markets. In this vein, the willingness of the banks to employ their branch network for the public good during World War I had a beneficial effect. On the other hand, the failure of the Home Bank in 1923 was further evidence that small banks could not survive. Only large and diversified organizations could survive and protect the small saver's deposit – a fundamental goal of public policy.[6]

The banks further adjusted to the new economic reality. The economic upheaval created by the war both shifted the centre of global capital markets to New York and created tremendous trade opportunities with a recovering Europe. The experience of the Canadian banks in New York combined with international networks, which were often better developed than their U.S. counterparts, had endowed the banks with the capabilities to profit from the new opportunities. With expansion came the base for the development of further specialization and even greater capabilities. However, the new reality was also reflected by the Bank of Montreal. In the era following World War I, experience in New York became a prerequisite for rising to CEO.

While not a year when there was a change in the Bank Act, 1929 was nonetheless an important year in economic history. Although the Canadian banks survived the Great Depression without a failure, the economic climate did have an impact. The banks tended to become increasingly liquid as there were few opportunities for asset growth, even while deposits still came in. As a result, there was a shift of attention to controllable costs and a rationalization of the branch networks. Economic necessity altered the wisdom of what had been a viable non-price, competitive service strategy in this regulated industry. The growth of deposits not only reduced bank profitability, but exposed the banks to public criticism. Why would they not lend the money that they had? The sport of bank bashing, which has a long history in Canada, reached new heights.[7]

NEW CORPORATE MARKETS AT
HOME AND ABROAD: 1934-67

Despite the best efforts of the banks to assure the public that the system was working, in 1934 the government created a central bank, the Bank of Canada. While the central bank had an effect on all banks, clearly it most dramatically affected the Bank of Montreal. Over the following years, the Bank of Montreal was forced to play catch-up as it now focused upon Latin America and the resource sector: strategies that had been previously pursued by its competitors.

The 1934–67 era was interesting for the Royal because it began to exert leadership. Under Morris Wilson, the first CEO to work his way up through the ranks, the bank took a public stand on various issues and encouraged the business community to follow. Seeing the threat of Social Credit in Alberta and some aspects of the New Deal in the United States, it recognized that it was time for corporations to realize the importance of an enterprise strategy. Business could no longer assume social legitimacy as a given.

World War II saw the banks engage in public service once again. However, the strictly economic impact of the war needs to be considered. The government's attempts to channel resources to the war effort led to cooperation among the banks. One aspect of this was the further rationalization of the branch system. While helping the government, the banks could cut back on a costly form of non-price competition. Second, personnel problems led to an increased focus both upon systems and the value of women as employees. Last, the condition of full employment and scarce consumer goods meant a significant build-up of deposits.

The postwar world offered tremendous opportunities for a system that had emerged strengthened rather than weakened by the war. War-ravaged countries needed North American exports and developing countries needed advice. Over the succeeding years, the bankers convinced the government to expand the scope of domestic operations and to leave the broad scope of international untouched. In fact, the neutral reputation of Canada established by such diplomats as Lester Pearson provided all banks with a competitive advantage over other foreign banks from imperialist powers in many host countries. The 1944 and 1954 Bank Act revisions allowed the banks to enter new fields in both corporate and personal lending.

The new playing field offered different ways for each bank to capitalize upon its advantages. The Royal, reflecting its size both domestically and internationally, announced in 1945 that its goal was "to serve all." The bank would protect its leadership position. In this context there were some interesting moves. Increasing attention was paid to the importance of the United States and to other non-domestic operations. In 1955, the bank signalled the importance of international as a differentiating strategy with the appointment of an assistant general manager for non-domestic. In 1961, the importance of the new information age was recognized with the appointment of an electronics officer in Toronto. This move further suggested the growing importance of Toronto. In 1966, the bank allied with the CIBC and the Toronto-Dominion to introduce Chargex. Even more interesting was the creation of a marketing division at head office. The Royal was out in front and intended to stay there.

The Bank of Montreal placed new importance on corporate and personal banking in 1946, while in 1958 it highlighted international operations when an international department was created. In 1964, it announced a new emphasis on foreign loans. In 1963, it also saw the need to market new information technology internally when it acquired IBM computers.

Scotiabank moved quickly to gain share in the new markets. Nicks' went "door knocking" on the Continent and in the United States to secure the large clients that it lacked in Canada. Relations with the Midland Bank were developed to assist operations in Britain while the increasing importance of the New York market was recognized and niches unattractive to the U.S. banks were targeted. A competitive advantage was the use of British tax expert, A.B. McKie. The bank could offer valuable assistance on how to go multinational from its own experiences. Among the emerging MNES targeted were the Japanese, and a Tokyo office was opened in 1962. The bank benefited further from its American experience when it copied a consumer-lending program from the Bank of America. The newly opened markets provided opportunities in the retail sector that were quickly pursued. By the end of the period, Scotiabank had a far stronger international presence and a developing retail franchise.

The CIBC developed its Western base and focused upon oil and gas with a new Calgary office while it also expanded into the United States. Other than some Caribbean Trust development and the introduction of Chargex, the McKinnon years gave the impression of a bank growing through the momentum established earlier. However, the acquisition of the Imperial Bank in 1961 created the largest branch network in Canada and emphasized the Canadian entity.

The period was interesting for a certain decline in relations with the government. The issue was "near banks." The banks believed that they were exposed to unfair competition for deposits from trust companies who were regulated provincially. The importance of deposit products and different levels of government regulation were both made manifest. The situation was alleviated with the 1967 Bank Act revision, which, following the recommendations of the Porter Commission, "loosened the straight jackets" on banks. While at times federal regulation had become hostile to the banks, it seemed that those regulations were now generally less restrictive. The banks affected the regulatory environment through their individual and cooperative strategies. This attention to the regulatory dimension was key to their success in Canada and abroad.

THE NEW INTERNATIONAL BANKING – THE EUROMARKETS: 1967–80

The emergence of the Euromarkets, which were the growth markets of the era, marked a new wave of international banking. The creation of these markets posed interesting problems for the theorist of the MNB. First, as Gray and Gray have asked, do we need a different theory to explain entry into markets that approximate perfect competition when most theories of the MNB are based upon assumptions related to imperfect competition?[8] Can the answer be that banks are trying to escape hostile regulation, as Grubel and others have suggested?[9] In this context, the nature of the hostile regulation should be considered. Is it regulation similar to taxes that restricts profitability, or is it restriction on product line that inhibits a bank from leveraging its knowledge-based assets? Or does the answer lie in internalization theory developed by Rugman, Goodman, and Khoury, among others, that has stressed the risk reduction possible through portfolio diversification?[10] Finally, could it be the simple profit motive, as Dean and Giddy found in their study of the United States and Canada?[11] The advent of the Euromarkets raised important new issues.

Throughout the era all banks attempted to develop the latent synergies in their geographic-based organizations through integrating mechanisms as capital markets became more closely linked. The two most international banks in the study, the Royal and Scotiabank, were showing the strains of previous growth and both were reorganized in 1967. What was most interesting about the reorganization was Scotiabank's recognition of the need to integrate its international operations to reflect the increasing globalization of capital markets. The Royal came to the same realization in 1970 with its creation of "teams." This strategy improved the capacity of both banks to pursue further growth among sophisticated customers in international markets.

The late 1960s and 1970s saw tremendous international growth on the part of all banks. However, it must be recognized that this was the era of the Euromarkets and syndicated lending. These were the growth markets. While this form of banking was obviously related to previously developed international skills, it was also sufficiently different to allow new entrants to compete in international in a manner that was new and different.

Another boost to international activity was domestic regulation that had a negative impact upon profits: the Winnipeg Agreement of 1972 and the Anti-Inflation Board legislation of 1976. It should be noted that this was general legislation and did not target the banks, even though it did have negative effects upon the banks.

It was via the Euromarkets that all banks entered into the well-publicized LDC sovereign debt market. It was also the market in which large, sophisticated MNES, such as IBM and Kodak, raise funds. As these MNES developed increasingly sophisticated treasury departments, they began to operate as MNBS. The threat of disintermediation by powerful buyers lowered margins in an increasingly competitive market and forced focus on efficiency. To some degree, the high-inflation environment masked some of the deeper developing problems.

In the world of the late 1960s, the Canadian banks were relatively large. In 1960, the Canadian banks, including those not part of this study, accounted for about 15 per cent of the international market in foreign currencies.[12] Moreover, three of the twelve largest banks in the world were Canadian.[13] The absence of a hostile anti-trust tradition had created companies capable of operating on a global scale.

The period was one of a new internationalization. The Canadian banks could capitalize in the global markets upon the intangible assets they had been building throughout their history. While the Royal and Scotiabank were better positioned, especially in Latin America, all banks increased their activities in the United States and London. The Bank of Montreal greatly increased its involvement with a new international banking division in 1976 and announced efforts in 1979 to become a leader in loan syndication. This fitted with the overall strategy of expanding the service line and increasing fee income. The bank sought differentiation through sophistication. However, in terms of sophistication it should be recognized that the Royal had established an important joint-venture merchant bank, Orion, in 1969. The Royal still saw advantages in being the leader.

A second area of interest was the implementation of new information technology. In 1968, while the CIBC was discussing plans for initiating on-line facilities, the Royal was discussing its ATMs. By 1971, this had expanded to discussions concerning automating the back room in order to provide better service. Scotiabank began to evaluate the impact of its new third-generation Honeywell equipment in 1969. Clearly, information processing was key to competition.

Interestingly, the era was equally marked by a downward spiral in business-government relations. The developing communications gap between the two is quite clear in the annual reports of Scotiabank from 1968 on. The bank was disenchanted with the government's policies, which discouraged foreign investment, and its inability to control the deficit. At the heart of the issue was the message that the country was not being run in a very businesslike fashion. This was a new and far more strident tone characterizing relations between the banks and the government.

GLOBAL COMPETITION
IN CANADA AND ABROAD:
1980-92

The passage of the 1980 Bank Act ushered in a new era of financial services and competition, as foreign banks were now officially allowed into the Canadian market. What was most striking during this period was the wave of reorganization among banks and the shift of emphasis to North America. Scotiabank increased the coordinating role of head office in 1979, recognizing the interdependence of the divisions. In 1980, the Royal reorganized to improve market effectiveness. Five executive presidents became the "chief operating officers of their respective banks." The "banks" and location of the COOS were:

1 Canada (Montreal)
2 National Accounts (Toronto)
3 International (Montreal)
4 World Trade and Merchant Banking (Toronto)
5 Finance and Investments (Montreal)

It is interesting to note that, in this reorganization the president was also located in Toronto. The growing importance of Toronto was evident.[14] The new marketplace rendered this organization ineffective and inefficient. In 1986, yet another reorganization took place: "An important change was to replace the traditional division of the Bank between International and Domestic groups with Bank-wide mandates for the management of each of our principal businesses." To be a bank was to be a global bank. Customer type, not geography, was the principle for organization.

The Bank of Montreal made sweeping changes under Mulholland. In 1982, a global structure to serve corporate and government clients was implemented and new initiatives in the use of computers were announced. It is again interesting to note that corporate banking, the core activity, was situated in Toronto. The following year, the bank acquired the Harris, an action that was explained in terms of developing a full North American operating capability, which was now essential to the new global strategy. From a strong North American base, global markets were scanned for new opportunities.

The CIBC reorganized in 1980 into international, corporate, and branch divisions. During the period, there was also a new emphasis on fee-based services. By 1986, it was time for another global organization. The bank now reorganized into a global SBU structure:

1 Individual
2 Corporate
3 Investment
4 Management Services

The global organization was diffusing through the industry.

In this context the 1986 organization of the Scotiabank was especially interesting. The bank was also pursuing the strategy of being a full-service financial institution and was acquiring world class information systems. The follower had time to appraise the competition and select the winning technologies. The new organization was broken down as follows:

1 Corporate Administration
2 Canadian Commercial and Retail
3 North American Corporate
4 Investment Banking
5 International

As had been the case throughout its history, Scotiabank moved in a similar, yet different manner with the retention of an international division. The structure recognized the linked, yet distinctive nature of international operations and perhaps the different nature of Scotiabank's operations which still included retail banking abroad.

The bank's aggressiveness in taking advantage of changing regulations in the Quebec securities industry was further proof of its "nonestablishment nature."

Considering the histories of the four banks together better allows us to identify some fundamental trends in both the banks and the industry. From a broad perspective, it is clear that as the importance of the Canadian banks in global terms has declined from the peak of the 1960s, their strategies and structures are becoming more similar. The reasons for this can be traced to fundamental shifts in markets. Regulation both in Canada and abroad had created segmented capital markets that allowed for more differentiated positions among major players. The globalization of markets tied to the re-regulation of many domestic markets led to a restructuring of the industry and changed the viable bases for differentiated positions. Separation into "four pillars" of financial services ceased being a global and competitive reality long before "the little bang" of 1987.

Other related forces drove the restructuring. Clearly the FTA, anticipation of NAFTA, General Agreement on Tariffs and Trade (GATT), and other trade arrangements affected industry structure.[15] While all the banks in our study desire a global presence, they are focused on one leg of the "triad": North America. The Asian markets of the 1990s are quite different from the markets initially explored by the banks, as is the EC of Europe 1992. The logic of a North American centre can be tied to a view that sees three large trading blocks: North America, Europe, and Asia. Moreover, the size of these three markets may preclude dominance in all three. Consequently, a strategic base must be selected. The selection of a strategic base does not equal withdrawal from other markets, but rather provides the focus for activities in other markets. The strategic relationship between target markets, product-market selection, and modes of entry must be considered. Appropriate modes of entry for multinational companies (MNCs) and various types of financial services firms are different. Interbank markets and alliances between financial services firms produce a complicated structure by forcefully raising the question of whether another player is a competitor or a customer.

The forces driving disintermediation and securitization were a further force toward greater strategic homogeneity. As corporate treasurers become more astute and have treasury departments that function as MNBs, they have diminishing needs for the knowledge assets that the banks can supply. Funds and information become commodities to be acquired at the lowest cost. If in the past strategy was based upon the sustainable competitive advantage of intangible assets, those assets of the banks may be losing value among the "prime" market segments. All banks who compete for prime clients must become increasingly concerned with controllable costs. For strategies of relationship banking to be successful, banks must be able to provide financial services more efficiently and effectively than their targeted customer segment(s) can do themselves. From this base, sustainable competitive advantages linked to specific customers and/or products can be developed.

To some degree, it should be recognized that interest costs are controllable. Even recognizing that banks are price-takers, a bank does make choices that can affect the risk premium attached to deposits. The advantages of high-leverage and high-return, risky loans must be weighed against their impact on funding costs. The effects of asset management on liability management are varied and complex. The focus on costs also leads us to understand the nature of organizational change taking place in Canada post-1980. In dynamic competitive markets, strategies tend to become more alike over time because the successful ones are copied. The same diffusion effects hold true for organizational form. In this price-competitive and transactions-costs driven industry, successful organizations must strive for organizational efficiency.

At the retail level, the blurring of boundaries between financial intermediaries is both a threat and an opportunity. The threat comes from new competitors who have expertise in different financial instruments, information sources, or distribution. Such competitors are both local and global. The opportunity comes from the market conditions that allow the creation of new bundles of services: a differentiated position. In this regard, the strong return to the retail market by all Canadian banks has been essential for maintaining and building their competitiveness.

Of overwhelming importance is the relationship between the new information technologies critical to competition in the financial-services industry and economies of scope. If multiple products do lead to a cost advantage, the number of defensible differentiated positions will be limited. However, success in squeezing scope economies from multiple product-lines will be a significant management challenge, just as is the achievement in corporate synergies. It is easy to create the basis for scope economies, but extremely difficult to implement the organizational changes necessary to achieve them. Successful financial-services institutions in the twenty-first century will have to be focused upon creating value for their customers. Market scope and organizational design will be dictated increasingly by customers' needs in this intensely competitive global industry.

CONCLUSION

All four banks have made important contributions to the competitiveness and development of the Canadian economy. All have done it in a distinctive manner. The case studies demonstrate the importance of trade for the development of the MNB since trade financing provided the original impetus for internationalization. In fact, the importance of an early international perspective created by trade financing and foreign born personnel may have been critical for the early recognition and pursuit of international opportunities.

However, the strategic importance of international connections for competing in the home market must also to be stressed. The Canadian banks needed the deeper capital markets of New York and London to assist in their asset-and-liability management problems. Once again, it is essential to understand the strategic role assigned to different international operations. Examining returns from international does not truly capture the contribution of international operations for bank profitability. Just as corporate strategy made a difference to overall performance, it became clear that this was as true for any single unit of the bank. All units must be assessed from the perspective of their strategic role in the whole. This is especially important as the banks are in the process of focusing their global networks to create and sustain competitive advantage principally in North America.

Second, while Richard Caves' theory leads us to expect cross-hauling, we need to consider the effect of barriers that prevent, or at least limit such practices.[16] The structure of the Canadian market and Canada's need for capital created tremendous opportunities for banks with international operations to bring clients into the protected Canadian market. It is important to note that just as the Bank Act protected the banks, tariff barriers created incentives for the entry of foreign firms. The effect of public policy upon the environment in which the banks operated was substantial. The banks recognized the importance of public policy and worked to secure legislation that was beneficial to the industry and, in general, for the Canadian economy.

The industrial structure of Canada and the industry was an especially important motive for internationalization prior to the extensive wave of internationalization via the Euromarkets in the 1960s and 1970s. If we are to understand the relatively early international success of the Canadian banks, we must follow their efforts to develop new competitive advantages as the marketplace changed. The banks pursued corporate strategies that selected domains, both in terms of geography and services, in order to provide a unique bundle of services to clients at home and abroad. International knowledge was an important competitive advantage for doing business in Canada, while knowledge of Canada was a key advantage in some foreign markets. This is as true today as it ever was in the past.

The success of the Canadian banks in international markets also leads us to consider some other sources of competitive advantage. First, the nature of regulation allowed the banks to develop an extensive branch system. Such a system forced the organization to develop the capacity to manage at a distance. The importance of such an organizational development must not be understated. A national system also meant that the banks dealt in virtually all sectors of the Canadian economy. The banks were able to develop expertise in assessing a number of major industries. In this context, Canada as an economy based upon the export of natural resources and the import of manufactured goods may have had a better understanding of developing economies that were replicating part of the Canadian experience. As other countries started to develop such industries, the knowledge capital produced a superior appraisal of the loan application at a lower cost. Knowing how to price is central to success in the banking industry.

In a similar vein, the close relations that all the banks maintained with the government may have helped to develop an expertise and a willingness for participation in public finance and megaprojects that combine both private and public participants. In the light of recent sovereign-debt problems, this may appear to be an advantage of dubious value. Perhaps even more important, however, was the public policy that encouraged the development of large banks early on. The Canadian banks were of sufficient size and reputation to compete as MNBS as the Euromarkets developed. A public policy that promoted the development of a concentrated and national industry created diversified banks that were able to compete globally.

The question has now arisen as to whether Canada needs larger banks. While Canadian banks are competitive, what are the implications of their smaller relative size in global markets, as shown in table 6.1? In the increasingly competitive global world, do we need banks closer to the size of the Japanese or major European banks? Determining the requisite size and product scope that will provide the information and financial flows needed by North American firms to be globally competitive remains a key question, to which shifting market dynamics preclude providing a facile answer.

Public policy concerns complicate the issue. While the recent reforms moved the Canadian regulatory framework toward an approach far more realistic than that of the United States, the same is not true for comparisons with Europeans or the de facto practices of Japanese banks and *keiretsus*. Europe is home to large universal services firms, known as *Allfinanz* in Germany and *bancassurance* in France. The recent government commitment to keeping insurance and banking separate angered bankers, and appropriately so, since bankers believe that explicit and implicit commitments to a new financial services approach were broken. Moreover, barriers impeding entry or prescribing the form of entry by banks into the retailing of insurance, life annuities, and car leasing deny the consumer benefits that arise from scope economies. It must also be asked whether such limitations inhibit the global competitiveness of our institutions vis-à-vis European and Japanese competitors. It is folly to compare overall size when different competitors can use different pathways to growth.

The issues surrounding competitiveness and public policy are complicated because of the number of public policy groups and regulators that impact upon the financial services industry. At the federal level, the Ministry of Finance, the Bank of Canada, the Office of the Superintendent of Financial Institutions, and Consumer and Corporate Affairs, in addition to committees of the House of Commons and the Senate, all come into play.[17] Many of these bodies also exist at the provincial level. Consequently, the financial services regulatory framework needs further revision, as public policy-makers realize.[18] There is still a pressing need to harmonize federal and provincial regulation as gaps and conflicts can adversely affect the competitiveness of the banks.

Unfortunately, the plethora of bodies provides special interest groups with numerous opportunities to capture public bodies, and the banks come under official scrutiny from a narrow perspective for their practices as they relate to access to networks, such as Interac or the payment system. The same is true for the banks' policies regarding investment outside Canada, service charges, interest rates on credit cards and mortgages, small business, hiring visible minorities, the handicapped, and so on. "Unfair" practices must be viewed and evaluated in light of broad global competitive realities.

Policies to promote "competition" have resulted in the failure of regional banks and many trust companies. Depositors have been protected by the Canada Deposit Insurance Corporation, but at what cost? The chartered banks and healthy trust companies are taxed to maintain sick institutions. In the long run, consumers pay in higher spreads between deposit and borrowing rates. Is it not time to take a harder look at the form of regulation that created healthy firms and thereby a healthy industry?[19] Making the healthy sick is an odd prescription for national competitiveness.

Perhaps even more important is the fact that in small markets, promoting multiple choice may not be the appropriate route. From Porter's approach, it is clear that if profits are excessive, entry will occur. Since 1980, foreign-based competitors provide the necessary competition and will increasingly do so as their field of operations is expanded. Just as the banks must develop their strategies in light of global competitors, so must public policy makers shift from promoting *competition* to *competitiveness*. Failure to do so will seriously hamper the ability of this enabling industry to foster Canadian competitiveness. In this context, it is imperative that our trade negotiators secure appropriate access to U.S. and Mexican markets under FTA and other markets under GATT and other multilateral processes.

It is important to recognize that as the four banks prepare to face a future that offers new challenge, strategies that were successful in the environments of the past may not be so in the future. The role of public policy in the recent trend toward strategic homogeneity should be analysed in this context. Globalization has diminished the ability of governments to promote arbitrary comparative advantage and to provide a domestic market structure that facilitates the pursuit of complementary differentiated positions. The rapid growth of new competitors and products has diminished the bases of differentiation that protected earlier strategic positions. Ironically, while globalization has opened up new markets, it has also served to emphasize the commodity nature of loans and thereby to promote price competition and strategic homogeneity. In this environment, attention to cost structure becomes all-important. Yet, the legacy of the past shows in commitments that affect the present and the future – whether the commitments be to branches, loans to troubled debtors, personnel, or whatever. The banks do have distinctive cultures and the "softer" areas of management will continue to have ramifications.

The performance of international banks from a country whose economy is trade-based and the host to significant levels of FDI advances our understanding of the MNB by focusing on how such banks choose to compete at home and abroad. In this context, the openness of the Canadian banking market relative to foreign markets is important. Only by seeing how all aspects of the firm's operations are integrated into its competitive position can the international activities be understood. This demands a thorough analysis of the firm's corporate strategy. From this analysis, we can see how such banks were not so much "leaders" or "followers," but rather key enablers for Canadian firms and the Canadian economy. Our banks have weathered many crises, and they will probably have to weather many more. It would be most unfortunate if the Canadian tradition of "bank bashing" kept us from recognizing and fostering the policies and initiatives that have created this powerful and globally competitive industry, which can and will play a key role in promoting the competitiveness of all Canadian firms.

Appendices

APPENDIX ONE
METHODOLOGICAL
CONSIDERATIONS:
THE VALUE OF CASE STUDIES

At the heart of this study was the quest to understand the competitive strategies of Canadian banks. Against the broad backdrop of economic analysis provided by the theory of the multinational enterprise (MNE) and the multinational bank (MNB), the efforts of individual banks to build and to defend competitive advantages were portrayed both in terms of domestic and foreign competitors. It was the success or failure of the banks in creating a sustainable competitive advantage that formed the basis for the financial performance analysed. The question asked was, how did the banks compete amongst themselves and with other banks?

The strategy of each bank was unique. Consequently, the nature of the research question demanded that the broader economic analysis of traditional industrial organization theory be enriched with historical accounts of the development of particular banks. In order to understand the development of each bank's strategy, an indepth analysis of each bank was undertaken. Chandler has shown the value of such an approach.[1]

While there was no desire to bore the reader with unnecessary historical detail, it was impossible to understand the behaviour of each bank in the late 1980s without an understanding of the endowments that each bank had created during its lengthy history. The strategic options available to the individual banks were to some degree a result of their past actions. The effects of the past also created a corporate culture that preconditioned the organization to pursue specific opportunities and to miss or to deny others.

ORGANIZATION OF THE CASE HISTORIES

Since the goal of the study was to understand the development of strategy in the banks, there was a natural focus on critical decisions and decision making.

The result of this was to organize chapter sections of each case around chief decision-makers. Unlike some industries, the leaders of the major banks were and are generally well known and many have left a distinct imprint on their banks, in much the same manner as Henry Ford, William Durant, or Thomas Watson did upon their companies. One reason for this impact may be that banks are multiproduct firms and an analysis of corporate strategy was essential for understanding individual business strategies. The role of the chief executive officer (CEO) was not only to manage the exposures created by the various growth strategies for different loan and deposit products, but also to ensure that certain services essential for the firms' strategic position were delivered. Balancing this diverse yet highly interdependent portfolio demanded centralized decision making.

A second organizing principal concerned the presentation of the cases. The banks were presented in the order of their founding. This was not due to historical whim, but rather to provide the reader with some sense of the competitive environment facing each bank as it entered the market.

While rivalry was an important competitive force, so too was the effect of government regulation. The banking industry has always been a regulated service industry. In virtually every country of the world, the financial services industry is regulated by governments and also increasingly by international bodies. Canadian banks have not been free to enter every market of their choosing because the Bank Act, which is revised every ten years, established limits, as do other jurisdictions. Initiatives must be seen not only in the light of the CEO, but in the light of the possible scope delimited by regulation.

On the other hand, it is important to realize that the effect of government regulation was not necessarily harmful to the industry. Regulation of the Canadian banks has been developed with the aim of aiding the economic development of Canada. It would be a mistake to see the relationship between the chartered banks and the governing bodies as inherently antagonistic. Rather, it can be asserted that the banks, at least until the 1960s, held that government regulation was meant to create a healthy banking industry. Government regulation can be both a source of opportunities and a comparative advantage.

The history of the role of the banks in developing banking legislation in Canada drew attention to the importance of understanding business-government relations in Canada and the role of the Canadian Bankers' Association (CBA). The banks have not passively accepted government restrictions placed upon their strategic choices, but have sought to guide the government's understanding of what is the appropriate competitive scope for their activities. By the late nineteenth century, the banks could see the advantages of cooperating to present their case to the government and to the public. Thus, the CBA was created to facilitate cooperation among the banks. The history of bank regulation provided not only the knowledge necessary to understand the economic effects of the Bank Act, but also the opportunity to see an important aspect of changing business-government relations in Canada.

The effect and probably intention of regulation was to create an oligopolistic industry that was Canadian-owned and internationally competitive, unlike many Canadian industries. Without an understanding of the role of government regulation and especially Canadian government regulation, it is impossible to understand the environment of bankers.

SYSTEMATIC ANALYSIS OF ANNUAL
REPORTS

A rich and as yet relatively unmined source for understanding corporate strategies and their implementation is the annual report. A systematic analysis of statements given by the executive officers in the annual reports over an extended period reveals a great deal concerning how each bank viewed its competitive environment as it scanned for opportunities and threats. In addition, discussions of the firm's strengths and weaknesses reveal how the executives assessed the capabilities of the organization in order to achieve its strategic intentions. This is especially true for the annual reports of the Canadian banks that have been judged by Lafferty Business Research to be among the best in the world.[2]

Disclosure in the previous year's document provided the opportunity to chart and analyse strategic intent. The results of 1992 must be interpreted in light of the promises of 1991. This is true for the CEO, as well as for the researcher. The researcher enjoys the great advantage of being able to look back upon events that are in the past to him but in the future for the CEO. Of course, the strategic intent revealed in 1991 will generally not be a completely accurate road map of what the company did during the year. The differences will frequently be the result of previously unforeseen opportunities. Consequently, we can use the statements of intent to separate *intended* from *emergent* strategies, reasonably secure in the level of strategic intent disclosed to the complex set of stakeholders.[3] However, the earlier statements provide a benchmark for analysis. In sum, the addresses in the annual statements provide us with valuable insights into strategy formulation and implementation.

There is no need to accept these statements at face value. Remarks concerning strategic directions that the bank wished to pursue were assessed against hard data taken from the financial statements, including data on portfolio structure and cost measures. It should also be recognized that changes may not be sudden. Rather, given the difficulty of adjusting bank portfolios and the costs of entering new markets, lags between statements of intentions and positive financial results should be expected. This illustrates the value of the historical perspective.

The use of case descriptions further served to open up the discussion of strategy formulation to consideration of process variables. That is, theories of the MNE that limit their views of decision-makers to *homo oeconomicus* may be excluding important behavioural considerations. While in the long run market discipline may force a certain degree of economic rationality upon strategists (at least upon those who wish to survive), in the short run, some other decision variables may exert considerable force. Historical studies allowed us to capture these unique elements and to enhance our understanding of the complexity of strategy making.

In case the above sounds too much like an encomium to the irrational or at least the arational, it should be noted that this was not the case. Rather, if we accept that decision making is inherently limited because of the impossibility of obtaining all relevant information, then it is important to analyse which factors account for some information being included in the process. To put this in strategic terms, it is essential to understand how strategists came to the recognition of opportunity. A consideration of the history of the different banks allowed us to raise questions concerning how individual opportunities came to be recognized and pursued.

In addition, there is a wealth of information concerning the banks because of virtually constant public scrutiny. The decennial review of the Bank Act involved exhaustive examination by committees of both the House of Commons and the Senate. During these hearings there were lively exchanges among officials from the Bank of Canada, the Department of Finance, bankers, businessmen, economists, and academics. The CBA also makes extensive efforts to keep the Canadian public and government well informed concerning the actions of the banks. As well, the banks are under the watchful eyes of the Inspector General of Banks, investment dealers, and bond-rating associations. The case can be made that one of the offshoots of the debt problem of less developed countries (LDCs) has been that banks have been forced to reveal more details concerning their asset portfolios in order to maintain a reasonable cost of capital. There is no dearth of publicly available information on the banks and this conditions the presentations made in the annual reports.

LIMITATIONS OF THE SOURCES

An obvious problem with the use of annual reports is the fact that they are written with the intention of putting the firm's best foot forward, which can result in both a biased and an incomplete account. It should be realized that this is not limited to the qualitative data taken from the body of the annual reports, but extends to the disclosure of financial information. The accounting policies that govern disclosure do allow banks latitude both in terms of what is reported and how it is reported. This can lead to problems not only when one compares one bank to another, but also in constructing reasonably consistent time-series data.

The above situation has led to the adoption of two policies. First, the more rigorous quantitative comparisons are limited to disclosures made since disclosure guidelines were altered by changes to the 1980 Bank Act. The Act, in conjunction with the increased attention focused on the banks because of fears arising from LDC-loan problems, have led to an improvement in the quality of available information. The adoption of common, or at least reasonably similar, reporting practices essential to ensure comparability both on a cross-sectional and longitudinal basis did not occur until 1983. Consequently, the data analysis is limited to what was reported in the 1983 and later annual reports and information from earlier reports that can be reconciled to 1983. Given the closure created by the 1980 Bank Act, this resulted in limited data losses.

Second, analysis of the banks by other financial experts has been considered. In this vein, it is important to recognize that reports by investment dealers and bond rating agencies impact upon the bank's cost of capital. Consequently, questions were asked and answers given beyond the confines of the annual reports.

While accepting that bias is an important limitation of the data base, there is also an important advantage. The bias that can be detected in the reports is a consistent bias. By discerning consistent, albeit biased, trends in the information, it is possible to develop a systematic interpretation. An analysis of "bias" can give important insights into the softer aspects of the organization that impact upon decision making.

The use of annual reports forces us to focus upon research design and to end the sterile debate over "quantitative" versus "qualitative" research. Context is the result of spatio-temporal situatedness. Hegel in his analysis of the "here and now" explored the difficulties of certainty in relation to perceptual objects. In part, this philosophic exploration demonstrated the impossibility of any description being totally complete. However, more important for our purposes was the attention paid to *being* as historical. Time and place condition the very existence of objects in this world. Since Hegel's work, it has been impossible for phenomenological researchers into human subjects to ignore the effects of history. Consequently, the analysis of annual reports must involve a reconstruction of the historical world from which the annual report comes. Bias is fundamental to historical being. It is important to note that this is as true for numbers as it is for words. A dollar in 1950 does not equal a dollar in 1991 and a simple inflation adjustment is not an adequate correction because the very meaning of money can change from time to time and from place to place. Careful research must deny the temptation to take the easy and *ahistorical* route.

This draws attention to the linkages between theoretical frameworks and analysis of states of the world. Annual reports do not tell the complete story, but completeness is an impossibility. Godel's incompleteness theorem addressed an important dimension by revealing the tension between completeness and consistency.[4] The importance of Godel's work was to illustrate that no system could be both complete and consistent because the language for evaluation must occur at a higher level. The point for scientific research is that to aim at completeness is to aim at an impossibility. What is important then is to set and to understand the importance of context. If we accept that all theories and narratives are inherently limited, then it becomes critical to be sensitive to the problem of theory-dependent statements[5] and to assess the appropriateness of any perspective. Annual reports provide a valuable perspective because of the multiple stakeholders that they address.

All data has limitations. With the recognition of the above limits, it is possible to support conclusions concerning the international development of the Canadian banks. On the other hand, some conclusions can only be reached with caveats concerning the reliability of the data. Every effort was made to inform the reader when this is the case.

CONCLUSION

Four chapters give the individual histories of the Bank of Montreal, Scotiabank, the Royal Bank of Canada, and the CIBC. Each history examines the course of each bank's growth and stresses its individuality, which creates a certain mosaic quality to the study. Each chapter seeks to emphasize how the bank responded to and changed the characteristics of the Canadian banking industry. The aim was to develop an understanding of each bank within the context of the industry, but also to emphasize how the conduct of each firm changed the industry context. A broad historical perspective not only allowed the various intricate interdependencies to be portrayed, but also allowed for an examination of singular events within a well-established qualitative methodology.

1871   Banks are allowed to "engage in and carry on such business generally as appertains to the business of banking."

Activities included issuing bank notes; accepting deposits; lending money on security; acting as a financial agent; and so on.

Prohibited activities included lending on real estate; buying, selling or bartering goods, and engaging in any activity other than banking.

The Act would be reviewed every 10 years, consequently each bank's charter was limited to 10 years. This would ensure that banks stayed attuned to changing economic conditions.

1881   Revision

Required reserves of Dominion notes were increased from a minimum of one-third to 40 per cent.

Concerns with bank failures led the government to give note holders first call on the assets of the bank.

1891   Revision

Required banks to send a list of deposits and dividends unpaid for more than five years to the minister of finance.

The Bank Circulation Redemption Fund was established to redeem the notes of failed institutions. A small percentage levy was imposed upon all banks to create this fund which in essence placed all bank notes on a similar footing.

Although not under the Act, the Canadian Bankers' Association (CBA) was formed in 1891 in recognition of the importance that industry cooperation had achieved in influencing public policy.

1900   The CBA was incorporated by an Act of Parliament.

1901   Revision

The passage of the new Bank Act in 1900 gave banks the right to issue bank notes in any British possession outside Canada. The Act simplified the mergers of banks as only the agreement of the banks and the approval of the governor-in-council upon receipt of the recommendation of the Treasury Board was required – not the previously required special act of Parliament. Banks were also now allowed to lend upon the security of standing timber and the right or license to cut it and to remove it. In addition, the Act made membership in the CBA compulsory.

Changes to merger requirements fostered national expansion. Banks could now merge by mutual consent of two-thirds of their shareholders and the approval of the Treasury Board and the governor-in-council. A specific act of Parliament was no longer required.

1913   Revision
A shareholders' audit by independent auditors responsible to the shareholders was required. The auditors were to be selected from a panel
selected by the CBA (delayed for political reasons). Government inspection
was not deemed necessary.
The management of central gold reserves under the CBA.

1923   Revision
Bank managers were prohibited from acting as agents for insurance
companies.
Shareholders' audits had to be carried out by two different firms of
auditors.

1924   Amendment
The Office of the Inspector General was established as part of the
Department of Finance.

1934   Revision
Bank cash reserves as a percentage of deposits set.
The 7 per cent ceiling on lending rates was retained.

1934   The Bank of Canada Act
The government established its own bank, the Bank of Canada, to issue
money. By 1945, it held this position exclusively.
The government now held effective control over the size of the banks
and the money supply.

1944   Revision
The interest ceiling on loans was reduced from 7 per cent to 6 per cent.
Par value of bank stocks were reduced from $100 to $10.
Provisions were made to transfer unclaimed balances to the Bank of
Canada after 10 years.

1954   Revision
Bank lending powers were expanded to include loans for residential
housing on the security of mortgages under the new National Housing
Act (NHA); chattel mortgages secured by household property including
automobiles; and loans secured by hydrocarbons in the ground.
An age limit of seventy-five was set for bank directors.

1967   Revision
The delay in passing the revision was in part due to the long awaited
Porter Commission which advocated free competition and flexibility. The
Commission held that banks should be freed from the 6 per cent ceiling
on loans in order to allow the banking system to become more responsive
to changing conditions. Deposit rates were also free to adjust.
Reserves on savings deposits were cut in half from 8 per cent to 4 per
cent to level the playing field with "near banks," such as trust companies,
who were not required to hold such reserves.

Banks were allowed to own leasing subsidiaries to compete with near banks and foreign competitors.

No shareholder could own more than 10 per cent of a bank nor could the aggregate of foreign shareholdings exceed 25 per cent. Foreign banks were effectively prohibited entry into the Canadian market. This was in response to Citibank's acquisition of the Mercantile Bank. While the Mercantile was grandfathered, limits were placed upon future growth.

1980   Bank Act Revision

Two categories of banks were established: the widely held and Canadian-owned chartered banks known as Schedule A banks and new closely held banks, mainly foreign, known as Schedule B banks. In order to gain entry, the bank had to convince the minister of finance that it would increase the competitiveness of the Canadian market and the bank's home government had to extend similar treatment to Canadian banks.

Schedule B banks were limited to lending 20 times their authorized capital. The total market share of the Schedule Bs was additionally limited initially to 8 per cent of the market. In addition, they were required to obtain the permission of the minister of finance to open a branch office. The new banks were effectively limited to a segment of commercial lending.

1980   Canadian Payments Association Act

This act removed responsibility for operating the clearing system from the CBA. The Canadian Payments Association membership included caisses populaires, credit unions, and the trust and loan companies.

1982   Fifty-seven "letters patent" had been granted to Schedule B banks. Banks were scrambling to get a license before the available allotment of capital were gone.

1984   The ceiling on foreign market share was lifted to 16 per cent.

1985   The failures of the Canadian Commercial and Industrial Bank and the Northland Bank again raised concerns over depositor safety.

1986   Quebec Securities Commission

The Quebec Securities Commission granted the Bank of Nova Scotia a license to create a full service underwriter, Scotia Securities. Aggressive action by Quebec and Scotiabank sounds the death knell of the classic four pillars.

1987   The Little Bang

Domestic and foreign commercial banks were allowed to engage in all types of securities dealings.

1988   The new nature of competition in financial services was made apparent when American Express applied for a banking license. Canadian bankers were outraged since they held that American Express was not regulated in its home country; the definition of "financial institution" had to be stretched to include a "financial corporation"; and a foreign company would be allowed to enter into activities prohibited to Canadian banks, such as marketing of goods and travel services.[2]

1989   The Canada-u.s. Free Trade Agreement

U.S. banks were exempted from restriction on foreign banks. The asset ceiling on other foreign banks was reduced from 16 per cent to 12 per cent to adjust to the new situation.

1990   American Express received its letter patent.

1991   Revision

Banks were allowed entry into the other pillars – they could now offer non-banking financial services such as trust or insurance through subsidiaries.

Banks were allowed to establish "networking" arrangements with other financial services providers. That is, they could now offer new services through their extensive retail branches. However, banks were prohibited from offering insurance services through their branches.

Powers to offer information services were expanded. While previously banks had offered some data processing related services, these powers were expanded to include:

• information processing;
• advisory services in the design, development and implementation of information management systems;
• design, development, manufacture and sale of ancillary computer hardware.

Banks were now permitted to hold, manage, and develop land through their real property corporations and to own real estate brokerage firms.

Specialized financing services were expanded as banks were allowed into a broader range of venture capital and merchant banking activities.

At the retail level, banks were allowed to provide investment counselling, portfolio management and financial planning.

Schedule A banks became known as Schedule 1 banks and Bs as Schedule 2 banks.

Notes

1 On the competitiveness of the financial services industry and the major Canadian banks, see Darroch and Litvak, "Diamonds and Money." Discussion of recent important trends concerning competitiveness can be found in Hirtle, "Factors Affecting the Competitiveness of Internationally Active Financial Institutions."

2 Nagy, *The International Business of Canadian Banks*, 4, discussed how the role played by the Canadian banks in international financial markets has far exceeded their role in the international economy.

3 In 1960, three of the twelve largest banks in the world were Canadian. See Franko, "Global Corporate Competition," and Darroch "Global Competitiveness and Public Policy." This pattern is not unusual for Canadian firms. See, e.g., Litvak, "Instant International."

4 A note on methodology appears in Appendix A.

5 For an interesting account of several key issues and episodes, see MacIntosh, *Different Drummers*.

6 See Darroch, "Global Competitiveness and Public Policy."

7 Schull and Gibson, *The Scotiabank Story*.

8 For a discussion of other regulatory regimes and issues, see the following and the bibliographies therein: Bryan, *Bankrupt*; Edwards and Patrick, eds., *Regulating International Financial Markets*; Kosters and Meltzer, *International Competitiveness in Financial Services*; Meerschwam, *Breaking Financial Boundaries*; and Pierce, *The Future of Banking*.

9 The "follower hypothesis" is strongly supported in the literature. See Darroch, "Strategic Management and Multinational Banking."

10 See Beck, "The Revolution in Financial Services." At various times, the Bank Act limited foreign ownership. However, it should be noted that "officially" foreign banks were allowed into Canada during this century

until the passage of the 1967 Bank Act. However, unofficially, the presence of *major* banks may have been discouraged: see Fayerweather, *The Mercantile Affair*. The 1980 Bank Act allowed for the entry of foreign banks, although there were limitations placed upon their growth.

11 See Baer and Pongracic, "The Development of Banking Structure in Five Countries."

12 U.S. regulation since 1929 has also sought to promote stability but through different mechanisms: see Pierce, *The Future of Banking*. However, U.S. regulation was averse to industry concentration and consequently focused on local markets. This prevented the diversification of loans that the Canadian approach encouraged. The resulting differences in the United States are discussed in Bryan, *Bankrupt*.

13 See Cline, "'Reciprocity.'"

14 Porter, *Competitive Strategy*. See Deutsch, "A Conversation with Michael Porter." For specific application to the banking industry, see Ballarin, *Commercial Banks Amid The Financial Revolution*. For different recent strategic perspectives, see de Carmoy, *Global Banking Strategy* and Gonzalez and Mintzberg, "Visualizing Strategies for Financial Services."

15 There are strategies for smaller markets called focus strategies, but the same general conditions hold.

16 If a firm could combine low cost with differentiation, the result would be incredible profitability. An example would be IBM in the early PC market. The same condition may hold for many other firms generally regarded as "excellent" and who display surprising levels of profitability.

17 It should be noted that American Express may not have been the low-cost producer in the financial services industry, but in a specific market segment. Whether that segment is sufficiently broad to be classified as an industry is a difficult question. However, as a practical matter of competitor analysis, it would have been folly to ignore American Express's considerable advantages in Travel and Entertainment cards.

18 In general, this is a complicated area. See Litvak and Maule, "Assessing Industry Concentration."

19 See Day, *Market Driven Strategy*.

20 This is generally true, although there is some leeway.

21 See the classic article on scope economies, Bailey and Friedlander, "Market Structure and Multiproduct Industries."

22 This is another complex issue. Changing environments can give competitive advantage to firms outside the traditional structure. This is often argued in the United States where regulation is far more restrictive on banks than upon "non-bank" financial firms, such as Sears or GMAC.

23 While this borders on caricature, it is broadly appropriate for some U.S. market segments.

24 "According to Jean Dermine of Insead, a European business school, European banks throw away a fifth of their profits each year because they do not know how to balance their asset and liability positions properly": "Time to Leave," 3.

25 The policy of Scotiabank has differed from its rivals: see Darroch, "Strategic Management in Turbulent Environments." The Royal also seems to be prepared to use this lever.

26 One manner of measuring the riskiness of a bank is compare credit ratings. However, this reflects asset quality in addition to other factors affecting income.

27 One proxy for the riskiness of a financial services firm is bond ratings by independent agencies such as Standard and Poor's or Moody's.

28 This mirrors the typical organizational split between commercial and retail in Canadian banks.

29 In an effort to create a global level playing field, the Bank for International Settlements has established that bank capital must equal 8 per cent of risk-weighted assets. Interestingly, even if banks have sufficient capital to be sound, they can still have liquidity problems created by perceptions that they are not sound. This was dramatically demonstrated by the failure of the Continental Bank of Illinois. It has been argued that the bank failed not because of excessive lending to the energy sector, but because of a run created by Japanese money managers who were responding to a mistranslated press report. See Murphy, "Power Without Purpose," 72–3.

30 In Porter's terms, the strategy would be characterized as Multidomestic rather than Global. Some background on the differences are discussed in Doz and Prahalad, "How MNCs Cope with Host Government Intervention."

31 There are risks in disintermediating. The shocks in the 1987 stock market clearly showed volatility in direct financial instruments. More recently, the Reichmann's problems at Olympia and York (O&Y) started with problems in the commercial paper market.

32 See Federal Reserve Bank of New York, "Recent Trends in Bank Profitability."

33 This figure appeared in Darroch, "Strategic Management in Turbulent Environments," 210.

34 For a fuller discussion, see Darroch and Litvak, "Gaps, Overlaps and Competition Among Jurisdictions."

35 This raises the issue of contestable markets in Canadian regulation. While U.S. banks could not "bank" in Canada, they affected industry dynamics by attracting CFOs of Canadian companies to their New York offices. The nature of the product or service renders the value of physical

distribution channels problematic. This is just one of the differences in this rather unusual industry.

36 In advanced capital markets, the bank could hedge its exposure in order to manage risk. An anonymous reviewer for this manuscript commented that this could characterize Canadian banks: "After all, the Canadian banks were operating as though LIBOR existed, even before it was formalized."

37 One of the advantages of employing Porter is his breadth. On managing value-added activities, see Porter, *Competitive Advantage*.

38 For some recent discussions linked to international banking, see Hultman and McGee, "Lending by U.S. Branches of Foreign Banks"; Sabi, "An Application of the Theory of Foreign Direct Investment to Multinational Banking in LDCS"; and Tschoegl, "International Retail Banking as a Strategy."

39 Internalization theory has been developed to explain the reasons for FDI. For a fuller discussion of the issues, see e.g., the works of Casson, Dunning, Hymer, and Rugman in the bibliography.

40 This is an incentive for banks to replicate and therefore search for similar, rather than dissimilar markets. This explains the rationale of the multidomestic strategy.

41 For example, see Scotiabank, "Competitiveness and the Regulation of Canadian Banks."

42 See Darroch, "Global Competitiveness and Public Policy," especially 162–70.

43 See "Japan's monetary implosion," 75–6. This position could be hedged in advanced capital markets.

44 See Murphy, "Power Without Purpose," 72–3.

45 Examples of commercial banks who made a strategic transition to this position include J.P. Morgan and even more especially, Bankers Trust.

46 While this sounds impossible, it became far easier with the development of large interbank markets, such as the Euromarkets.

47 Location is generally a critical element in the strategies of service firms.

48 This issue has received considerable discussion in the strategy literature. See, e.g., Hofer and Schendel, *Strategy Formulation*, chap. 5.

49 See Williamson, "The Modern Corporation."

50 See Bailey and Friedlander, "Market Structure and Multiproduct Industries" and Williamson, "The Modern Corporation."

51 However, by selling fee-based services, banks can increase the overall profitability of its dealings with successful clients.

52 See Porter, "From Competitive Advantage to Corporate Strategy."

53 Anecdotal evidence concerning the earnings multiple paid for investment banks whose major assets go out the door every night suggests that this might not be the case. However, the success of a new competitor in the

financial services industry, GE Capital, is based upon their willingness to manage companies when loans go sour.

54 Porter, "From Competitive Advantage to Corporate Strategy," 53.

55 See Pennings and Harianto, "The Diffusion of Technological Innovation in the Commercial Banking Industry," and Steiner and Teixeira, *Technology in Banking*.

56 The market share of Schedule B, or Schedule 2 banks as they are now known under the Bank Act, was limited by legislation.

57 The failure of Drexel and the need to verify the status of various global transactions provided clear evidence of some of the practical difficulties caused by these seemingly academic concerns.

58 Doz, "Strategic Management in Multinational Companies"; Doz and Prahalad, "An Approach to Strategic Control in MNCs"; and, Prahalad and Doz, "Headquarters Influence and Strategic Control in MNCs." Bartlett and Ghoshal, *Managing Across Borders*, offers an insightful discussion of the problems of managing in the global environment of the 1990s.

59 See Lush, "'Bank-brokerage' deal proves costly winner."

60 Hout, Porter, and Rudden, "How Global Companies Win Out", argue that as businesses become global, the emphasis must shift to centralization. For financial services, this was and is true if the company seeks to intermediate between two different types of regions.

61 As does the theory of the MNB developed by Caves. See, e.g., "Discussion of Henry S. Terrell and S. Key" or *Multinational Enterprise and Economic Analysis*.

62 On this point, see Armour and Teece, "Organizational Structure and Economic Performance."

63 See Williamson, *Markets and Hierarchies*.

64 On this topic, see Stanbury, *Business-Government Relations in Canada*.

CHAPTER TWO

1 This section draws upon the fine scholarly work of Denison, *Canada's First Bank*.

2 It should be noted that relations between the two trading companies were not cordial.

3 Denison, *Canada's First Bank*, vol I, chap 3, offered an extensive critique of Breckenridge's work, who attributed significant Scottish influence during the early years of the bank.

4 Moffat served for only one year, but returned to the board in 1822 and served until 1835. Other founding directors were Austin Cuvillier (1817–25), F.W. Ermatinger (1817–26), John Forsyth (1817–20), George Garden (1817–26), John Gray (1817–21), James Leslie (1817–29), John McTavish (1817–18), George Moffat (1817–18), Hiram Nichols (1817–19), George

Platt (1817–18), Zabdiel Thayer (1817–18), and Thomas Turner (1817–18). See Denison, *Canada's First Bank*, vol. 2, Appendix B for a complete listing of directors of the bank from its founding until 1967.

5 The other employees were the cashier, Robert Griffin, the second teller, James Jackson, the accountant, Robert Dupuy, the discount clerk and future cashier, Benjamin Holmes, the second bookkeeper, Allan McDonnell, and the porter, Alexander McNiven.

6 Bank directors made frequent trips to New England to maintain these connections. Another indication of the importance of U.S. investors was that the currency of account was dollars, not pounds.

7 Denison, *Canada's First Bank*, vol. 1, chap. 4, believed that problems associated with the Second Bank of the United States led to the sale of Bank of Montreal shares by U.S. citizens. The bank's success in Canada meant that these shares were repatriated.

8 Gerard had violated the by-laws of the bank.

9 A more liquid portfolio would also provide lower yields.

10 Denison, vol. 2, 92 notes that this was the origin of important and unique pledge aspects of Canadian banking legislation.

11 The volatility of U.S. real estate has frequently posed problems for lenders. History does repeat itself.

12 Denison, *Canada's First Bank*, vol. 1, 160.

13 According to Denison, *Canada's First Bank*, vol. 2, 172, both branch and agency were the terms used in the minutes of the meetings that discussed the London venture.

14 King returned to manage the London branch in 1879, a position he held until 1888.

15 Denison made a most interesting case for the role of bankers in the orderly settling of the Canadian West in comparison to the U.S. West.

16 The new Act also required that bank mergers have the approval in writing of the minister of finance.

17 This was possible because the Glass-Steagall Act separating investment and commercial banking was not passed until 1933. On the history of U.S. regulation and important current issues, see Meerschwam, *Breaking Financial Boundaries* or Pierce, *The Future of Banking*.

18 Cited in Denison, *Canada's First Bank*, vol. 2, 355.

19 See the 119th (1936) Annual Report, 8 and 11, the 120th (1937) Annual Report, 8, and the 121st (1938) Annual Report, 12.

20 See 120th (1937) Annual Report, 11.

21 See Denison, *Canada's First Bank*, vol. 2, appendix B, for a list of the chairmen of the board. After Vincent's departure in 1929, there was no other chairman until Drummond, who held the position from 1942–6. There were only two chairmen between 1946 and 1959: B.C. Gardner

in 1952 from 1952 to 1954 and Arthur C. Jensen from 1959 to 1964.
G. Arnold Hart succeeded Jensen in 1964.

22 The 124th (1941) Annual Report reports that Mr. Spinney had been lent to the government to coordinate various programs.

23 One receives the strong impression that most of the new employees were women and considered temporary, since the staff in the military were essentially regarded as being on a leave of absence. The 128th (1945) Annual Report, 17 offers thanks to the temporary women employees. See also the 123rd (1940) and 129th (1946) Annual Reports.

24 See the 125th (1942) Annual Report.

25 The 130th (1947) Annual Report, 20.

26 The 134th (1951) Annual Report. A similar statement was made by Arthur C. Jensen in the 136th (1953) Annual Report: "The high level of foreign trade and the active interest in Canada shown by external capital has resulted in a full use of our services in connection with such business."

27 The 131st (1948) Annual Report, 26.

28 The 137th (1954) Annual Report, 24.

29 The 139th (1956) Annual Report, 30.

30 Ibid., 27.

31 The 143rd (1960) Annual Report, 16.

32 For example, Mulholland in the 144th (1961) Annual Report revealed a concern with controllable costs.

33 For example, the 142nd (1959) Annual report discussed how the drop in assets was related to improved clearing procedures.

34 The 143rd (1960) Annual Report, 26–7.

35 The 146th (1963) Annual Report, 28. A divisional office to supervise business in Quebec other than in Montreal was created.

36 Ibid., 19–21 and 29.

37 Ibid., 27.

38 The 143rd (1960) Annual Report, 29.

39 The 144th (1961) Annual Report, 30.

40 The 145th (1962) Annual Report, 28.

41 See the 147th (1964) Annual Report, 18. See also the 156th (1973) Annual Report with its discussion of the creation of six divisional board committees to increase decentralization.

42 The 149th (1966) Annual Report, 36.

43 The 152nd (1969) Annual Report, 39 and 16–17.

44 The 156th (1973) Annual Report, 14–15 discussed the success of Master Charge.

45 See the 149th (1966) Annual Report, 18

46 The 152nd (1969) Annual Report, 14.

47 The 147th (1964) Annual Report, 36, discussed trade promotion. The increase in loans was discussed in the following Annual Reports: 148th (1965), 28; 152nd (1969), 15; 156th (1973), 39; and 158th (1975), 4.

48 See the 154th (1971) Annual Report, 13–15.

49 The 158th (1975) Annual Report, 4.

50 The 153rd (1970) Annual Report, 14.

51 The 158th (1975) Annual Report, 9.

52 The 148th (1965) Annual Report, 19.

53 The 149th (1966) Annual Report, 17.

54 On decentralization, see the 147th (1964) Annual Report, 18; the 149th (1966), 22 and 35–7; and, the 152nd (1969), 16.

55 The 153rd (1970) Annual Report, 15.

56 The 148th (1966) Annual Report, 36–7.

57 The 150th (1967) Annual Report, 39.

58 The 151st (1968) Annual Report, 33.

59 The 165th (1982) Annual Report, 14.

60 The 162nd (1979) Annual Report, 5.

61 See for example the 165th (1982) Annual Report, 17. The sophistication and size of the bank's real-time computer system is a source of pride in virtually every annual report.

62 The 160th (1977) Annual Report, 21 reported an increase of 11.8 per cent in other operating revenue and the 161st (1978) Annual Report an increase of 19 per cent. In addition, the 164th (1981) Annual Report discussed the refinement of non-credit services, such as cash management, as cash generators.

63 The 159th (The 1976) Annual Report, 10.

64 Ibid., 12. See also the 162nd (1979) Annual Report, 16 and the 163rd (1980) Annual Report, 4.

65 See the 164th (1981) Annual Report, 24, where recent changes to the Bank Act were discussed.

66 The 162nd (1979) Annual Report, 7, stated that the bank was the only Canadian bank ranked among the top few in loan syndication.

67 The 159th (1976) Annual Report, 12.

68 See the 161st (1978) Annual Report, 17.

69 The 160th (1977) Annual Report, 14.

70 The 162nd (1979) Annual Report, 23.

71 The 159th (1976) Annual Report, 6.

72 The 162nd (1979) Annual Report, 4.

73 The 165th (1982) Annual Report, 5.

74 Brinco was a client of Mulholland's at Morgan Stanley. The company, which was responsible for building the billion dollar Churchill Falls project in Labrador, was hit with disaster when a plane carrying six key

executives crashed. Mulholland, who was a director of Brinco, stepped into the void left by the deaths of the senior executive team and became CEO and president of Brinco in 1970. The following month he became a director of the Bank of Montreal. After the Churchill Falls project was completed in 1974, Mr. Mulholland was elected president of the Bank of Montreal in 1975.

75 The 166th (The 1983) Annual Report, 3–4.

76 Ibid., 4. See also Horvitch, "Harris gives B of M competitive advantage," 12.

77 Ibid., 18.

78 Clearly this was the extreme. In practical terms, it meant getting as much business with each customer as possible. This recognized the marketing truism that it is far less costly to sell additional services to existing customers than to develop new customers.

79 The 168th (1985) Annual Report, 19.

80 The 167th (1984) Annual Report, 26.

81 See the 166th (1983) Annual Report, 30.

82 The 168th (1984) Annual Report discussed the bank's role as financial advisor to the Ministry of Water Resources and Electric Power of the People's Republic of China.

83 The 166th (1983) Annual Report, 14. As an intermediary, a bank must be as concerned with liability as asset management. See also ibid., 4.

84 Ibid. The mortgage company and the Brazilian subsidiary were separated as much for legal reasons as for any other.

85 The 1984 Annual Report, 36.

86 A bank must be familiar with innovations on capital markets in order to stay competitive. For example, the debt-to-equity conversion scheme proposed by Mulholland is discussed by Foster, "Mulholland proposes scheme to help Brazil's debt problem," B2; or, Mittelstaedt, "B of M to swap Brazilian debt for equity," B1.

87 Only 75 per cent of Nesbitt Thomson was acquired.

88 For example, see the discussion of integrating the functions of the International Banking Group with Treasury and Corporate and Government Banking in the 166th (1983) Annual Report, 12.

89 For example, see Mittelstaedt, "Resignations at Bank of Montreal fuel speculation about low morale," B5; or, Gordon, "B of M," 15. In the press coverage, there were also comments about Mulholland's tough management style as well as that he had been brought in "to shake the bank up" in the mid-1970s.

90 In the 171st (1987) Annual Report, 24, it was noted that Nesbitt had strength in the petroleum sector, too.

91 See the 169th (1986) Annual Report, 7.

92 See the 170th (1987) Annual Report, 20.

93 See "Third World exposure cases downgrading of B of M ratings," B5. This was a problem throughout the 1980s. Recently, Dominion Bond Rating Services lowered the ratings on the big three auto makers. In reporting the cuts, a spokesperson made the following remark, the downgrade is "the biggest cumulative single cut since the banks in 1982." See Milner, "DBRS slashes ratings of Big 3's finance arms," B1.

94 See the 170th (1987) Annual Report, 18.

95 Ibid., 14.

96 Ibid., 13.

97 Immediately prior to becoming president, he had been executive vice-president and group vice-president, personal banking. Before moving to personal banking, Barrett had been senior vice-president and deputy group executive, treasury group. Interestingly, F.A. Comper, the future president, was senior vice-president of treasury while Barrett was there and in 1987 was appointed executive vice-president, operations.

98 However, Barrett has discussed the importance of the Advanced Management Program at Harvard upon his development as a manager.

99 Chisholm, "The Youngest Chairman," 29.

100 See the 171st (1988) Annual Report, 9.

101 See Newman, "A survival strategy at the B of M" 40.

102 See McNish, "B of M unit sets stage for expansion," B1.

103 See 173rd (1990) Annual Report, 4. The video "Excellence: Making the Commitment" that unveiled the strategic plan to employees took a bronze medal at the 1990 International Film and TV Festival in New York.

104 Chisholm, "The Youngest Chairman," 29.

105 See Ip, "B of M – champion of cheaper money," 1.

106 See Milner, "B of M lowers rate on small-business loans," B9.

107 See Roseman, "Bank issues lower-rate card," B7.

108 McNish, "Bank of Montreal seeking its consumer roots," B1.

109 See Gibb-Clark, "B of M erasing barriers to women," B1, and the lead editorial, "Striving for equality at the banks," D6. It should be noted that Marnie Kingsley was head of the task force. To put the issue in context, it should be noted that the banks had been criticized by a coalition of women's groups. See Allen, "Banks criticized for lagging on job equity for women," A6. The bank has also worked to increase native hiring. See Heinrich, "Bank pledges native focus," 42.

110 See Whyte, "Nesbitt to retain separate identity," 21.

111 See Enchin, "Bank chases after big business," B18.

112 See Ip, "B of M has 24-hour currency trading," 5.

113 See McQueen, "Banking executive slams U.S. system," 6.

114 See the 173rd (1990) Annual Report, 8.

115 See Whyte, "B of M clears path into trust industry," 42.
116 See Crichtley and Gittins, "Off the Record," 40.
117 See *Financial Post*, "B of M board to meet in U.S.," 20, and *Financial Times*, "BMO's break with the horsy set," 2.
118 See, e.g., Barrett, "A new, revitalized Canada is not an impossible dream," 7, and the report of Barrett's speech at the 1991 annual meeting by Gibbon, "Ottawa advised to finance new jobs," A1. Not all parties were enamoured by the speeches. John McDermid, minister of state for finance, was clearly not impressed by a recent Barrett speech, see *Globe and Mail*, "Banker told to take own advice," B2.
119 Due to rounding, the area graphs sometimes do not always exactly total 100 per cent.
120 See Ip, "TD, Nat Bank down in ratings; B of M upgraded," 40.
121 Horvitch, "B of M the beloved of small business," 44.
122 For a more thorough examination of this topic see Darroch, "Strategic Management in Turbulent Environments," especially Appendix 1.

CHAPTER THREE

1 Schull and Gibson, *The Scotiabank Story*, 381.
2 The charter was based upon the charter granted to the Bank of New Brunswick in Saint John.
3 This is, of course, typical of service organizations and applies to banks insofar as the strategy is one of replication. See Carman and Langeard, "Growth Strategies for Service Firms."
4 Schull and Gibson, *The Scotiabank Story*, 60.
5 The bank announced it was open for business and was ready to negotiate loans, handle foreign exchange, and make collections "in all parts of Canada on the most favourable terms." See Galles, "The Bank of Nova Scotia in Minneapolis, 1885–1892."
6 There was also a fear that the tax situation in Minnesota would change. The bank had had an informal agreement that it was taxed only on capital employed in Minnesota, but there were rumours that a tax would be levied on total capital.
7 Schull and Gibson, *The Scotiabank Story*, 70.
8 Neufeld, *The Canadian Financial System*, 99. The Big Nine are the Bank of Montreal, the Royal Bank of Canada, the Canadian Bank of Commerce, the Imperial Bank of Canada, the Bank of Nova Scotia, the Bank of Toronto, the Dominion Bank, La Banque Provinciale du Canada and La Banque Canadienne Nationale.
9 Prior to 1898, the operating head of the bank held the title "cashier." In 1898, the title was changed to "general manager." The Toronto office had been opened in 1897.

10 C.A. Kennedy, the manager in Winnipeg, had called on the client of the Merchants Bank of Canada, but the importance of the incident seems to have been exaggerated by the CBA. See Schull and Gibson, *The Scotiabank Story*, 84–7.

11 See Neufeld, *The Canadian Financial System*, 99.

12 The three largest banks were the Bank of Montreal, the Royal Bank of Canada, and the Canadian Bank of Commerce. This is, of course, consistent with oligopoly theories of international banking, which suggests that banks from the same countries will have congruent networks. However, it should be borne in mind that it would be virtually impossible to be an international bank and not be represented in London at that time and later in New York.

13 See also Schull and Gibson *The Scotiabank Story*, 206–10 and the discussion in the 128th (1959) Annual Report, 19.

14 See the 109th (1940) Annual Report, 17 and the 127th (1957) Annual Report.

15 See the 116th (1947) Annual Report, 26.

16 See the 127th (1958) Annual Report, 22.

17 See the 129th (1960) Annual Report, 3.

18 There is a discussion of this product in the 127th (1958) Annual Report, 22.

19 See the 126th (1957) Annual Report, 19–20.

20 See the 117th (1948) Annual Report, 22–3.

21 In real terms the growth was 10.5 per cent foreign and 7.5 per cent domestic.

22 The 131st (1962) Annual Report, 18.

23 Of course, there were potential dangers, as was made evident by U.S. President Johnson's guidelines of February 1965 concerning capital flows. Suddenly, the bank found its U.S. clients were discouraged from maintaining large deposits with the bank. See the 134th (1965) Annual Report, 14. The Euromarkets still offered a viable source of U.S. dollars.

24 The increasing sophistication of the corporate treasurers was an important force driving product innovation as the 134th (1965) Annual Report, 15 makes clear.

25 See the 133rd (1964) Annual Report, 7.

26 This was an interesting move in light of later concerns with disintermediation.

27 See the 133rd (1964) Annual Report, 16.

28 Discussion of the computer first takes place in the 133rd (1964) Annual Report.

29 Bankers essentially view the reserve requirements imposed by federal regulation as a tax. There is nothing like an unfair tax to affect competition and infuriate people.

30 The 134th (1965) Annual Report, 11.

31 Seven of these were in the Caribbean, one in Belfast, one in Edinburgh and two in Greece. See the 138th (1969) Annual Report, 19. As before, the bank was prepared to close foreign offices, as was revealed by the 140th (1971) Annual Report.

32 See the 140th (1971) Annual Report, 18.

33 The 139th (1970) Annual Report, 18–19 reveals the following connections: a 30 per cent equity position in Maduro & Curiels, West India Merchant Bankers Ltd, Bank Mees and Hope of Holland, and participation in Unibank with eight other banks. Joint ventures could be attractive when the bank lacked expertise or for regulatory reasons.

34 The 139th (1970) Annual Report made clear the extent of decentralization – only 1 per cent by number of commercial credits required head office approval.

35 See the 140th (1971) Annual Report, 17.

36 There was a change-over to a third generation Honeywell computer in 1969 as well as the installation of some on-line terminals in branches and the transfer of the data-processing facility from head office to Don Mills. See the 138th (1969) Annual Report, 19–20.

37 The 136th (1967) Annual Report contains an interesting discussion of changes in international banking. There was more attention being paid to term structure because there was a shift to longer term lending and term deposits as banks increased intermediary services.

38 See the 137th (1968) Annual Report, 15.

39 One reason for the closing of foreign branches could have been the increasing integration of foreign capital markets that made it not only practical but desirable to limit the degree of decentralization as market forces demanding decentralization decreased.

40 See the 137th (1968) Annual Report, 19 and the 139th (1970) Annual Report, 16.

41 See the 139th (1970) Annual Report, 18. Given that much of the operation in Jamaica would be retail, it would be easier to separate this operation than some offices that would be more closely integrated with global operations.

42 The 140th (1971) Annual Report, 18.

43 See the 136th (1967) Annual Report, 12. Stronger complaints concerning the unfair advantages of near banks in consumer lending were voiced in the 138th (1969) Annual Report, 16.

44 Whether this was because Canadian policy combined with reciprocity clauses in other countries was limiting the scope of the bank's international operations, or it preferred to have competition with foreign agencies in the open, since it was not difficult for a Canadian firm to deal with a New York or other international bank anyway. Given the

changes in the market, new regulation could serve to level the playing field.

45 See the 137th (1968) Annual Report, 10–11. There is an interesting discussion of parliamentary reform on page 8. In the previous year, the 136th (1967) report, there was mention of the hard work but not altogether satisfactory results of the government.

46 The 139th (1970) Annual Report, 19.

47 See especially the 137th (1968) Annual Report, 10–11 and the 140th (1971) Annual Report, 7.

48 See the 141st (1972) Annual Report, 14 and the 1979 Annual Report, 13.

49 See the 141st (1972) Annual Report, 12.

50 Ibid. McQueen, "Scotiabank Comes Out of the Shadow," discussed how a similar strategy was employed in ABMS.

51 Attention to liability management was developed in international and in 1979 was extended to domestic. See the 1979 Annual Report, 13.

52 The 1973 Annual Report, 23 had a section stressing the importance of education and expanding the role of women for the future. The 1979 Annual Report, 7, reported that women were becoming more prominent.

53 The 1979 Annual Report, 5.

54 See the 1977 Annual Report, 3 where it was asserted that the international scene was not as bad as some said. At the same time, the u.s. market was not without its dangers as problems in REITS showed, 1977 Annual Report, 23.

55 See the 1974 Annual Report, 19; 1975 Annual Report, 10; 1977 Annual Report, 11; 1978 Annual Report, 21; and, 1979 Annual Report, 16. The 1973 Annual Report, 20 noted that roughly 50 per cent of foreign liabilities came from the u.s. wholesale market.

56 The 1979 Annual Report, 18.

57 The 1980 Annual Report, 19.

58 The 141st (1972) Annual Report, 14 and 21. See also, the 1973 Annual Report, 4, and the 1978 Annual Report, 7.

59 For example, see the 1973 Annual Report, 7.

60 The 1973 Annual Report, 22–3.

61 Scotiabank acted as an intermediary and offered a variety of deposit and related activities to central banks and investors. The scope of activities can be seen by the fact that the bank purchased 65 per cent of total Canadian gold production.

62 This is not to suggest that one partner exploits the other. Rather, a partnership may be mutually beneficial but would not be expected to be permanent.

63 The 1974 Annual Report, 11.

64 The 1974 Annual Report discussed a consolidated cash plan for Canadian firms. Essentially, this allowed the firm to net balances across Canada. While the complexities of doing this internationally were significant, it was still an extension of the basic hardware and software in principal.

65 The 1975 Annual Report, 15.

66 The 1978 Annual Report, 4.

67 See the discussion of new products for small business and strong denials that the bank favoured large clients in the 1973 Annual Report, 18–21.

68 the 141st (1972) Annual Report, 12.

69 See the 1974 Annual Report, 15 and the 1977 Annual Report, 15–16.

70 The 141st Annual Report, 14.

71 See the 1973 Annual Report, 22–3 and the 1976 Annual Report, 5–6.

72 The 1978 Annual Report, 9.

73 See the 1979 Annual Report, 6. It was noted that since that time the bank had become more aggressive in seeking out new opportunities.

74 The 1981 Annual Report, 8.

75 The details of the changes made it easier to tap into international capital markets that would also be of importance to the bank given its international orientation.

76 Presumably one could compete domestically, but the price of upsetting the orderly Canadian financial markets might have been too high.

77 The 1988 Annual Report, 6.

78 The 1990 Annual Report, 11.

79 Howlett, "Scotiabank to set up trust unit," B7.

80 Emphasis added, 1989 Annual Report, 5. In the essay, "Canadian Banks: A National Asset," included in the 1988 Annual Report, it was pointed out that seven of the ten largest auto leasing firms were foreign owned.

81 The 1991 Annual Report, 11.

82 The 1989 Annual Report, 12.

83 See the 1985 Annual Report, 1.

84 See the 1986 Annual Report, 12–13.

85 The 1989 Annual Report, 15.

86 The 1986 Annual Report, 10.

87 The 1985 Annual Report, 15.

88 The 1987 Annual Report, 11 and the 1990 Annual Report, 19.

89 Galt, Lush, Robinson and Slocum, "Power plays opened securities industry," B1.

90 The 1987 Annual Report, 11.

91 The 1989 Annual Report, 18.

92 The 1987 Annual Report, 4.

93 The 1987 Annual Report, 15.

94 The 1986 Annual Report, 13; and the 1987 Annual Report, 14.

95 The 1988 Annual Report, 19.
96 The 1990 Annual Report, 5.
97 The 1991 Annual Report, 5.
98 See Whyte, "Scotiabank's Ritchie wins over the critics," 8.
99 The 1987 Annual Report, 24.
100 Due to rounding, the area graphs sometimes do not always exactly total 100 per cent.
101 See the discussion in the 1991 Annual Report, 4.
102 The transition is not complete as at the request of the board, Mr. Ritchie will remain chairman of both the board and the executive committee for at least one more year.

CHAPTER FOUR

1 This chapter draws heavily upon Ince, *The Royal Bank of Canada*.
2 The 76th (1945) Annual Report, 9.
3 This, unfortunately includes myself: see Darroch, "Strategic Management in Turbulent Environments." Turbulence created difficulties for researchers as well as bankers.
4 See chapter five: The Canadian Imperial Bank of Commerce, "William McMaster and the Founding of the CIBC: 1867–70".
5 Kinnear's short tenure was the result of his extensive business dealings. He simply lacked the time to oversee the bank. Kenny had the novel view for the time that the president should be at the bank full time, but as Ince notes, this did not happen until the tenure of M. W. Wilson (1934–46).
6 The branch was closed in 1889.
7 Ince, *The Royal Bank of Canada*, 11, holds that the agency was the first real break from being a provincial bank.
8 On benefit packages, see ibid., 13.
9 See ibid., appendix 5.
10 The West was studied prior to this expansion by C.A. Crosbie, the supervisor of Vancouver. Representation in the Yukon and Northwest Territories did not begin until 1948.
11 Later the bank was acquired by the Commerce. See chapter five: The Canadian Imperial Bank of Commerce, "Sir Edmund Walker: 1907–24".
12 The move was surprising because of Neil's position, which was relatively junior.
13 Towers was succeeded by E.C. Common and O'Halloran of the Foreign Trade department until 1925 when the publication was placed under the editorship of the newly hired economist, Dr. D.M. Marvin (1925–38), then under his successor, F.J. Hornung (1938–42) and then under the bank's librarian, Miss M. Turnbull for one year, 1942. At that time it

was decided to appeal to broader interests and John R. Heron, Public Relations Adviser, took charge.

14 From 1869–1905, the dividend rate fluctuated between 6 per cent and 8 per cent. By 1911, the rate had climbed to 12 per cent. Throughout the 1920s, there was a 2 per cent bonus. By 1934, the rate fell to 8 per cent and remained there until 1942 when it fell to 7.5 per cent and then 6 per cent the following year, where it remained until the end of the war when an upward trend could be seen.

15 Branch rationalization was done in cooperation with other banks, as discussed earlier. An interesting aspect of the cooperative-competitive stance of the Canadian banks vis-à-vis one another was revealed in these years. All had an interest in maintaining an industry with the reputation for stability.

16 See the 65th (1934) Annual Report, 6 and the 66th (1935) Annual Report, 7.

17 The new spirit of cooperation shown in the rationalization of the branch system which may have lessened the need for non-price competition.

18 On the CBA, see the 69th (1938) Annual Report, 6–7. The association issued 11 articles on banking hoping to explain the role of the chartered banks and the Bank of Canada. The basic argument was that the Bank of Canada, not the chartered banks, was responsible for controlling credit operations.

19 The loss of note-issuing privileges was further justification for rationalization of the branch system, see the 65th (1934) Annual Report, 6.

20 For example, see ibid., 6–8.

21 See the 68th (1937) Annual Report, 10.

22 "Again" since labour unrest in the 1920s, exemplified by the Winnipeg General Strike, had led to similar attacks. In the 74th (1943) Annual Report, 7–9, Wilson discussed proposals to nationalize the banks and argued that even New Zealand, a socialist model, had private banking.

23 See the 74th (1943) Annual Report, 9.

24 See the 71st (1940) Annual Report, 7.

25 See the 70th (1939) Annual Report, 9. Interestingly, mention of tourism goes back as far as the 67th (1936) Annual Report.

26 For example, see the 71st (1940) Annual Report, 6, or the 76th (1945) Annual Report, 7.

27 The 76th (1945) Annual Report, 9.

28 See the 81st (1950) Annual Report, 18–19.

29 See the 86th (1955) Annual Report, inside front cover, and 24.

30 The 82nd (1951) Annual Report, 25.

31 The 79th (1948) Annual Report, 19, discussed how head office officials travelled in order to develop and to maintain personal contacts in foreign markets.

32 This was ongoing theme following the discussion in the 85th (1954) Annual Report, 20ff.

33 See the 77th (1946) Annual Report, 10.

34 See the 77th (1946) Annual Report, 8.

35 See the 82nd (1951) Annual Report, 20, the 85th (1954) Annual Report, 17, and the 90th (1959) Annual Report, 14–15.

36 For example, see the 81st (1950) Annual Report, 22–3.

37 The 1967 Annual Report, 29.

38 See the 91st (1960) Annual Report, 19.

39 See the 92nd (1961) Annual Report, 17.

40 See the 97th (1966) Annual Report, 24.

41 The 97th (1966) Annual Report, 22.

42 The 1972 Annual Report, 18.

43 See the 97th (1966) Annual Report, 15ff.

44 See the 1978 Annual Report, 17. It should be noted that "largest and most complex organizations" could, and most likely would, include government clients.

45 Ibid.

46 Ibid.

47 See the 1979 Annual Report, 31, 33.

48 See the 1980 Annual Report, 9.

49 The 1980 Annual Report, 9.

50 See the 1983 Annual Report, 23.

51 The 1983 Annual Report, 2–3.

52 Ibid., 3.

53 For example, see the discussion in Gordon, "Feisty Orion tries to get back on track," 19, or Gooding, "Royal Bank seeks stellar role for Orion," 1.

54 See the 1985 Annual Report, 20 and the 1986 Annual Report, 26.

55 See the discussion of the financing of the AMC plant in Brampton in the 1984 Annual Report, 24.

56 See the 1986 Annual Report, 24.

57 See the 1985 Annual Report, 25–30.

58 See the 1983 Annual Report, 27.

59 The 1986 Annual Report, 23.

60 Ibid., 4.

61 Ibid., 1–2.

62 The 1991 Annual Report, 10.

63 The 1989 Annual Report, 7 and the 1991 Annual Report, 11.

64 The 1989 Annual Report, 25.

65 The 1989 Annual Report, 11.

66 The 1991 Annual Report, 10.

67 The 1990 Annual Report, 11.

68 The 1987 Annual Report, 14.
69 The 1989 Annual Report, 9, 11.
70 1990 Annual Report, 19.
71 See Horvitch,"'High noon' at the Royal Bank," 1.
72 The 1987 Annual Report, 18–19.
73 To understand the customer side, see Hageman, "Should Your Company Be a 'Corporate Bank'?" 4.
74 The 1991 Annual Report, 16. See also the 1987 Annual Report, 20.
75 The 1990 Annual Report, 3 and the 1991 Annual Report, 3.
76 The 1989 Annual Report, 22.
77 The 1990 Annual Report, 14.
78 The 1991 Annual Report, 16.
79 The 1987 Annual Report, 20.
80 The 1989 Annual Report, 15.
81 The 1990 Annual Report, 18.
82 See, e.g., Taylor, "Business, Politics and Politicians."
83 Due to rounding, the area graphs sometimes do not always exactly total 100 per cent.
84 Changed treatment for loan-loss provisions was responsible for Figure 4.6 showing more than 100 per cent as the loan-loss provisions are deducted from the overall portfolio. LDCs account for most of the problem.

CHAPTER FIVE

1 This chapter draws heavily upon Ross, *A History of the Canadian Bank of Commerce* and St L. Trigge, *A History of the Canadian Bank of Commerce with an account of the other banks*.
2 For those who find this an odd concept, follow the problems of Lloyd's of London and the role played by "names" who guarantee that Lloyds will be able to meet any insurance claims.
3 See Ross, *A History of the Canadian Bank of Commerce*, vol. 2, 21. Given a knowledge of later history, it is interesting to note the early complaints of "western" Canada. Perhaps as long as there is a lag between the development of commerce and financial institutions, such complaints are an inevitable feature of economic life.
3 Cited in Ross, *A History of the Canadian Bank of Commerce*, vol. 2, 21.
4 See ibid., vol. 2, 54.
5 For a history of the Gore Bank, see ibid., vol. 1, chap 4.
6 Readers familiar with the current U.S. scene may find comparisons interesting.
7 The London and County Bank was not receptive. A previous deal negotiated with the Union Bank would have been acceptable but was rejected by the Union Bank at the last minute. E.H. King may have played a role

here. See Ross, *A History of the Canadian Bank of Commerce*, vol. 2, 60.

8 The Royal is the best example for this line of argument.

9 The branch was closed in 1886.

10 Focus upon educational efforts by Canadian bankers is one of the key reasons for their international competitiveness. See Darroch and Litvak, "Diamonds and Money."

11 This was closed in 1900 because of changes in the tax laws and the business was transferred to the Commercial National Bank of New Orleans. The relationship between regulation and the economic viability of a branch should never be forgotten.

12 See Ross, *A History of the Canadian Bank of Commerce*, vol. 2, 122.

13 Ibid., Chap 3, "The Yukon Adventure," and Chap 5, "The Romance of Banking," provide interesting reading on the human side of banking.

14 Denison, *Canada's First Bank*, made a similar point.

15 A major promoter of Western expansion in the early 1900s was Sir John Aird, a future president. When Aird was manager of the Winnipeg branch, he made forceful presentations to the board concerning opportunities in the West.

16 On the very interesting development of British international banking, see the works by Geoffrey Jones in the bibliography. Of particular interest was the lack of links between domestic and international operations. The historic separation of the two has had important implications for British bank mergers, even in the 1990s.

17 This early recognition of potential liabilities should be heeded by bankers in these early days of expanding financial services.

18 In 1909, another product was added – safety-deposit boxes.

19 Interestingly, in many ways this is the problem facing account managers now.

20 Later, bonuses for study as well as recreation rooms were added for the staff in order to improve working conditions.

21 See St L. Trigge, *A History of the Canadian Bank of Commerce*, 35.

22 Given the general unrest following the war, attacks on the banks were no surprise.

23 See the 67th (1933) Annual Report, 14. The report discusses the joint actions taken by the bank and its rivals, but does not discuss how the decisions came to be, nor if the CBA was involved.

24 See St L. Trigge, *A History of the Canadian Bank of Commerce with an account of the other banks*, 158; 63rd Annual Report, 17–18; 70th Annual Report, 16.

25 See St L. Trigge, *A History of the Canadian Bank of Commerce with an account of the other banks*, 177–8.

26 See the 70th (1936) Annual Report, 18. It is noted that construction is unusually low. I cannot account for the missing 9 per cent.

27 The 70th (1936) Annual Report, 17.

28 Times change, as any reader following the problems caused by protection of agricultural sectors for current trade negotiations will know.

29 See the 69th (1935) Annual Report, 34.

30 See the 78th (1944) Annual Report, 16.

31 See the 83rd (1949) Annual Report and the 87th (1953) Annual Report.

32 See the 98th (1964) Annual Report.

33 For example, see 105th (1971) Annual Report, 9–10.

34 See the 97th (1963) Annual Report.

35 96th (1962) Annual Report, 15.

36 The CIBC has maintained an excellent reputation in this area. Today, Donald J. Worth, vice-president, mining specialist group is highly respected by the mining industry.

37 See the 97th (1963) Annual Report, 27ff.

38 MacIntosh, *Different Drummer*, 122–3.

39 For example, the 112th (1978) Annual Report, 11, discussed how companies were turning to the Euromarkets. This is a variant of the follower hypothesis that should be recognized.

40 See ibid., 11.

41 See the 110th (1976) Annual Report, 10 and the 112th (1978) Annual Report, 11.

42 See the 108th (1974) Annual Report, 18.

43 See ibid., 11.

44 See Wong, "Heir Today, Gone Tomorrow," B1. The story reported that ties between Harrison and Fullerton were never that close and that Harrison's reluctance to give up control over day to day operations was one source of the CIBC's problems.

45 The 1983 Annual Report, 9–10.

46 See ibid., 11ff.

47 The 1986 Annual Report, 13.

48 Ibid., 17.

49 Ibid., 21.

50 Horvitch made the interesting observation that the new structure also freed Fullerton from appointing a successor. The structure allowed the further testing of internal candidates.

51 The 1986 Annual Report, 25.

52 See the 1984 Annual Report, 3.

53 See the 1986 Annual Report, 5.

54 See the 1987 Annual Report, 7–8.

55 The 1990 Annual Report, 6. Association with Bell's Alex system may have limited market penetration.

56 See the 1990 Annual Report, 12.

57 The 1987 Annual Report, 4.

58 See ibid., 4.

59 CIBC was the first Canadian investment dealer to receive a license in Japan. See the 1990 Annual Report, 13.

60 Bruck, *The Predators' Ball* provides an excellent discussion of the changing role of ownership in financial services institutions as the phrase British phrase "merchant banking" became popular in New York and Beverly Hills.

61 There were 78 in Canada, 11 in the United States, 6 in Europe, 4 in Asia, 3 in Australia, and 2 in Latin America.

62 See the 1986 Annual Report, 21.

63 The 1989 Annual Report, 4–5.

64 The 1991 Annual Report, 11.

65 The 1987 Annual Report, 16

66 See Fullerton, "Changing a Bank."

67 Howlett and Milner, "CIBC chief changing 'country club' system," B1.

68 Occasionally problems and negative publicity were created. See, e.g., Gibb-Clark, "CIBC's behaviour in firing 'inexcusable'," B8.

69 Flood is not completely clear of the Olympia and York problem. See Jorgenson, "Street Talk," B6. See also Kilpatrick, "Help Wanted," 18–19.

70 Due to rounding, the area graphs sometimes do not always exactly total 100 per cent.

71 The numbers do not total 100 because the bank uses a global adjustment figure to update the date from 30 September to 31 October.

72 See, for example, Reguly, "CIBC seeks healthy U.S. investment," 5 and Whyte, "CIBC says Mexico venture possible," 3.

73 A position paper entitled "The Constitutional Debate: A Straight Talking Guide for Canadians" was circulated with newspapers.

CHAPTER SIX

1 For example, see Davis, *Excellence in Banking*.

2 The TD is excluded as it did not acquire an investment bank. However, while the TD has long been highly regarded, other Canadian banks have been improving the manner in which they are perceived in international markets.

3 See Ip, "Banks stocking up on liquid assets," 3.

4 Ryval, "'Hard times' means special lending rates," B6.

5 There is an important tension between regulation and competitiveness. Public policy and regulation can be a source of competitive advantage or can damage competitiveness depending upon market conditions and market perceptions. Given the importance of the issue, it is imperative that regulated industries work with public policy-makers to secure regulation appropriate to their market environment.

6 In this context, the relative decline of the retail investor in Canadian stock markets should be noted.

7 See Critchley, "Off the Record," 5.

8 From the perspective of the percentage composition of their asset portfolio.

9 These changes pose important issues for regulators. See, e.g., Courchene, "Grappling with Mobility."

10 On this topic, see the insightful work of Steiner and Teixeira, *Technology in Banking*. I am grateful to Tom Steiner for his help in understanding this area.

11 See Darroch, "Stability as Virtue," and "Strategic Management in Turbulent Environments"; Darroch and Litvak, "Canadian Banks," and "Strategies for Canada's New North American Banks"; and, Farnsworth, "Canada's mighty banks on a march to the south," A6.

12 *The Economist*, "Foreign banks in America," 86.

13 See Siklos, "Banks at low risk in Eastern Europe," 6.

14 The TD was named one of the excellent banks in the world by an independent panel of experts. See Davis, *Excellence in Banking*.

15 Terry, "T-D Bank a surprise in Japan," B1.

16 I write this with trepidation as the future has the habit of making fools of forecasters, but so be it. See e.g., Farnsworth, "Canada's mighty banks on a march to the south," A6.

17 In fact, rates on credit cards were often cited as being too high while there were concerns over the rates that seniors could receive for their deposits. Commentators typically focused on the gaps between the two different prices but pay little attention to the costs incurred. This has been an ongoing source of concern for the banks.

18 See Darroch, "Strategic Management in Turbulent Environments" where correlations between movements in key borrowing rates and net interest margins of the banks revealed basic differences between Scotiabank and the others.

19 Superior credit rankings have been and continue to be a source of competitive advantage to Canadian banks, especially in the United States. See Darroch, "Stability as Virtue," and "Leaders of the Pack," and "Horses for Courses."

20 See *Financial Post*, "Bank Service charges jump," 4.

21 See Whyte, "Big Six eye U.S. credit card market," 6.

22 McKenzie, "Shopping around can trim outrageous bank charges," 23.

23 On a balance of $1,001, the National Bank, which is not part of this study, was actually lower than the CIBC.

CHAPTER SEVEN

1 See Pierce, *The Future of Banking*, for analysis of similar issues in the United States.

2 In this context it is interesting to consider the role played by financial services institutions in the large Japanese trading houses.

3 For a short history of the Act, see appendix 2. See also, Capes and Raynor, *Orientation to Banking*, 54–63.

4 Cline, "'Reciprocity,'" provided important insights into this topic.

5 This is interesting in light of current discussion of Canadian competitiveness. See Darroch and Litvak, "Diamonds and Money."

6 This important lesson was forgotten when the small Western banks were created. The Estey Commission demonstrated that despite significant economic changes, the early vision of Canadian branch banking was correct.

7 For example, see the 1982 parliamentary investigation into bank profits.

8 Gray and Gray, "The Multinational Bank: A Financial MNC?"

9 Grubel, "The New International Banking."

10 Goodman, "Bank Lending to Non-Opec LDCs," Khoury, *Dynamics of International Banking*, and Rugman, *International Diversification and Multinational Enterprise*, or Rugman and Kamath, "International Diversification and Multinational Banking."

11 Dean and Giddy, "Strangers and Neighbours."

12 Nagy, *The International Business of Canadian Banks*, 31 and 35. While this is an imperfect measure, it does serve to indicate the international orientation of the Canadian banks relative to others. The share now would be considerably less.

13 See Franko, "Global Corporate Competition."

14 The movement to a single centre is not unique to Canada. See the Economist, "A Survey of Financial Centres."

15 On this topic see Walter, *Barriers to Trade in Banking and Financial Services*.

16 Caves, "Discussion of "Henry S. Terrell and S. Key, 'The U.S. Activities of Foreign Banks.'"

17 A more extended discussion of the regulatory complexities can be found in Darroch and Litvak, "Gaps, Overlaps and Competition among Jurisdictions."

18 See Kelly, "Major financial reforms looming."

19 Pierce, *The Future of Banking*, provides an interesting commentary on problems created by trying to prevent the failure of small institutions.

APPENDIX ONE

1 See Chandler, *Strategy and Structure* and *The Visible Hand*. Williamson, "The Modern Corporation" has already demonstrated how the work of business historians such as Chandler can be fruitfully married to industrial organization. More recently, Tschoegl, "International Retail Banking as a Strategy," 70, remarked:

In this paper we cite historical and anecdotal evidence in addition to more "scientific" evidence. We do this for three reasons. One is that "scientific" evidence is often unavailable; the examples make the arguments concrete and establish their plausibility. Obviously examples lack generalizeability; the samples are small and not random. Nevertheless, such evidence is appropriate to an exercise in economic rhetoric (McCloskey 1983). Our second reason is that we are interested in understanding the behaviour of unique firms, with individual names and histories, which find themselves in unique circumstances. We therefore combine the generality of theory with the richness of cases. Our third reason for citing history is to draw attention to some fascinating firm histories and descriptions of banking systems.

An appreciation of the uniqueness of each firm is a prerequisite for understanding its strategy.

2 See Scotton, "Royal and B of M reports judged best in the world," 27.

3 See Mintzberg and Waters, "Tracking Strategy in an Entrepreneurial Firm," "Researching the Formation of Strategies," and "Of Strategies, Deliberate and Emergent."

4 More formally the principle is "in any class of non-contradictory formulae there are undecidable propositions." The result is the incompleteness of any formal logical system. See Kneale and Kneale, *The Development of Logic*, for a good discussion of Godel's place in the history of logic.

5 Serious limitations in explanatory power of theories can arise from theory dependency. For example, some critics in discussions of Kuhn, *The Structure of Scientific Revolutions*, have asserted that under certain conditions the dominance of the generally accepted paradigm could preclude statements of nonconforming events being uttered. This raises interesting problems as to when the new paradigm starts to surface. It would seem that paradigms, much as natural language, allow for change by not limiting themselves to purely denotative structures that would limit connotative richness. For a seminal study on counter-factuals, see Goodman, *Fact, Fiction, and Forecast*, especially 3–27.

APPENDIX TWO

1 This appendix draws upon chap. 3, "The Bank of Canada and The Bank Act," in Capes and Raynor, *Orientation to Banking*; Ince, *The Royal Bank of Canada*; and MacIntosh, *Different Drummers*. MacIntosh provides a fascinating account of the relationship between banking and politics in Canada.

2 See MacIntosh, *Different Drummers*, 181–8.

Bibliography

"A New Awakening: A Survey of International Banking." *Economist*, 24–30 March 1984.

"A Survey of Financial Centres: Can the Centre Hold?" *Economist*, 27 June 1992.

Adams, Nigel. "The Gloom That Envelopes Canadian Banks." *Euromoney*. September 1982.

– "Philadelphia: The Teenagers of International Banking." *Euromoney*. August 1983.

Aharoni, Yair. *The Foreign Investment Decision*. Boston: Harvard University Press, 1966.

Aliber, Robert Z. "International Banking: Growth and Regulation." *Columbia Journal of World Business*. Winter 1975.

– "Toward a Theory of International Banking." *Economic Review of the Federal Reserve Bank of San Francisco*. Spring 1976.

– *The International Money Game*. 3d ed. New York: Basic Books, 1979.

– "The Integration of the Off-Shore and Domestic Banking System." *Journal of Monetary Economics* 6 (1980).

Allen, Gene. "Banks criticized for lagging on job equity for women." *Globe and Mail*, 26 September 1991.

Amano, A. "Specific Factors, Comparative Advantage and International Investment." *Economica* 44 (1977).

Anderson, Erin, and Hubert Gatignon. "Modes of Foreign Entry: A Transaction Cost Analysis and Propositions." *Journal of International Business Studies*. Fall 1986.

Armour, H.O., and David J. Teece, "Organizational Structure and Economic Performance: A Test of the Multidivisional Hypothesis." *Bell Journal of Economics* 9 (1978).

Baer, Herbert, and Elizabeth Pongracic. "The Development of Banking Structure in Five Countries." Unpublished paper. Federal Reserve Bank of Chicago, 1984.

Bailey, Elizabeth E., and Ann F. Friedlander. "Market Structure and Multi-product Industries." *Journal of Economic Literature* 20 (September 1982).

Baker, James C., and M. Gerald Bradford. *American Banks Abroad, Edge Act Companies and Multinational Banking*. New York: Praeger, 1974.

Ballarin, Eduardo. *Commercial Banks Amid the Financial Revolution: Developing a Competitive Strategy*. Cambridge, MA: Ballinger, 1986.

Barrett, Matthew. "A new, revitalized Canada is not an impossible dream." *Financial Post*, 20 May 1992.

Bartlett, Christopher, and Sumantra Ghoshal. *Managing Across Borders: The Transnational Solution*. Boston, Mass.: Harvard Business School Press, 1989.

Baum, Daniel Jay. *The Banks of Canada in the Commonwealth Caribbean: Economic Nationalism and Multinational Enterprises of a Medium Power*. New York: Praeger, 1974.

Beck, Stanley M. "The Revolution in Financial Services," Speech to the Empire Club of Canada, 20 February 1986.

Bhattacharya, Anindaya. "Offshore Banking in the Caribbean by U.S. Commercial Banks: Implications for Government Business Interaction." *Journal of International Business Studies*. Winter 1980.

Binhammer, H.H. *Money, Banking and the Canadian Financial System*. 4th ed. Toronto: Methuen, 1982.

Blanden, M. "Why Banks Choose to Work Together." *The Banker*. March 1981.

Bleeke, Joel A., and Lowell L. Bryan. "The Globalization of Financial Markets." *McKinsey Quarterly*. Winter 1988.

Bleeke, Joel A., and Brian A. Johnson. "How to Survive in the Age of the Global Investor." *McKinsey Quarterly*. Summer 1988.

Bloch, Henry S. "Foreign Risk Judgment for Commercial Banks." *Bankers Magazine*. Autumn 1977.

Blount, Edmon W. "New Directions in the Financial Services Industry." *Journal of Business Strategy* 2 (Spring 1982).

Boddewyn, J.J., Marsha Baldwin Halbrich, and A. C. Perry. "Service Multinationals: Conceptualization, Measurement and Theory." *Journal of International Business Studies*. Fall 1986.

Brecher, Charles, and Vladimir Pucik. "Foreign Banks in the U.S. Economy: The Japanese Example." *Columbia Journal of World Business*. Spring 1980.

Bronte, S. "Japanese International Finance: The Dilemma of Japan's City Banks." *Euromoney*. September 1979.

Brown, Hugh M. "Canadian Chartered Banks – Where Do We Go From Here?" Investment Report. Toronto, Burns Fry Ltd., 11 April 1983.

– "Updated Outlook for Chartered Bank Earnings. Are Canadian Banks Undercapitalized?" Investment Report. Toronto, Burns Fry Ltd., 25 July 1983.

Brucker, Eric. "A Microeconomic Approach to Banking Competition." *Journal of Finance* 25 (1970).

Bryan, Lowell L. "Breaking Up the Bank." *McKinsey Quarterly*. Summer 1988.

– *Bankrupt: Restoring the Health and Profitability of Our Banking System.* Toronto: HarperCollins Books, 1991.

Bryan, Lowell L., and Paul Allen. "Geographic Strategies for the 1990s." *McKinsey Quarterly.* Winter 1988.

Buckley, P.J., and Mark Casson. *The Future of the Multinational Enterprise.* London: Macmillan, 1976.

– *The Economic Theory of the Multinational Enterprise.* New York: St. Martin's Press, 1985.

Canadian Bankers' Association. "Corporate Concentration in the Financial Services Sector." Briefing Paper. October 1986.

– "Regulating 'Networking': A Proposed Approach." Briefing Paper. May 1988.

Canadian Life and Health Insurance Association Inc. "Where We Stand on the Legislative Reform of Canada's Financial Services Sector." Briefing Paper. February 1989.

– "The Position of Canada's Life and Health Insurance Industry on National Treatment for International Trade in Insurance and Financial Services." Briefing Paper submitted to the OECD, 27 October 1989.

– Capes, John (M.E.) and Thomas E. Raynor. *Orientation to Banking.* Scarborough, Ont.: Prentice-Hall, 1986.

Carman, James M., and Eric Langeard. "Growth Strategies for Service Firms." *Strategic Management Journal* 1, no. 1 (1980).

Casson, Mark C. "Transaction Costs and the Theory of the Multinational Enterprise." In *New Theories of the Multinational Enterprise*, edited by A.M. Rugman. New York: St. Martin's Press, 1982.

Casson, Mark C., ed. *The Growth of International Business.* London: George Allen and Unwin, 1983.

Caves, Richard E. "International Corporations: The Industrial Economics of Foreign Investment." *Economica* 38 (1971)

– "Discussion of Henry S. Terrell and S. Key, 'The U.S. Activities of Foreign Banks: An Analytical Survey.'" In *Key Issues in International Banking.* Boston: Federal Reserve Bank of Boston, 1977.

– *Multinational Enterprise and Economic Analysis.* Cambridge: Cambridge University Press, 1982.

Cechetto, Seth M. "A Comparative Analysis of the Internationalization of United States and Canadian Banks." M.A. thesis, Norman Patterson School of International Affairs, Carlton University, Ottawa, 1979.

Centre on Transnational Corporations. *Transnational Banks: Operations, Strategies and Their Effects in Developing Countries.* New York: United Nations, 1981.

Chandler, A.D., Jr. *Strategy and Structure: Chapters in the History of the Industrial Enterprise.* Cambridge, Mass.: MIT Press, 1962.

– *The Visible Hand: The Management Revolution in American Business.* Cambridge, Mass.: Belknap Press, 1977.

- "The Functions of the HQ Unit in the Multibusiness Firm." *Strategic Management Journal* 12, Special Issue (Winter 1991).
Channon, Derek F. *British Banking and the International Challenge.* London: Macmillan, 1977.
- *The Service Industries: Strategy, Structure and Financial Performance.* London: Macmillan, 1978.
- *Bank Strategic Management and Marketing.* New York: Wiley, 1986.
Chisholm, Patricia. "The Youngest Chairman: Matthew Barrett Faces a Tough Challenge." *Maclean's*, 30 July 1990.
Clendenning, E. Wayne. *The Euro-Currency Markets and the International Activities of Canadian Banks.* Ottawa: Information Canada for the Economic Council of Canada, 1977.
Cleveland, Harold van B., and Thomas F. Huertas. *Citibank: 1812–1970.* Cambridge, Mass.: Harvard University Press, 1985.
Coase, R.H. "The Nature of the Firm." *Economica* 4 (1937).
Cline, William R. "'Reciprocity': A New Approach to World Trade Policy?" *Policy Analysis in International Economics* 2 (September 1982).
Coleman, William D. "The Banking Policy Community and Financial Change." In *Policy Communities and Public Policy in Canada: A Structural Approach*, edited by William D. Coleman and Grace Skogstad. Toronto: Copp Clark Pitman, 1990.
Coulbeck, Neil. *The Multinational Banking Industry.* New York: New York University Press, 1984.
Courchene, Thomas D. "Grappling with Mobility: The Role of the State as Regulator of Financial Institutions." 42nd Annual Conference of the Institute of Public Administration of Canada, 27 August 1990.
Crane, Dwight B., and Robert G. Eccles. "Commercial Banks: Taking Shape For Turbulent Times." *Harvard Business Review*. November-December 1987.
Crane, Dwight B., and Samuel L. Hayes, III. "The New Competition in World Banking." *Harvard Business Review*. July–August 1982.
Critchley, Barry. "Off the Record: Banks find another way." *Financial Post*, 30 January 1992.
Critchley, Barry, and Susan Gittins, "Off the Record." *Financial Post*, 25 June 1991.
Curtin, Donal. "Japanese Banking – The International Retreat." *Euromoney*. March 1983.
- "The Bank of Tokyo Counts the Cost of Leadership." *Euromoney*. February 1983.
DRT International. "Business Issues for Financial Services: The Changing Role of Technology." Briefing Paper. DRT International. June 1991.
Dalbey, Homer. "Planning on Both Sides of the Atlantic." *The Bankers Magazine*. March-April 1986.

Dale, Richard S. "Country Risk and Bank Regulation." *The Banker*. March 1983.

Darroch, James L. "Strategic Management and Multinational Banking: The Case of the Canadian Banks." Ph.D. dissertation, 1989.

– "The Changing Face of International Banking: Institutional Transformation and Innovation in Product Design." *Banking & Finance Law Review* 4 (April 1990).

– "Changing Markets, Changing Competitors and New Information Technologies." Toronto: Insight Seminar Services, Section 8, 1990.

– "Stability as Virtue: The Competitive Advantages of Canadian Banks in the United States." *Business in the Contemporary World*. Spring 1991.

– "Global Competitiveness and Public Policy: The Case of Canadian Multinational Banks." *Business History* 34, no. 3 (July 1992).

– "Strategic Management in Turbulent Environments: The Canadian Banks in the 1980s." *Research in Global Strategic Management* 3 (1992).

Darroch, James L., and Isaiah A. Litvak. "Canadian Banks: New Strategic Initiatives." *Business Quarterly* 56, no. 2 (Fall 1991).

– "Diamonds and Money: Porter and Canadian Financial Services Firms." *Business Quarterly* 56, no. 3 (Winter 1992).

– "Strategies for Canada's New North American Banks." *Multinational Business*. Spring 1992.

– "Gaps, Overlaps and Competition among Jurisdictions: Evolving Canadian Financial Services Policies and Regulations." *Journal of World Trade*. April 1992.

Davis, Steven I. "How Risky Is International Lending?" *Harvard Business Review*. January-February 1977.

– "Why Strategic Planning Is the Key to Eurobanking." *Euromoney*. August 1980.

– "International Bank Expansion: Time for a Reassessment?" *The Banker*. May 1981.

– *Excellence in Banking*. London: Macmillan, 1985.

– *Managing Change in the Excellent Banks*. New York: St Martin's Press, 1989.

Day, George S. *Market Driven Strategy: Processes for Creating Value*. New York: The Free Press, 1990.

de Carmoy, Herve. *Global Banking Strategy: Financial Markets and Industrial Decay*. Oxford: Basil Blackwell, 1990.

Dean, James, and Ian H. Giddy. "Strangers and Neighbours: Cross-Border Banking in North America." *Banca Nazional del Lavoro Quarterly Review* no. 137 (1981).

– *Averting International Banking Crises*. New York University Monograph Series in Finance and Economics, no. 1. New York: New York University, 1981.

Dean, James, and Herbert G. Grubel. "Regulatory Issues and the Theory of Multinational Banking." In *Issues in Financial Regulation*, edited by Franklin R. Edwards. Toronto: McGraw-Hill, 1979.

Dematte, C. "International Financial Intermediation: Implications for Bankers and Regulators." *Banca Nazionale del Lavoro Quarterly Review* 136 (1981).

Denison, Merrill. *Canada's First Bank: A History of the Bank of Montreal.* Toronto: McClelland and Stewart, 1966.

Deutsch, Barry I. "A Conversation with Michael Porter." *Bank Marketing.* May 1990.

Dod, David P. "Bank Lending to Developing Countries." *Federal Reserve Bulletin.* September 1981.

Donaldson, T.H. *International Lending by Commercial Banks.* New York: Wiley, 1979.

Doz, Yves L. "Strategic Management in Multinational Companies." *Sloan Management Review.* Winter 1980.

Doz, Yves L., and C.K. Prahalad. "How MNCs Cope with Host Government Intervention." *Harvard Business Review.* March–April 1980.

– "Headquarters Influence and Strategic Control in MNCs." *Sloan Management Review.* Fall 1981.

Dufey, Gunter, and Ian H. Giddy. *The International Money Market.* Englewood Cliffs, N.J.: Prentice Hall, 1978.

– "Innovation in International Financial Markets." *Journal of International Business Studies.* Fall 1981.

Dunning, John H. "Trade, Location of Economic Activity and the MNE: A Search for an Eclectic Approach." In *The International Allocation of Economic Activity*, edited by Bertil Ohlin, et al. Proceedings of a Nobel Symposium held in Stockholm. London: Macmillan, 1977.

Eccles, Robert G., and Dwight B. Crane. "Managing Through Networks in Investment Banking." *California Management Review*, Fall 1987.

– *Doing Deals: Investment Banks at Work.* Cambridge, Mass: Harvard Business School Press, 1988.

Economic Council of Canada. *A New Frontier: Globalization and Canada's Financial Markets.* Ottawa: Canadian Government Publishing Centre, 1989.

Edminister, R.O. *Financial Institutions: Markets and Management.* New York: McGraw Hill, 1980.

Edwards, Franklin R., ed. *Issues in Financial Regulation.* Toronto: McGraw Hill, 1979.

– The New International Banking Facility: A Study in Regulatory Frustration." *Columbia Journal of World Business.* Winter 1981.

Edwards, Franklin R., and Hugh T. Patrick, eds. *Regulating International Financial Markets: Issues and Policies.* Boston: Kluwer, 1992.

Edwards, Franklin R., and Jack Zwick. "Activities and Regulatory Issues: Foreign Banks in the United States." *Columbia Journal of World Business.* Spring 1975.

Einhorn, J.P. "International Bank Lending: Expanding the Dialogue." *Columbia Journal of World Business*. Fall 1978.

Eiteman, David K. "The Spread of Foreign Banks into the United States: Far Eastern Bank Operations in California." In *International Business in the Pacific Basin*, edited by R. Hal Mason. Lexington, Mass.: D.C. Heath, 1978.

Enchin, Harvey. "Bank chases after big business." *Globe and Mail*, 6 March 1991.

Euromoney. "The Puzzling International Approach of Nat West." July 1981.

– "Foreign Banks in America." August 1983.

– "Leaders of the Pack." December 1990.

– "Horses for Courses." January 1992.

– "Euromoney 500: Meltdown? What Meltdown." June 1992.

Fairlamb, D. "Savings and Co-operative Banks Become Increasingly International." *The Banker*, November 1980.

Farnsworth, Clyde H. "Canada's mighty banks on a march to the south." *New York Times*, 5 April 1992.

Fayerweather, John. *The Mercantile Affair: A Case Study of Canadian Nationalism and a Multinational Firm*. New York: New York University Press, 1974.

Federal Reserve Bank of Boston. *Key Issues in International Banking*. Boston: Federal Reserve Bank of Boston, 1977.

Federal Reserve Bank of New York. "Recent Trends in Bank Profitability." *Federal Reserve Bank of New York*. September 1986.

Fellows, J.A. "Theory of the Banking Firm." *American Economist* 22 (1978).

Fieleke, Norman. "The Growth of U.S. Banking Abroad: An Analytical Survey." In *Key Issues in International Banking*. Boston: Federal Reserve Bank of Boston, 1977.

Financial Post. "B of M board to meet in U.S.." 20 September 1991.

– "Bank service charges jump." 3 April 1992.

Financial Times of Canada. "BMO's break with the horsy set." 27 May 1991.

Fleming, A.E. "Arab Bank: Origins and Recent Developments in Capital Markets." *IMF Survey*. 8 February 1982.

Flowers, E.B. "Oligopolistic Reaction in European and Canadian Direct Investment in the United States." *Journal of International Business Studies*. Fall/Winter 1976.

"Foreign Banks in America." *Economist*, 23 May 1992.

"Foreign Banks Sense Progress Toward National Treatment in Canada." *ABA Banking Journal*. October 1983.

Foster, Richard. "Mulholland proposes scheme to help Brazil's debt problem." Report on Business, *Globe and Mail*, 13 March 1987,

Frankel, Allen. "International Banking, Part 1." *Federal Reserve Bank of Chicago Business Conditions*. September 1975.

Franko, L.G. "Global Corporate Competition: Who's Winning, Who's Losing and the R&D Factor as One Reason Why." *Strategic Management Journal* 10, no. 5 (September–October 1989).

Freedman, C. "Micro-theory of International Financial Intermediation." *American Economic Review: Papers and Proceedings* 67 (1977).

Frenkel, Allen. "The Lender of Last Resort Facility in the Context of Multinational Banking." *Columbia Journal of World Business*. Winter 1975.

Friedman, I. "Evaluation of Risk in International Lending: A Lender's Perspective." *Federal Reserve Bank Of Boston*. October 1977.

Friedman, Irving S. *The Emerging Role of Private Banks in the Developing World*. New York: Citicorp, 1977.

Friedman, K.J. "The 1980 Canadian Banks and Banking Law Review Act: Competitive Stimulus or Protectionist Barrier?" *Law and Policy in International Business* 13 (1981).

Frowen, Stephen F. *A Framework of International Banking*. Guildford, U.K.: Guildford Educational Press, 1979.

Frydl, E.J. "The Debate Over Regulating the Eurocurrency Markets." *Federal Reserve Bank of New York Quarterly* 4 (1979–1980).

Fullerton, R. Donald. "Changing a Bank." *Business Quarterly* 55, no. 3 (Winter 1991).

Gagnon, J.E. "The New Merger Guidelines: Implications for the New England Banking Markets. *New England Economic Review*. July–August 1982.

Galbraith, Jay R., and Rober K. Kazanjian. *Strategy Implementation: Structure, Systems and Process*. St. Paul, Minn.: West Publishing Co., 1986.

Galles, D.L.C. "The Bank of Nova Scotia in Minneapolis, 1885–1892." *Minnesota History*. Fall 1971.

Galt, Virginia, Patricia Lush, Allan Robinson, and Dennis Slocum. "Power plays opened securities industry." *Globe and Mail*, 31 December 1988.

Gardner, Mona J. and Dixie L. Mills. "Women's Banks – Where to Now?" *The Bankers Magazine*. January-February 1983.

Gibb-Clark, Margot. "B of M erasing barriers to women." *Globe and Mail*, 6 December 1991.

– "CIBC's behaviour in firing 'inexcusable'." *Globe and Mail*, 24 February 1992.

Gibbon, Ann. "Ottawa advised to finance new jobs." *Globe and Mail*, 21 January 1992.

Giddy, Ian H. "The Theory and Industrial Organization of International Banking." In *Internationalization of Financial Markets and National Economic Policy*, edited by Robert G. Hawkins, R. Levich, and C. Wihlborg. New York: J.A.I. Press, 1983.

Giddy, Ian H., and D.L. Allen, "International Competition in Bank Regulation." *Banca Nazional del Lavoro Quarterly Review* 130 (1979).

Globe and Mail. "Investment News: Third World exposure cases downgrading of B of M ratings," 13 May 1987.

– "Bank moves to increase native hearing," 25 June 1991.

– "Striving for equality at the banks," 7 December 1991.

– "Banker told to take own advice," 7 February 1992.

Goldberg, Lawrence G., and Anthony Saunders. "The Growth of Organizational Forms of Foreign Banks in the U.S." *Journal of Money, Credit and Banking*, August 1981.

Gonzalez, Maria, and Henry Mintzberg. "Visualizing Strategies for Financial Services." *McKinsey Quarterly*. 1991, no. 2.

Gooding, Wayne. "Royal Bank seeks stellar role for Orion." *Financial Post*, 8 February 1986.

Goodman, Laurie S. "Bank Lending to Non-Opec LDCs: Are Risks Diversifiable?" *Federal Reserve Bank of New York Quarterly Review*. Summer 1981.

Goodman, N. *Fact, Fiction, and Forecast*. 2d ed. Indianapolis: Bobbs-Merrill, 1965.

Gordon, Andrea. "B of M: Can't tell players without a program." *Financial Times of Canada*, 31 December 1984.

– "Feisty Orion tries to get back on track." *Financial Times of Canada*, 10 February 1986.

Gray, Jean M., and H. Peter Gray. "The Multinational Bank: A Financial MNC?" *Journal of Banking and Finance* 5 (1981).

Griffith-Jones, Stephany. "The Growth of Multinational Banking, The Eurocurrency Market and Their Effects on Developing Countries." *Journal of Development Studies*. January 1980.

Green, Christopher. *Canadian Industrial Organization and Policy*. 2d ed. Toronto: McGraw-Hill, 1985.

Group of Thirty. "How Bankers See the World Financial Market." Briefing Paper, New York: Group of Thirty, May 1982.

Grubel, Herbert G. "A Theory of Multinational Banking." *Banca Nazional del Lavoro Quarterly Review* 123 (1977).

– "The New International Banking." *Banca Nazional del Lavoro Quarterly Review* 146 (1983).

Hageman, Helmut. "Should Your Company Be a 'Corporate Bank'?" *McKinsey Quarterly*, 1991:4.

Hale, David D. "Global Finance and the Retreat to Managed Trade." *Harvard Business Review*. January–February 1990.

Hall, David J. and Maurice A. Saias. "Strategy Follows Structure." *Strategic Management Journal* 1, no. 2 (1980).

Haslem, J.A., A. Christofi, J.P. Bedingfield, and A.J. Stagliano, "A Statistical Analysis of International Banking Measures and Relative Profitability." *Management International Review* 26, no. 2 (1986).

Hawkins, Robert G. *The Internationalisation of Financial Markets and National Economic Policy*. Toronto: McMillan, 1981.

Hayes, Samuel L., III, and Philip M. Hubbard. *Investment Banking: A Tale of Three Cities*. Boston: Harvard Business School Press, 1990.

Hegel, G.W.F. *The Phenomenology of Mind*. Translated by J.B. Baillie. New York: Harper & Row, 1967.

Heimann, John. "The Problem of Confidence in Domestic and International Banking Sysems." *Journal of Banking and Finance* 6 (1982).

Heinrich, Erik. "Bank pledges native focus." *Financial Post*, 7 May 1992.

Hirtle, "Factors Affecting the Competitiveness of Internationally Active Financial Institutions." *FRBNY Quarterly Review*. Spring 1991.

Hofer, Charles W., and Dan Schendel. *Strategy Formulation: Analytical Concepts*. St. Paul: West Publishing Co., 1978.

Horvitch, Sonita. "Harris gives B of M competitive advantage." *Financial Post*, 15 October 1983.

– "'High noon' at the Royal Bank." *Financial Post*, 9–15 November 1987.

– "B of M the beloved of small business." *Financial Post*, 26 June 1992.

Hout, Thomas, Michael E. Porter, and Eileen Rudden. "How Global Companies Win Out." *Harvard Business Review*. September–October 1982.

Howlett, Karen. "Scotiabank to set up trust unit: Wealth of aging population seen as new source of business." *Globe and Mail*, 27 March 1992.

Howlett, Karen, and Brian Milner. "CIBC chief changing 'country club' system." *Globe and Mail*, 21 January 1991.

Hultman, Charles W., and L. Randolph McGee. "Lending by U.S. Branches of Foreign Banks." *Journal of Commercial Bank Lending*. August 1989.

Hutton, H.R. "The Regulation of Foreign Banks – A European Viewpoint." *Columbia Journal of World Business*. Winter 1975.

Hymer, Stephen. *The International Operations of National Firms: A Study of Direct Foreign Investment*. Cambridge, MA: The MIT Press, 1976.

Ince, Clifford H. *The Royal Bank of Canada: A Chronology: 1869–1969*. No Publisher, No date.

Ip, Greg. "B of M has 24-hour currency trading." *Financial Post*, 1 April 1991.

– "B of M – champion of cheaper money." *Financial Post*, 6 May 1991.

– "TD, Nat Bank down in ratings; B of M upgraded." *Financial Post*, 8 May 1991.

– "Banks stocking up on liquid assets." *Financial Post*, 8 September 1992.

Ireland, J. "International Banking Facilities: The Bahamas Eyes Its Future." *The Banker*, July 1981.

Jacobs, Klass Peter. "The Development of International and Multinational Banking in Europe." *Columbia Journal of World Business*. Winter 1975.

Jain, Arvind K. "International Lending Patterns of U.S. Commercial Banks." *Journal of International Business Studies*. Fall 1986.

Jamieson, A.B. *Chartered Banking in Canada*. Toronto: Ryerson Press, 1953.

"Japan's Monetary Implosion." *Economist*, 31 October 1992.

Jordan, William. "Producer Protection, Prior Market Structure and the Effects of Government Regulation." *Journal of Law and Economics* 15 (1972).

Jorgensen, Bud. "Street Talk: Flood figures in CIBC disaster file." *Globe and Mail*, 24 April 1992.

Kalymon, Basil A. *Global Innovation and The Impact on Canada's Financial Markets*. Toronto: John Wiley & Sons in association with the National Centre for Management Research and Development, 1989.

Kelly, Doug. "Major financial reforms looming." *Financial Post*, 30 October 1992.

Kessler, Geldolph A. "The Need to Control International Bank Lending." *Banca Nazionale del Lavoro Quarterly Review* 132 (1980).

Key, S.J. "International Banking Facilities." *Federal Reserve Bulletin*. October 1982.

Khoury, Sarkis J. "International Banking: A Look at Foreign Banks in the u.s." *Journal of International Business Studies*. Winter 1979.

– *Dynamics of International Banking*. New York: Praeger, 1980.

Kilpatrick, Lynne. "Help wanted: A ceo to purge the mediocrity at cibc." *Financial Times of Canada*, 9 March 1991.

Kim, Seung H., and Stephen W. Miller. *Competitive Structure of the International Banking Industry*. Toronto: Heath Books, 1983.

Kindleberger, Charles P. "International Banks as Leaders or Followers in International Business." *Journal of Banking and Finance* 7 (1980).

Klein, Michael A. "Theory of the Banking Firm." *Journal of Money, Credit and Banking* 3 (1971).

Kneale, William, and Mary Kneale, *The Development of Logic*. London: Oxford University Press, 1962.

Knickerbocker, F.T. *Oligopolistic Reaction and Multinational Enterprise*. Boston: Division of Research, Graduate School of Business Administration, Harvard University, 1973.

Korth, Christopher M. "The Evolving Role of u.s. Banks in International Finance." *The Bankers Magazine*. July–August 1980.

– "Risk Minimization for International Lending in Regional Banks." *Columbia Journal of World Business*. Winter 1981.

Kosters, Marvin H., and Allan H. Meltzer, *International Competitiveness in Financial Services*. Boston: Kluwer, 1991

Kraft, John W. "What an American Bank Can Do for You: A Banker's Guide to China." *Columbia Journal of World Business*. Summer 1979.

Kryzanwoski, L., and G.S. Roberts, "Bank Structure in Canada." In *Banking Structure In Major Countries*, edited by George G. Kaufman. Boston: Kluwer, 1992.

Kuhn, T.S. *The Structure of Scientific Revolutions*. Chicago: The University of Chicago Press, 1962.

Kvasnicka, Joseph G. "International Banking: Part II." *Federal Reserve Bank of Chicago Business Conditions*. March 1976.

Langhor, Herwig. "Alternative Approaches to the Theory of the Banking Firm: A Note." *Journal of Banking and Finance* 6 (1982).

Lees, Francis A. *International Banking and Finance*. New York: Wiley, 1974.
– *Foreign Banking and Investment in the United States: Issues and Alternatives*. New York: Halsted Press, 1976.
Lehr, Dennis J., and Benton R. Hammond. "Regulating Foreign Acquisition of u.s. Banks: The CBCA and the BHCA." *Banking Law Journal*. February 1980.
Litvak, Isaiah A. "Instant International: Strategic Reality for Small High-Technology Firms in Canada." *Multinational Business*. Summer 1990.
Litvak, Isaiah A., and Christopher J. Maule. "Competition Policy and Newspapers in Canada." *The Antitrust Bulletin* 28 (Summer 1983).
– "Assessing Industry Concentration: The Case of Aluminum." *Journal of International Business Studies*. Spring–Summer 1984.
Lush, Patricia. "'Bank-brokerage deal proves costly winner." *Globe and Mail*, 25 February 1988.
Ma, Frederick. "Canadian Multinational Banks: Opportunities and Risks of International Banking Exposure." Investment Report. Toronto: Pitfield Mackay Ross, July 1981.
– "A Closer Look at the Quality of International Earnings – Bank P/E Multiples Are Higher Than They Appear To Be." Investment Report. *International Banking Quarterly*. Pitfield Mackay Ross, 6 June 1983.
– "Will Loans to Brazil Become Non-Performing? What is a Problem Loan Revisted." *International Banking Quarterly*. Pitfield Mackay Ross, 7 September 1983.
MacIntosh, Robert. *Different Drummers: Banking and Politics in Canada*. Toronto: Macmillan, 1991.
Mathis, F. John. "International Banking: An Outlook for the 1980s." *Journal of Commercial Bank Lending* 62 (1980).
Mathis, F. John, ed. *Offshore Lending By u.s. Commercial Banks*. 2d. ed. Washington: Robert Morris Associates, 1981.
Mathis, F. John, and D.C. Maslin. "RMA Survey of the Management of International Loan Portfolio Diversification." *Journal of Commercial Bank Lending* 63 (March 1981).
Maxwell, Charles E., and Lawrence J. Gitman. "Risk Transmission in International Banking: An Analysis of 48 Central Banks." *Journal of International Business Studies*. Summer 1989.
Maxwell, Mark L. "Databanks: Valuing Canadian Bank Stocks with Three Key Measures." Investment Report. Gordon Capital, 30 April 1992.
McDonald, W. Scott. "World Banking Beyond the Tempest." *Canadian Banker and ICB Review* 90 (April 1983).
McKenzie, George W. "Regulating the Euromarkets." *Journal of Banking and Finance* 5 (1981).
McKenzie, Rob. "Shopping around can trim outrageous bank charges." *Financial Post*, 9 December 1991.

McNish, Jacquie. "Bank of Montreal seeking its consumer roots." *Globe and Mail*, 19 March 1990.
- "B of M unit sets stage for expansion." *Globe and Mail*, 3 September 1991.
McQueen, Rod. "Scotiabank Comes Out of the Shadow." *Report on Business Magazine*. November 1985.
- "Banking executive slams U.S. system." *Financial Post*, 21 June 1990.
Meerschwam, David M. *Breaking Financial Boundaries: Global Capital, National Deregulation, and Financial Services Firms*. Cambridge, MA: Harvard Business School Press, 1991.
"Metamorphosis: A Survey of International Banking." *Economist*, 25 March 1989.
Milner, Brian. "B of M lowers rate on small-business loans." *Globe and Mail*, 12 December 1991.
- "DBRS slashes ratings of Big 3's finance arms." *Globe and Mail*, 30 January 1992.
Mintzberg, H., and J.A. Waters, "Tracking Strategy in an Entrepreneurial Firm." *Academy of Management Journal*. 25, no. 3 (September 1982).
- "Researching the Formation of Strategies: The History of Canadian Lady, 1939–1976." In *Competitive Strategic Management*, edited by Robert Boyden Lamb. Englewood Cliffs, NJ: Prentice-Hall, 1984.
- "Of Strategies, Deliberate and Emergent." *Strategic Management Journal* 6, no. 3 (July–September 1985).
Mittelstaedt, Martin. "Resignations at Bank of Montreal fuel speculation about low morale." *Globe and Mail*, 13 October 1984
- "B of M to swap Brazilian debt for equity." *Globe and Mail*, 3 April 1987.
Monti, Antonio. "Recent Trends in International Banking." *Journal of Banking and Finance* 6 (1982)
Morse, J. "Control of Multinational Banking." *The Banker*. August 1977.
Moskowitz, W.E. "Global Asset and Liability Management at Commercial Banks." *Federal Reserve Bank of New York Quarterly Review* 4 (1979–1980).
Murphy, R. Taggart. "Power Without Purpose: The Crisis of Japan's Global Financial Dominance." *Harvard Business Review*. March–April, 1989.
Nagy, Pancras. *The International Business of Canadian Banks*. Montreal: Centre for International Business Studies, Ecole des Hautes Etudes Commerciales, 1983.
Naidu, G.N. "Differences in International Financial Practices: Implications for Foreign Lending." *Journal of Commercial Bank Lending*. April 1983.
Neufeld, E.P. *The Canadian Financial System: Its Growth and Development*. Toronto: Macmillan, 1972.
Newman, Peter C. "A Survival Strategy at the B of M." *Maclean's*, 9 April 1990.
Nigh, Douglas, Kang Rae Cho, and Suresh Krishman, "The Role of Location-Related Factors in U.S. Banking Involvement Abroad: An Empirical Examination." *Journal of International Business Studies*. Fall 1986.

OECD. *International Trade in Services: Banking*. Paris: OECD, 1984.

Park, Yoon S., and Jack Zwick. *International Banking in Theory and Practice*. Reading, Mass.: Addison-Wesley, 1985.

Pastre, Olivier. "International Bank – Industry Relations: An Empirical Assessment." *Journal of Banking and Finance* 5 (1981).

– *Multinationals: Bank and Corporate Relationships*. Contemporary Studies in Economic and Financial Analysis no. 28. Greenwich, CT: JAI Press, 1981.

Pennings, J.M., and F. Harianto, "The Diffusion of Technological Innovation in the Commercial Banking Industry." *Strategic Management Journal* 13, no. 1 (January 1992).

Pesant, J.M. "The Third Force in International Banking." *The Banker*. April 1980.

Phalen, George E. "Discussion of Norman S. Fieleke, 'The Growth of U.S. Banking Abroad: An Analytical Survey.'" In *Key Issues in International Banking*. Boston, Federal Reserve Bank of Boston: 1977.

Pierce, James L. *The Future of Banking*. New Haven and London: Yale University Press, 1991.

Poniachek, Harvey A. "U.S. International Banking and the Latin American Market." *The Bankers Magazine*. September-October 1983.

Porter, Michael E. *Competitive Strategy: Techniques for Analyzing Industries and Competitors*. New York: Free Press, 1980.

– "Contributions of Industrial Organization to Strategic Management." *Academy of Management Review* 6, no. 4 (1981).

– *Competitive Advantage: Creating and Sustaining Superior Performance*. New York: Free Press, 1985.

– "From Competitive Advantage to Corporate Strategy." *Harvard Business Review*. May–June 1987.

– *The Competitive Advantage of Nations*. New York: Free Press, 1990.

Porter, Michael E., and Monitor Corp. *Canada at the Crossroads: The Reality of a New Competitive Environment*. Ottawa: Business Council on National Issues and Minister of Supply and Services, October, 1991.

Porzecanski, Arturo. C. "The International Role of U.S. Commercial Banks: Past and Future." *Journal of Banking and Finance* 5 (1981).

Poterba, James M. "Comparing the Cost of Capital in the United States and Japan: A Survey of Methods." *FRBNY Quarterly Review*. Winter 1991.

Prahalad, C.K., and Yves Doz. "An Approach to Strategic Control in MNCs." *Sloan Management Review*. Summer 1981.

Price Waterhouse. *Management Challenges in the Financial Services Industry: Senior Executives' Viewpoint*. January 1992.

Reguly, Eric. "CIBC seeks healthy U.S. investment." *Financial Post*, 1 April 1991.

Reidenbach, Eric R. and Robert E. Pitts. *Bank Marketing: A Guide to Strategic Planning*. Englewood, Cliffs, NJ: Prentice-Hall, 1986.

Revell, J.R.S. *Costs and Margins in Banking – An International Survey*. Paris: OECD, 1980.
– *Banking and Electronic Fund Transfers*. Paris: OECD, 1983.
Rhoades, S.A. "Structure – Performance Studies in Banking: An Updated Summary and Evaluation." *Federal Reserve Bulletin* 68 (1982).
Roseman, Ellen. "Bank issues lower-rate card." *Globe and Mail*, 16 January 1992.
Ross, Victor. *A History of the Canadian Bank of Commerce with an account of the the other banks which now form part of its organization*. Toronto: Oxford University Press, 1920 and 1922.
Rudy, John P. "Global Planning in Multinational Banking." *Columbia Journal of World Business*. Winter 1975.
Rugman, Alan M. "Motives for Foreign Investment: The Market Imperfections and Risk Diversification Hypotheses." *Journal of World Trade Law* September-October 1975.
– "Risk Reduction by International Diversification." *Journal of International Business Studies*. Fall/Winter 1976.
– "International Diversification by Financial and Direct Investment." *Journal of Economics and Business*. Fall 1977.
– *International Diversification and Multinational Enterprise*. Lexington, MA: Lexington Books, 1979.
– *Inside the Multinationals: The Economics of Internal Markets*. New York: Columbia University Press, 1981.
Rugman, Alan M., and Shyam J. Kamath. "International Diversification and Multinational Banking." In *Recent Developments in International Banking and Finance*, edited by Sarkis J. Khoury and Alo Ghosh. Lexington, MA, and Toronto: Lexington Books, D. C. Heath and Company, 1987.
Rumelt, Richard B. *Strategy, Structure and Economic Performance*. Boston: Division of Research, Harvard Business School, 1974.
– "Diversification Strategy and Profitability." *Strategic Management Journal* 3, no. 4 (1982).
Ryval, Michael. "'Hard times' means special lending rates." *Globe and Mail*, 9 November 1992.
Saade, Nicholas A., Jr. "How Banks Can Live with Low Spreads." *Euromoney*. November 1981.
Sabi, Manijeh. "An Application of the Theory of Foreign Direct Investment to Multinational Banking in LDCs." *Journal of International Business Studies*. Fall 1988.
Sakakibara, Eisuke. "The Japanese Financial System in Transition." In *The Future of the International Monetary System*, edited by Tamior Agmon, et al. Lexington, MA: Heath Books, 1984.
Sarmet, M. "Recent Trends in International Project Financing." *The Banker*. September 1981.

Saxe, Jo W. "Concessionary Lending to Developing Countries." *Journal of Banking and Finance* 5 (1981).

Schull, Joseph, and J. Douglas Gibson. *The Scotiabank Story: A History of The Bank of Nova Scotia, 1832–1982*. Toronto: Macmillan, 1982.

Scotiabank. "Competitiveness and the Regulation of Canadian Banks." Briefing Paper. Toronto, Bank of Nova Scotia, October 1986.

Scotton, Geoffrey. "Royal and B of M reports judged best in the world." *Financial Post*, 16 June 1992.

Shain, Melanie Maxwell. "You Buy Money to Sell at a Spread, Can You Do It with Goods Too?" *ABA Banking Journal*. October 1983.

Siklos, Richard. "Banks at low risk in Eastern Europe." *Financial Post*, 21 August 1991.

Stanbury, W.T. *Business-Government Relations in Canada: Grappling with Leviathan*. Toronto: Methuen, 1986.

Steiner, Thomas D. and Diogo B. Teixeira, *Technology in Banking: Creating Value and Destroying Profits*. Homewood, Ill.: Business One Irwin, 1990.

Sterling, J.F., Jr. "A New Look At International Lending by American Banks." *Columbia Journal of World Business*. Fall 1979.

Stuhldreher, Thomas J. and James C. Baker. "Bankers' Attitudes Toward U.S. Foreign Bank Regulation." *The Banker*. January 1981.

Suzuki, Yoshio. *Money and Banking in Contemporary Japan*. New Haven: Yale University Press, 1980.

Synnott, W.R. "Total Customer Relationships in International Banking." *MIS Quarterly*. September 1978.

Swoboda, Alexander K. "International Banking: Current Issues in Perspective." *Journal of Banking and Finance* 6 (1982).

Taylor, Allan R. "Business, Politics and Politicians." *Business Quarterly*. Spring 1991.

Terrell, Henry S., and Sydney J. Key. "The U.S. Activities of Foreign Banks: An Analytical Survey." In Federal Reserve Bank of Boston, *Key Issues in International Banking*. Boston, 1977.

Terrell, Henry S., and John Lemoine. "The U.S. Activities of Foreign-Owned Banking Organizations." *Columbia Journal of World Business*. Winter 1975.

Terry, E. "T-D Bank a surprise in Japan." Report on Business, *Globe and Mail*, 6 August 1990.

Theobald, Thomas C. "Offshore Branches and Global Banking – One Bank's View." *Columbia Journal of World Business*. Winter 1981.

Thoman, G. Richard. "International Banking Can Be Profitable for U.S. Regional Banks." *Columbia Journal of World Business*. Winter 1975.

"Time To Leave: A Survey of World Banking." *Economist*, 2 May 1992.

Trigge, A. St L. *A History of the Canadian Bank of Commerce with an account of the other banks which now form part of its organization*. Vol. 3. Toronto: The Canadian Bank of Commerce, 1934.

Tschoegl, Adrian E. "Concentration Among International Banks: A Note." *Journal of Banking and Finance* 6 (1982).
- "International Retail Banking as a Strategy: An Assessment." *Journal of International Business Studies*. Summer 1987.
Vernon, Raymond. "Commentary on James Dean and Herbert G. Grubel, 'Regulatory Issues and the Theory of Multinational Banking'." In *Issues in Financial Regulation*, edited by Franklin R. Edwards. Toronto: McGraw-Hill, 1979.
Walter, Ingo. "Country Risk, Portfolio Decisions and Regulation in International Bank Lending." *Journal of Banking and Finance* 5 (1981).
- *Barriers to Trade in Banking and Financial Services*. London. Trade Research Centre, 1985.
- *Global Competition in Financial Services: Market Structure, Protection, and Trade Liberalization*. Cambridge, Mass. An American Institute/Ballinger Publication, 1988.
Walter, Ingo, and H. Peter Gray. "Protectionism and International Banking." *Journal of Banking and Finance* 7 (1983).
Wellons, Philip. "International Bankers: Size Up Your Competitors." *Harvard Business Review*. November–December 1982.
Wels, A. "How Citicorp Restructured for the 'Eighties'." *Euromoney*, April 1980.
Whyte, Heather D. "B of M clears path into trust industry." *Financial Post*, 15 January 1991.
- "CIBC's Mexico venture possible." *Financial Post*, 26 July 1991.
- "Nesbitt to retain separate identity." *Financial Post*, 27 February 1992.
- "Big Six eye U.S. credit card market." *Financial Post*, 23 March 1992.
- "Scotiabank's Ritchie wins over the critics." *Financial Post*, 26 October 1992.
Williamson, Oliver E. *Markets and Hierarchies: Analysis and Antitrust Implications*. New York: Free Press, 1975.
- "Transaction Cost Economics: The Governance of Contractual Relations." *Journal of Law and Economics* 22 (1979).
- "The Economics of Organization: The Transaction Cost Approach." *American Journal of Sociology* 87 (1981).
- "The Modern Corporation: Origins, Evolution, Attributes." *Journal of Economic Literature* 19 (1981).
- "Credible Commitments: Using Hostages to Support Exchange." *American Economic Review* 83 (1983).
- *The Economic Institutions of Capitalism*. New York: Free Press, 1985.
Wong, Jan. "Heir Today, Gone Tomorrow." *Globe and Mail*. 16 May 1987.
Wright, Richard W., ed. *International Dimensions of Canadian Banking*. Toronto: Addison-Wesley, 1983.
Wright, Richard W., and Gunter A. Pauli. *The Second Wave: Japan's Global Assault on Financial Services*. New York: St Martin's Press, 1987.

Yannopoulos, George N. "The Growth of Transnational Banking." In *The Growth of International Business*, edited by Mark C. Casson. London: George Allen and Unwin, 1983.

Zimmer, Steven A., and Robert N. McCauley. "Bank Cost of Capital and International Competition." *FRBNY Quarterly Review*. Winter 1991.

Index